Creating an Australian School Literacy Policy

A Research-Informed Guide to Designing a Policy That Fits Your School

Dr Margaret K. Merga

amba press

Published in 2023 by Amba Press, Melbourne, Australia.
www.ambapress.com.au

Previously published in 2023 by Hawker Brownlow Education.
This edition replaces all previous editions.

Designer: Matthew Harrod

ISBN: 9781923116061 (pbk)
ISBN: 9781923116078 (ebk)

A catalogue record for this book is available from the National Library of Australia.

Acknowledgements

This book would not exist without the support and encouragement of many people. First, I would like to thank Caroline Hartley from Hawker Brownlow Education (HBE) and Olivia Tolich (formerly at HBE) for reaching out and expressing interest in publishing my work when it was still very much at idea stage. Thank you Caroline for guiding me through the process at HBE and for being so supportive. I'd also like to thank Lauren Mitchell for her editorial and formatting work, and Sarah Handscomb for her consideration of my work.

I would also like to thank Trish Hepworth and Jacqui Lucas from the Australian Library and Information Association (ALIA) for being early enthusiasts, and imagining how the book could potentially be used to inform professional learning. This early injection of optimism from ALIA buoyed my writing and gave me a sense of purpose. I would also like to thank the Australian School Library Association and the Western Australian School Library Association for making me your Patron and sustaining me with ongoing encouragement and support.

I wish to thank Professor Susan Ledger at the University of Newcastle for facilitating an Honorary Adjunct appointment at this university. The academic literature cited in this book was accessible to me due to this appointment, so thanks for your invaluable support of my work.

I would like to thank Fiona Walker and Vicki Briggs from the Department of Education in Western Australia for kindly sharing some of their co-created materials on whole-school literacy planning that are not publicly available, and for the stimulating exchanges of ideas we have had on this topic over the years. I would also like to thank Fiona Walker for being an early reader of the manuscript for this book; your expert feedback and generous support were gratefully received.

As usual, I would like to thank Marián Merga, whose ongoing support enables me to chase my interests, and Gabriel and Samuel Merga for being on my team. Thanks again to Gabe for taking time out from your very busy study and work schedule to be an early critical reader of all of my books.

Table of contents

About the author

Dr Margaret K. Merga is an author and consultant at Merga Consulting, supporting schools and professional associations seeking to build school reading cultures and enhance school library advocacy. Margaret is an honorary adjunct at the University of Newcastle, Australia, and a senior researcher in literacy, library, and research communication.

Margaret has extensive teaching experience across K–12 and higher education and is the leading Australian researcher in school-based literacy policy research.

Abbreviations

AC	Australian Curriculum
ACARA	Australian Curriculum, Assessment and Reporting Authority
AITSL	Australian Institute for Teaching and School Leadership
APST	Australian Professional Standards for Teachers
DoEWA	Department of Education Western Australia
EAL/D	English as an additional language or dialect
GATE	Gifted and talented education
HoLA	Head of learning area
ICT	Information and communication technology
ILNNP	Improving Literacy and Numeracy National Partnership
LAC	Language Across the Curriculum (movement)
LNNP	Literacy and Numeracy National Partnership
NAPLAN	National Assessment Program – Literacy and Numeracy (Australian national high-stakes testing programme)
OCBs	Organisational citizenship behaviours

OECD	Organisation for Economic Co-operation and Development
OFSTED	Office for Standards in Education, Children's Services and Skills (UK)
PD	Professional development
PE	Physical education
PISA	Programme for International Student Assessment
SAE	Standard Australian English
SAER	Students at educational risk (Australia)
SENCO	Special Educational Needs Co-ordinator (UK)
WSLP	Whole-school literacy policy

Introduction

If you are reading this book, it is likely that you either need to write a brand new whole-school literacy policy (WSLP), or update your existing policy so that it meets the needs of your school.

It might be hard to know where to start in order to create a policy that works for you. While there has been research on school-based policy development in other areas such as attendance policy (Rood, 1989) and information and communication technology (ICT) policy (Vanderlinde et al., 2012), there has been very little work done on how to design and implement an effective school literacy policy, though there has been some recent work on writing policy for specific literacy areas (see Snow et al., 2021, on a reading instruction and support policy). This is unfortunate given the importance of literacy to students and schools, which I explore in detail in this book.

While I am convinced that there is no single perfect policy for all schools and contexts, the diversity in available policies is surprising. When I first started analysing school literacy policies back in 2017, I was struck by just how different individual school literacy policies were in terms of length, complexity, scope, structure and areas of focus.

On one hand, this is a good thing. Despite the popularity of one size fits all approaches to education solutions cooked up by politicians, educators know that schools and their students have widely varying cultures, needs and contexts, so this approach rarely works in education. What works well for a school down the road may not be a good fit where you are. The great variety in content in available school literacy policies gives you a wide range of possibilities to draw upon, many of which I present in this book.

On the other hand, the differences in quality, depth, clarity and consideration in the policies are concerning. Some Australian schools turn out a one or two page document that is titled a WSLP or similar, that offers very little to their educators and leadership teams. Some of these documents seem to be created as a box ticking exercise rather than as a document that will guide the collective understandings of literacy within a school, articulate clear literacy learning goals and detail a clear whole-school direction for attaining them.

Given the constraints on contemporary schools' time and resources, and the constantly evolving expectations and needs in relation to literacy that they must be responsive to, I can understand why many Australian policies are less than comprehensive. Furthermore:

> school leaders and staff are not always resourced or qualified to meet the demands required to effectively write or update school policy. In general, school staff report not having enough time to engage in policy writing and suggest they lack the required expertise. Moreover, training and professional development available for policy writing are variable or non-existent for many school staff. (Allen et al., 2021, p. 2)

If you have to write a WSLP anyway, getting some guidance on how to make a document that can serve the students and educators in your school seems worthwhile. It is great that you are taking the time to explore your options through reading this book, and I hope that your research culminates in the creation of a useful policy that has practical value in your school.

In addition to my previous published and peer-reviewed work on WSLP analysis (Merga, 2021a; Merga & Gardiner, 2018), for this book I have dedicated substantial time and attention to closely analysing available literacy policy documents from both Australia and the UK in order to bring you options and possibilities that you can draw on while crafting or revising your own policy. Awareness of what is being produced in both contexts is useful because in some cases, we can learn from what others are doing elsewhere. This book includes some insights from UK policies, as well as useful facets of Australian policies across contexts. Despite the acknowledged differences in education systems and limitations inherent in some of these UK works, drawing on UK documents offers potential benefit for Australian leaders who seek to enhance their capacity to articulate some aspects of their WSLPs given that UK documents are typically more comprehensive.

When delivering keynotes at national conferences I have asked the educator audience if their school has a literacy policy or not. There is often ambiguity around the existence of such documents, particularly if they were never meaningfully used by the school. You might not know if your school has historically developed a WSLP.

In addition, your school may have given their WSLP an unusual name. Sourcing Australian WSLPs is challenging due to the many different names Australian policies go by. In contrast, the majority of UK documents sourced were titled 'literacy policy'. As you are reading this book, you may wish to have current and previous iterations of your school's WSLP to hand (if they exist). If you are new to your school and looking to see if such a document has been created at your school, here are just some of the many titles that Australian WSLPs are known as: Literacy Policy; Literacy or English Agreement; Literacy Plan; Whole-school Literacy or English Plan; Literacy and Numeracy Policy or Plan; Whole-school Literacy or English Agreement; English Policy; Continuity of Learning Plan: Literacy; Whole-school Literacy Policy; Literacy Programme; Language Policy; Whole-school Approach to Literacy; and, Literacy Curriculum Guide. A WSLP is also often hidden in a School Business, Site, Improvement or Operational Plan. For the sake of ease of discovery for your future colleagues, it would be wonderful if there was greater uniformity in the naming of Australian documents.

Throughout this book, I make direct reference to the WSLPs that I analysed without naming any schools, referring to them as AU(#) or UK(#) so that you can keep track of where policy was generally generated.

The main reason to do this is to provide you with practical examples of how the possibilities I describe in this book can be actualised. By familiarising ourselves with the good ideas of others and learning from their omissions, we can build school literacy policies that are valuable and that make a meaningful contribution to student learning, while being practical in their orientation.

You can start to get a feel for what might work for you, and the choices are considerable. WSLPs range from a one- or two-page document (for example, AU66), to far more lengthy works of over twenty pages. Shorter works are more common in Australia (Merga, 2021a). Some documents show very little originality or tailoring to school needs, being primarily cut and pasted from other curricular documents, often without attribution, as I explore further in this book. In contrast, there are also carefully planned, detailed documents that are closely tailored to school needs. Some documents have avoided pinning down any real targets or implementation plans. Others may risk being too prescriptive in their approach.

One of the key issues will be to decide what literacy means to you, in your context, and that is why I have discussed some of the key considerations in relation to this in the second chapter of the book. Literacy itself is a huge amorphous blob that refuses to be pinned down, and even once it's defined, everyone keeps arguing over it, wanting to make it bigger or smaller, simpler or more complex, more inclusive or more specific. Actually daring to define literacy takes a little bravery, given some of the controversies that I describe later in this book. Students' literacy needs are more variable than their shoe sizes, and as their individual literacy needs continue to expand with the growing communicative affordances of the modern world, at the same time, both internal and external accountabilities on school literacy performance seem to burgeon every year. A literacy policy should not be a mirror or a cut and paste of the curriculum, though it of course needs to be responsive to mandated curriculum and other external requirements. A literacy policy needs to detail how literacy is going to be taught and learned within your school, how it is going to be supported and by whom. It needs to be a useful supporting document for sustaining and improving strong student literacy performance in your school, but it also needs to encourage students' adoption of lifelong literacy identities and practices that will support their literacy needs beyond school.

Another issue will be pinning down who exactly your policy is for. Who is your intended audience? While it is probably a given that teachers and school leadership will be expected to read and use your document, will students be reading it (or parts of it) to understand expectations of them and how the school is going to support them? Will parents be given a copy? You need a document that meets your needs and is accessible both within and beyond the school community, that answers requirements that diverse stakeholders dictate, and at the same time resonates with your core beliefs and research-supported understandings about literacy, student learning and broader student needs. While you do need to look both forward and backward in composing a literacy policy, there will be limitations in your capacity to future-proof the policy. You are going to do the best you can for now, and future revisions and iterations can cover unanticipated future needs. Tailor your expectations and the expectations of others accordingly by creating a scope early in the process that acts like a cell wall; while it is a semipermeable membrane that will allow some things both in and out of the cell, it is very selective.

I hope that you find this book useful. Any feedback you may have around your experiences using the book to lead or support literacy policy development or revisions within your school will be gratefully received, as I can use this to inform and strengthen future editions of this work.

CHAPTER 1

Why does your school need a whole-school literacy policy?

Why does your school even need another policy, and why a whole-school literacy policy (WSLP)?

Contemporary schools may seem to be awash with policies. These are designed to demonstrate compliance with regulatory requirements, create standards to promote quality teaching and learning, and provide opportunities for engagement between staff, their students and communities (Allen et al., 2021).

Whether you are using this book to write or revise your WSLP, you may have to justify why giving time and resourcing to working on a WSLP is worthwhile. That it is in the best interests of your school may need to be argued with leadership and other stakeholders, particularly given the competing demands on time and resourcing already on your plate. Recent times have seen a shift in focus from individual teacher change and development to more sweeping whole-school and system reforms (te Riele et al., 2021), and a resurgence in attention on school literacy policies is responsive to this shift.

While you should theoretically have vital leadership support for this endeavour, I am aware that many school leaders do not have the keen focus on literacy that might be expected, given the importance of literacy for schools and students. For example, our recent research with secondary

English teachers found that 'leadership support for ensuring that struggling literacy learners have their literacy skills developed across all learning areas in their school … indicated room for improvement', with only 56.51 per cent of our respondents feeling that their leaders were committed to this goal (Merga, Mat Roni & Malpique, 2021a, p. 545).

As such, this book does not assume that you have leadership support from the outset, though I will provide a wealth of information around how to foster this going forward. Schools that are still reeling from newly introduced changes or large staff turnovers may be particularly reluctant to introduce anything new. However, I am confident that if you can establish a clear argument, supported by the research and analysis in this book, this will help you to win over the support you need, and I cover gaining stakeholder support further in Chapter 5. Ultimately, a well-crafted WSLP should make everyone's lives easier, by putting everyone on the same page, engaging support from across the school, and facilitating induction of new staff.

The background details in this chapter can help you to convince your school leadership team to commit time and support for work on the WSLP by detailing the importance and precarity of literacy. It gives a brief history of the WSLP and also raises the possibility that school library professionals could take a leadership role in this area. Finally, the chapter invites all readers to consider how the literacy policy communicates the values and priorities of their school.

The importance and precarity of literacy

Investment in school literacy planning and policy development can be seen as valuable as it can strengthen a school's literacy offerings and encourage a unified approach across year levels and subject areas.

The importance of individual literacy in the contemporary world cannot be overstated, and it is well known that young people need strong literacy skills in order to thrive in school and beyond. While as I explore further herein, literacy is much more than the traditional literacy skills of reading, writing, listening and speaking, these skills are all valuable, with perhaps the most research attention given to reading. As a result, we know that children with stronger reading skills not only achieve higher academic attainment in school. They also experience better health, are less likely to experience poverty or imprisonment, experience better vocational outcomes such as a higher likelihood of employment, and have a higher salary beyond school when compared with children who lack reading proficiency (McIntosh & Vignoles, 2001; Sanfilippo et al., 2020). In this way, building student literacy can play a key role in mitigating the uneven socio-economic prospects that young people experience.

The smaller body of research into the benefits of writing skills contends that writing is critical in fostering students' success in school and beyond (Graham, 2019), with the quality of writing instruction implicated in student attainment (Christensen, 2005; Malpique et al., 2020).

As a facilitator of ongoing academic attainment, the importance of strong literacy skills only grows as children move through the years of schooling, and success at secondary school level relates to a student's ability to understand and employ the specific language requirements of subjects (Fenwick, 2010). Students with low literacy skills will begin to experience disadvantage even earlier than that. By the age of eight, children spend up to half of the school day involved in writing tasks, so those who struggle with writing will be disadvantaged (Mackenzie & Hemmings, 2014).

Just as strong literacy skills confer advantage, adults who lack functional literacy skills can face significant limitations in their ability to perform crucial daily tasks that their more literate counterparts take for granted, such as the ability to read street signage and fill out forms (Ferguson & Merga, 2021). Furthermore, low reading comprehension can exclude adult Australians from understanding potentially life-saving written public health information produced by the government during the pandemic (Ferguson et al., 2021), and thus it is unsurprising that literacy can impact not only on quality of life, but also potentially life expectancy (Gilbert et al., 2018). While further research is needed, recent research has found a significant association between vaccine hesitancy and low health literacy in the context of the COVID-19 pandemic (Montagni et al., 2021), and given the relationship between traditional literacy skills such as reading comprehension and health literacy, this further highlights the dire need for strong literacy skills in current times.

Both students and adults will also need a wealth of additional literacies such as critical and information literacy in order to make sound decisions in a post-truth world. It can be contended that 'we live in an environment that is drenched in misinformation, "fake news", and propaganda not because of an unavoidable accident but because it has been created by political actors in pursuit of political and economic objectives' (Lewandowsky & van der Linden, 2021, p. 27). Given that internet users increasingly rely on social media as a key information source (Suarez-Lledo & Alvarez-Galvez, 2021), focusing sole attention on traditional literacies in schools could be a mistake with far reaching consequences.

In many schools throughout the world, literacy is closely measured at individual, state, national and international levels to report on student achievement as well as to determine literacy performance and the meeting of accountabilities. High-stakes testing is one of the most commonly discussed ways that this measurement is undertaken. This close scrutiny of school literacy performance maintains firm pressure on schools to constantly improve student literacy test performance. Australian children begin to participate in high-stakes testing from around Year 3, past the point where they are expected to demonstrate independent reading skills as part of the National Assessment Program – Literacy and Numeracy (NAPLAN; Merga, 2018). Of course, many students are being tested before they have strong independent reading skills in English, for a range of reasons. Such high-stakes testing begins even earlier in the UK, when children are typically only six or seven years old (Standards and Testing Agency, 2018).

Australian declines tracked in international testing theoretically keep public attention on the need for greater support for improvement in students' literacy skills. However, I have reservations about the use of scores from the Programme for International Student Assessment (PISA) as indicators of students' literacy achievement, particularly when used in isolation as definitive literacy indicators. The many deficiencies of PISA have been raised and then summarily ignored over time (see Zhao, 2020, for a detailed review). This does not change the fact that regardless of their legitimacy, PISA results are seen as key indicators, with accountability for nations raised accordingly as they strive to better their positioning on the Organisation for Economic Co-operation and Development (OECD) league table. Indeed, while criticism raised against PISA contends 'that the entire enterprise is problematic' and that 'its flawed view of education, flawed implementation, and flawed reasoning are sufficient to discredit its findings and recommendations', nonetheless, 'its influence continues to expand' (Zhao, 2020, p. 261). Furthermore, where politicians and policy makers draw on declines in students' literacy test scores to justify changes, these changes often are not particularly useful or research supported.

Significant concerns have also been raised about the NAPLAN testing in Australia (for example, Perelman, 2018), including misgivings around how transitioning to online writing assessment is taking place, 'without sufficiently accounting for how wealthier children with more access to keyboards may find their advantage compounded by such a shift, with the reverse experience for disadvantaged students' (Merga, Malpique et al., 2021, p. 1147). The building of student literacy is a core goal of education systems (Spichtig et al., 2022), so even without the impetus given by declines in national literacy performance, it is likely that literacy would still be on the agenda. High-stakes testing results keep attention on a narrowed conceptualisation of literacy.

While these tests clearly have significant limitations, they have given some insights into the spread of achievement within mainstream classrooms. Research findings from Victorian students in Australia contend that this spread of student literacy achievement more than doubles as students move through school, and by Year 9, the spread of attainment for students is 5.5 years, with the top 10 per cent of students around eight years more advanced than the bottom 10 per cent (Goss & Sonnemann, 2016). In results from international high-stakes testing in the PISA, Australia's performance in reading literacy has decreased over time (Thomson et al., 2019), with the number of low performers 'increasing by 7 percentage points between 2000 and 2018' (p. 32), and in recent times, Australia has seen declining scores in international high-stakes testing of writing (Thomas, 2020).

Concerning literacy scores on international testing are not just a problem for Australian students. There is also growing concern about students' writing development internationally (Graham & Rijlaarsdam, 2016), and there has been an average increase in the proportion of low literacy performers across OECD countries (Schleicher, 2019). Around 17 per cent of Australian teenagers could be considered a struggling literacy learner according to the results of the most recent NAPLAN tests, which found that 82.9 per cent of Year 9s tested at or above the national minimum standard for writing, 89.7 per cent for reading, 91.1 per cent for spelling, and 87.7 per cent for grammar and punctuation (Australian Curriculum, Assessment and Reporting Authority [ACARA], 2021a).

The times that we are currently living through also hold unique challenges for student literacy. It is predicted that the education interruptions caused by the pandemic will have a significant negative impact on students' literacy attainment (Kuhfeld et al., 2020), and may have 'intensified existing inequities pertaining to digital access, further impacting people already socially and financially disadvantaged' (Wise et al., 2022, p. 3). Research already suggests that there have been major adjustments to instruction that can impact on student learning, and unequal resourcing to support home learning where necessary, with remote instruction offering an inferior experience to face to face schooling for many students (Domina et al., 2021; Merga, Malpique et al., 2021; Reimers, 2022). In Chapter 4, I will address the importance of considering the flow-on impacts of the pandemic on literacy policy, but my main point here is that any declines or stagnations in student literacy that have resulted from education interruption during the pandemic will compound students' disadvantage as they move through the years of schooling, given that literacy skills seem to be influenced by a Matthew Effect, where the rich in literacy skills get richer and the poor get poorer over time (Stanovich, 2009).

With these expectations and pressures, the question of who is responsible for supporting student literacy gains within schools is an important one. Though it has been a catch phrase for years, we are increasingly moving toward an understanding that literacy needs to be a *whole-school responsibility*. This means that every educator within a school is responsible for fostering student literacy gains across the curriculum.

In Australia, literacy as a whole-school responsibility arguably made its biggest jump toward becoming an expectation in 2014. Since this time, to varying extents, all Australian states and territories of Australia have used the Australian Curriculum (AC) devised by the ACARA, and this curriculum clearly situates literacy as a general capability to be taught across subject areas and year levels. As noted previously:

> while the notion that literacy should be a priority outside of subject English is not new (Humphrey & Robinson, 2012), national recognition of its importance across all areas, mandated in a cohesive curriculum, was a significant development. As such, all teachers across all disciplines and years of schooling must take responsibility for building their students' capacities in both literacy as conceived more generally, and the specific literacy needs of their learning area(s). (Merga & Gardiner, 2018, p. 37)

However, just because this is an expectation does not mean that it is happening in all schools, and your WSLP can be a key step towards realising this goal beyond the aspirational. Any WSLP needs to materially position literacy as a whole-school responsibility, and not just play lip-service to this idea. Your policy is a chance to be responsive to the external accountabilities on schools in relation to literacy, while at the same time articulating your own context-responsive vision of literacy going forward, and I will provide more background on the origins of the WSLP next.

The whole-school literacy policy

Positioning literacy as a whole-school responsibility in a school policy is responsive to the need to give close consideration to the fostering of students' literacy skills and attitudes across learning areas. Curriculum positioning of literacy as a whole-school responsibility is not exclusive to Australia. For example, in Scotland it is deemed that the core skills of literacy (alongside numeracy and health and wellbeing) will underpin all learning, and there is an expectation that teachers be knowledgeable in planning for literacy learning in all subject areas (Campbell et al., 2020). Similarly, the AC positions literacy as a whole-school priority and a general capability, noting that 'success in any learning area depends on being able to use the significant, identifiable and distinctive literacy that is important for learning and representative of the content of that learning area' (ACARA, 2022c, para. 3). I explore these expectations further in Chapter 2, but it is important to establish here that literacy *beyond* the subject English is an Australian curricular expectation.

Some of the Australian policies I analysed for this book drew on descriptions of whole-school literacy from versions of the AC verbatim. For example, AU76 includes the following:

> While much of the explicit teaching of literacy occurs in the English learning area, literacy is strengthened, made specific and extended in other learning areas as students engage in a range of learning activities with significant literacy demands. Paying attention to the literacy demands of each learning area ensures that students' literacy development is strengthened so that it supports subject-based learning. This means that:
>
> - all teachers are responsible for teaching the subject-specific literacy of their learning area/s
> - all teachers need a clear understanding of the literacy demands and opportunities of their learning area/s.

This is a direct quote from AC version 8.4 (ACARA, n.d.-b, paras. 1–2), showing awareness of the importance of this curricular component, though no quotation marks are used, and no attribution is given. It is also important to note that within AU76 there is no further consideration of how this whole-school approach will actually be enacted within disciplines beyond English.

Even where school policies give a nod to this facet of the curriculum, implementation planning is needed to take this notion beyond the aspirational to the actual (and I also explore this issue further in Chapters 2 and 5). The expectation that literacy be a whole-school responsibility should be formalised and planned for in the creation of a WSLP that goes beyond simply including a cut and paste from the curriculum. Ideally, a WSLP is a document that articulates an expectation that literacy be developed across subjects and year levels, clearly articulating how this will be done, with associated responsibilities and goals assigned, and this book will support you to do this.

While further research is needed, there are certainly indications that school literacy policies may be associated with literacy improvements within schools (for example, Hill & Crevola, 1999; Ofsted, 2013). Hill and Crevola (1999) found that 'substantial, measurable improvements in early literacy outcomes can be achieved when schools adopt a whole-school, design approach' (p. 10). There is a paucity of large-scale studies that compare literacy outcomes for 'like' schools with or without WSLPs, and given the remarkable difference in policy quality and focus found across Australian schools (Merga, 2021a; Merga & Gardiner, 2018), findings on such studies could be questionable anyway. There is also a lack of research that situates literacy policy as an intervention with pre- and post-assessment to determine its efficacy on student achievement, controlling for the impact of other factors that can shape literacy attainment.

This means that while you are now reading a book on WSLPs, there is a lack of research-tested best-practice models in existence, so while I cite the best available research, there are significant gaps that really need to be addressed to support schools to design the most effective WSLPs. We have found that while 'schools may design and enact plans, agreements and policies to formalise the position of literacy as a whole-school priority and guide how this priority is to be enacted in daily practice', nonetheless, 'there is limited research literature exploring or detailing best practice in designing or enacting a whole-school approach to literacy in peer-reviewed research sources' (Merga & Gardiner, 2018, p. 38). However, I am not suggesting that we are ever likely to find the one perfect model, applicable in all contexts. As I mentioned in the introduction, the lack of a rigid one-size fits all model is likely to persist into the future, as schools and students are so different.

Just because there is a relative lack of research in this area does not mean that school literacy policies and whole-school approaches to literacy are new concepts. The movement toward a whole-school approach to literacy that underpins the need for school policy is the result of a reconceptualising of literacy from being conflated with subject English, to involving knowledge and skills that need to be enacted to learn and demonstrate learning across all subject areas.

A whole-school approach to literacy was partly a product of the Language Across the Curriculum (LAC) movement (Goodwyn & Findlay, 2003), and the slogan 'every teacher is a teacher of language' comes from this movement. This LAC movement originated in London in 1966 at the gathering of a group of secondary English teachers who were considering the role of verbal communication in English lessons, a conversation that expanded to encompass the role of language and literacy more broadly across the curriculum (Parker, 1985) . The LAC promoted a student-centred focus on language learning across all discipline areas (Alford & Windeyer, 2014), and the key aspects of this movement were:

- language has a central role in learning;
- students need to be actively engaged in meaning-making;
- teachers need to foster student-centred learning (as opposed to didactic approaches);
- active learning involves four key modes of language: reading, writing, speaking and listening, and
- students' own language should be the principal tool for working through curriculum content. (May & Wright, 2007, p. 371)

As per below, one of the seminal though controversial works of this period, the *Bullock Report – A Language for Life* (Bullock, 1975; see Beverton & Sewell, 2002 for detail on controversy) was still being quoted in a relatively recent UK school literacy policy (UK43) that was included in the body of policies analysed in this book, showing its enduring influence:

> > If standards of achievement are to be improved, all teachers will have to be helped to acquire a deeper understanding of language in education. This includes teachers of other subjects than English, since it is one of our contentions that every school should have an organised policy for language across the curriculum, establishing every teacher's involvement in language and reading development throughout the years of schooling.
>
> This advice still stands. These materials and the 'Whole School Literacy Policy' have been produced in order to assist all department areas in the development improved whole school literacy levels. (UK43)

Use of this quote in a relatively current WSLP also suggests that some schools are reflecting on the origins of the whole-school approach to literacy when devising their WSLP. Other relevant recommendations from this UK report (Bullock, 1975) included the requirement that schools have a policy for language across the curriculum.

The LAC movement spread in Canada and Australia during the 1970s, bolstered by further theory development and research, and by the late 1970s, it was fashionable for Australian schools to create language policies with cross-curriculum focus (Boomer, 1992). In the 1980s, the LAC movement further progressed as knowledge became 'increasingly constructed as the result of a complex interaction between individuals and their environments and textual exposure' (Parker, 1985, p. 173). The influence of the LAC movement in the UK was significant during the 1980s, and 'the introduction of coursework and speaking and listening into the curriculum' during that time 'can be seen as a direct result of LAC' (Goodwyn & Findlay, 2003, p. 22). There was subsequent resurgent interest in WSLPs in the late 1990s due to the 1997 UK *National Literacy Strategy* (Beverton & Sewell, 2002).

Clearly, the possibilities of the LAC have refused to fade away over time, and while successful *practical* implementation of whole-school approaches to literacy has never been realised across every Australian school, the sentiments of the LAC have continued to influence literacy planning and curriculum to some extent. As noted previously:

> the positioning of literacy as a general capability to be expressed as an underpinning facet of all disciplinary learning in the AC can be seen as part of this broader shift in understandings around language, disciplinary literacy and the value of literacy as a gateway skill for learning in other areas. (Merga & Gardiner, 2018, p. 38)

Today, just as the positioning of literacy as a whole-school priority varies depending on context, whether or not you are expected to have a WSLP or plan in place depends on where you are. Some nations or regions mandate the creation of school-level literacy policies in order to meet perceived educational needs.

For example, in Flanders, the Flemish Region of Belgium, schools are required by the government to implement school-based language education policies to enhance student proficiency in Dutch, and this mandate was responsive to a literacy performance gap between migrant and non-immigrant students that became visible through PISA results (Vanbuel, 2021). In this context, a school language policy is 'a document/policy compiled by the members of the school team (for example, teachers, the principal)', that 'identifies the linguistic needs of students, and provides school-based solutions that the entire team agrees upon' (Vanbuel, 2021, p. 4).

In the UK, 'literacy remains at the heart of the latest policy documents and Ofsted's framework for inspection (in both schools and ITE). These insist that every school needs a whole-school literacy policy which is implemented systematically across the curriculum' (National Literacy Trust, 2018, p. 4). The most recent version of the Ofsted (2022) *School Inspection Handbook* includes the expectation that inspectors will 'draw on information from the school's policy for teaching reading, phonics assessments, phonics screening check results and lesson visits' (p. 77).

This expectation of external scrutiny of school literacy policies may be one of the reasons why the UK documents are generally more comprehensive than their Australian counterparts, and consciousness of Ofsted scrutiny is apparent at policy level. For example, the first page of UK54 is heavily populated by direct quotations from Ofsted literature: specifically, the aforementioned Ofsted (2022) *School Inspection Handbook* and *Improving Literacy in Secondary Schools: A Shared Responsibility*, an Ofsted (2013) survey report. This should not be read as an endorsement of Ofsted and its school inspections; indeed, recent analysis by Hofer et al. (2020) found 'no strong indication for positive inspection effects on school processes as well as input and context variables', bringing into doubt 'if inspection in its current form considerably contributes to sustainable school improvement that goes beyond an alignment of teaching practices and content with performance standards' (p. 17). Rather, it should be read as a potential explanation of why WSLPs seem so common in the UK, and why they may typically be more detailed than their Australian counterparts, with accountability pressures related to inspections (Hofer et al., 2020) a potential causative factor.

In Australia, while there is no national mandate that all schools have literacy policies, expectations for school level literacy policies are articulated differently between the states and territories. Where there are state or territory expectations of school literacy policies, this is often part of a broader education reform agenda, such as in Australian public schools in Queensland in 2002 (Lynch, 2009). One of the four key themes of the *Literate Futures* project in Queensland was concerned with 'the involvement of teachers, parents and, potentially, other stakeholders in the development of a whole-school literacy plan', and this was the 'focus of the whole-school planning theme' (Freebody, 2007, p. 19).

In some areas and times, expectations have existed or were inferred, though it is more typical for expectations to remain unspecified. For example, in the context of Tasmania, the 2018 *Tasmanian Literacy and Numeracy Framework* involves a whole-school approach to literacy and numeracy improvement:

- The leadership team leads the development of whole school improvement planning using inquiry cycles.
- The Good Teaching Literacy and Numeracy guides form the basis of practice.
- All teachers are responsible for the literacy and numeracy growth of students within English and Mathematics and across the curriculum.
- Literacy and numeracy are prioritised in school planning.
- Teachers understand and use agreed models and practices to support literacy and numeracy learning. (Tasmanian Government, 2018, p. 1)

Clearly, all of the above could be at least in part facilitated through school literacy policies, though an expectation for them is not explicitly stated in this document. Perhaps the Tasmanian Government is reluctant to burden schools with additional expectations, however given the link between these dot points and a WSLP, at least suggesting that a WSLP be created could be prudent, particularly given the need to address the serious literacy issues facing the Tasmanian population. According to the most recent available data on adult literacy in Australia, only 52.8 per cent of Tasmanian males (Australian Bureau of Statistics [ABS], 2013, para. 17) have a functional literacy level sufficient 'to cope with a varied range of material found in daily life and at work' (ABS, 1997, para. 20). Tasmanian women have the lowest levels of functional literacy in all of Australia (46.9 per cent; ABS, 2013, para. 17), meaning that functionally literate females in this state are in the minority, though these 2012 data are now somewhat dated. When I was collecting Australian school literacy policies and plans for analysis between 2017 and 2021, as I describe in Chapter 3, I could not readily source a single one from Tasmania, suggesting that either these plans do not exist, are not publicly available, or go under completely different names. The possibilities of the WSLP may need to be explicitly introduced to the Tasmanian Department of Education and Tasmanian schools; perhaps it will be part of the upcoming Framework due for release in March 2023 (Tasmanian Government, 2022).

Currently, the Department of Education (DoE) in Western Australia (WA) also does not mandate creation of whole-school literacy planning documents. However, the DoEWA provides professional development for schools looking to develop and improve their whole-school literacy planning, supported by a framework produced by Fiona Walker and her former colleague Vicki Briggs that is not published for external views, but was kindly provided to me on request. I was familiar with their work in this area having discussed whole-school literacy planning with the DoEWA team previously. As such, there is a history of expectations for whole-school literacy planning even where mandates for such plans or policies were not in place.

Whole-school planning for literacy and numeracy was also expected of Australian schools involved in the 2013 *Improving Literacy and Numeracy National Partnership* (ILNNP). This was a project that involved substantial Australian Government funding 'to help states and territories improve the performance of students who are falling behind in literacy and/or numeracy, with a particular emphasis on students from disadvantaged backgrounds and Aboriginal and Torres Strait Islander students', designed to bridge the gap between the end of the Literacy and Numeracy National Partnership (LNNP) in December 2012 and implementation of school funding reforms in January 2014 (Department of Education, 2014, p. 4). It also focused on a whole-school approach to literacy and numeracy improvement, and made specific reference to the use of 'whole school plans'.

> This approach focused on assisting schools with the process of collaborative planning; the coordination of the provision of opportunities for professional learning for school leaders and specialist teachers; and in the setting of improvement targets. The approach was developed around the three components of the school improvement cycle:
>
> - assessing data and other school evidence related to student achievement and school operations – On-entry (Pre-primary – Year 2), NAPLAN data and school self-assessment via milestones and the Monitoring Review Framework (MRF) (Attachment 3).
> - planning to improve the standards of student achievement through whole school plans, setting challenging yet realistic improvement targets and selecting evidence-based strategies; and
> - acting to implement strategies. (Department of Education, 2014, p. 20)

As such, planning for whole-school literacy in Australia has a history of direct and indirect expectations, some of which I have briefly outlined here.

I will now shift the focus to more pragmatic considerations in relation to the WSLP, starting with the selection of a leader for the initiative.

Leading from the library

A WSLP needs a leader heading up an enthusiastic and cross-curricular literacy team. I go into additional detail about assembling the right literacy team in Chapter 5.

In the secondary school context, it might be automatic to assume that the leader of a WSLP initiative would be head of learning area (HoLA) for subject English. While the English HoLA is a literacy expert, they are not the only school-based educator who can take on this role, and I would like to broaden the pool of potential candidates. Those of you who are already familiar with my work will know that my research has focused on the influence of diverse social agents on young people's literacy engagement and skills. These agents include but not limited to primary teachers, secondary English teachers, teacher librarians and parents. I have not focused on just one or two influences, so when I consider the leadership of a WSLP, I do not automatically assume that the HoLA is always the right person for the job.

A WSLP initiative can be led by any capable, qualified and experienced literacy expert within a school, whether they be a classroom or library-based educator. While teacher librarians may typically be underutilised as a potential leader of WSLP development and revision initiatives, in this section I propose that teacher librarians could also be given consideration for the WSLP leadership role. I am not suggesting that they are the right person for the job in every case and context; every school is different, and every educator brings different strengths to such a role. I am however suggesting that when the decision is being made, that their potential not be overlooked for the following reasons.

Qualified. First, teacher librarians are up to the job as dual qualified library staff with expertise in *both* education and library and information sciences. Surprisingly, it is relatively common for teacher librarians to note that their classroom teachers and school leaders may be unaware of their status as qualified educators (as explored in Merga, 2019a). It is an unfortunate reality that teacher librarians might be one of the last educators within the school that comes to mind when seeking a literacy leader for an initiative such as this. Classroom teachers may not be aware that the teacher librarian is dual qualified, and teacher librarians may also feel that they lack recognition and support from the school leadership team (Merga, 2019b).

The Australian School Library Association (ASLA, 2018) details the required qualification expectations of teacher librarians in Australia.

> A teacher librarian holds recognised teaching qualifications and qualifications in librarianship, defined as eligibility for Associate (i.e. professional) membership for the Australian Library and Information Association [ALIA].
>
> Within the broad fields of education and librarianship, teacher librarians are uniquely qualified. This is valuable because curriculum knowledge and pedagogy are combined with library and information management knowledge and skills. (paras. 1–2)

As such, teacher librarians are qualified to lead whole-school literacy initiatives such as the development or revision of whole-school literacy policies.

Knowledgeable. Furthermore, teacher librarians are expected to have expertise in literacy. The ASLA (2014a) *Evidence Guide for Teacher Librarians in the Highly Accomplished Career Stage* (which is reflective of the Australian Institute for Teaching and School Leadership [AITSL] Professional Standards for Teachers) details these literacy educator expectations.

> Highly accomplished teacher librarians have a sound understanding of how children and young adults become independent readers and have a detailed knowledge of how to promote and foster reading. They have a comprehensive understanding of literacy and literature for children and young adults. They are active participants in the design, resourcing and implementation of literacy and numeracy programs within their schools. (p. 8)

Classroom-based English teachers are not the only qualified literacy experts within a secondary school. Leading a WSLP allows teacher librarians to display and further develop the literacy teaching knowledge and skills that are part of their role.

Beyond professionals standards, literacy education is a key facet of the role and professional expectations of Australian teacher librarians (Merga, 2020a). Research suggests that all teacher librarians are expected to be educators. Analysis of job description documents of Australian teacher librarians in Australia yields insight into a literacy educator role that encompasses a breadth of facets that are explicitly detailed in 90 per cent of these documents. These expectations included but were not limited to the following:

> Plan and facilitate contemporary student-centered reading programs. Link literary texts with curriculum units where appropriate. Collaborate with other teaching staff to promote literacy and literature. Provide training and information for staff and parents in reading, literacy and literature. Support teachers to enhance student literacy skills. Develop strategies to foster a love of reading and literature for leisure. Promote a diverse range of text types and themes, from varied cultural perspectives. Conduct book talks, make recommendations and guide students' recreational reading choices. Promote the benefits of regular reading for academic performance. Plan, promote and conduct displays and events to encourage reading. Promote literature to staff. Draw on a range of resources to make informed choices about collection development and publicize and promote new acquisitions. Possess an extensive knowledge of children's literature across a breadth of genres. Read junior and young adult fiction acquisitions. Foster and maintain a school culture that promotes reading and literature. Provide an environment conducive to reading. Model reading engagementand enjoyment. (Merga, 2020a, pp. 894–895)

My interviews with teacher librarians at thirty Australian schools also found that these literacy professionals provide support for struggling literacy learners. Teacher librarians' role in supporting struggling readers included:

> providing targeted support for struggling readers by identifying them, providing them with age and skill-appropriate materials, undertaking skill scaffolding supporting choice, supporting students with special needs, providing one-to-one matching, promoting access to books, enhancing the social position of books and reading, reading aloud to students, facilitating silent reading, and preparing students for high-stakes literacy testing. (Merga, 2019c, p. 156)

As such, teacher librarians can play a key role in supporting the diverse literacy needs of students with varying skill and engagement levels.

This multi-faceted literacy educator role has led to literacy benefits for students. As I have established in my extensive recent research on teacher librarians, 'librarians in schools can be highly effective literacy and reading advocates' (Merga, 2019a, p. v), and thus unsurprisingly, the research linking qualified school library staff and student literacy benefits is growing over time. Research suggests that there is a strong positive relationship between high-quality library programmes and student performance in literacy (as reviewed in Lance & Kachel, 2018). Recently, the influential International Literacy Association published a brief strongly in support of the literacy leadership role played by school library professionals within schools (Ness et al., 2022).

Cross-curricular. Teacher librarians exist outside the silos around subject areas that can often exist in secondary schools in particular (Merga, 2022a). They are also adept at communicating across subject areas within secondary schooling contexts, as they work with teachers from subject areas beyond English to support students' literacy and information literacy needs.

As I explore further in Chapter 6, it is imperative that the WSLP be easily read and understood by all teachers within a school, not just English subject or literacy experts. Given their experience communicating with educators across the curriculum, it is possible that teacher librarians may be less inclined to use complex technical terms in relation to literacy, and may be more familiar with disciplinary literacies from these other curricular areas than a secondary classroom English teacher or their English HoLA counterparts.

Furthermore, some past failures in efforts to implement a whole-school approach to literacy have been attributed to 'a justifiable anxiety that one will be told how to teach by members of the English Departments' or literacy advisors (Beverton & Sewell, 2002, p. 24). Where the initiative is led from the library, there is less likely to be a sense that one subject area within the school is being given precedence over the others, potentially alleviating anxieties of teachers of curriculum areas beyond English.

Collaborative. Furthermore, teacher librarians are typically highly collaborative, and used to working closely with other staff. They network across the school, with the ASLA and ALIA (2016) *Statement on Teacher Librarians in Australia* recognising that they 'lead and provide services and programs developed collaboratively with the principal, curriculum leaders, teaching colleagues, members of cultural, linguistic, indigenous and other unique groups in the school, including the professional development of staff' (pp. 1–2). Given that opportunities for collaboration and networking are associated with lower attrition rates of staff in schools (Borman & Dowling, 2008), good collaborators who can build these networks and strengthen these relationships can do much to support the morale of staff while leading a WSLP. Internationally, the professional learning of the school library professionals includes collaborative skills (Newsum, 2020).

In addition, the collaborative role of the teacher librarian is evident in analysis of the job description documents of teacher librarians, with 92.5 per cent of roles seeking a collaborative and team oriented staff member (Merga, 2020a). Recurring expectations for collaboration were as follows:

> Assist staff with resourcing, and plan units of work with colleagues. Incorporate information literacy and literacy skills into units of work. Collaborate to create and resource reading programs. Work as part of a team with other library staff. Model strong collaborative skills for the learning of colleagues. (Merga, 2020a, p. 894)

It is already a common part of their role to collaborate with teaching staff specifically to promote literacy learning (Merga, 2020a). As such, collaborating with staff across the school around the WSLP is not a stretch for the teacher librarian.

Leaders. Teacher librarians can be instructional leaders (Branch & Oberg, 2001), and as with other school library professionals, they are expected to show leadership and build their leadership skills. In this regard, school library professional leadership is both 'an expectation and a mandate', and internationally, 'professional librarian and technology organizations include leadership as a component of school library standards' (Newsum, 2020, p. 224). As contended by McPherson (2020):

> A teacher librarian needs to be a leader to develop a school library programme, ensure visibility in the school, and show the wider school community the importance of the library to the school by building awareness in the school community of the teacher librarian's role and the benefits of the school library. (p. 139)

Therefore, teacher librarians may typically show leadership across many facets of their role. For example, many teacher librarians already have extensive literacy leadership experience as heads of their libraries, and more than a third of their job description documents articulated leadership expectations (Merga, 2020a). They may also commonly provide leadership through facilitating professional development, where they may 'provide ongoing professional development for staff in areas such as literacy, information literacy and literature', and 'support the establishment of a vibrant professional learning community' (Merga, 2020a, p. 896). As such, even if it has not been well-recognised within their schools, teacher librarians typically have the leadership skills and experience to justify their leadership of a WSLP.

Final note. The WSLP does not need to be led from the library; any enthusiastic and knowledgeable educator can perform this role, however the teacher librarian should not be discounted from consideration. Given the importance of the policy and the inevitable investment of time and resourcing involved, taking the time to find the right leader for this initiative from a broad range of sufficiently qualified and experienced possibilities is prudent. I explore this further in Chapter 5.

Projecting the school's values and priorities

The final observation I want to make in this first chapter is that you need to be aware that the WSLP that you create tells a story about your school. It is going to project your school's values and priorities, and both inclusions and exclusions may come under scrutiny. This scrutiny may be from within the school or from the broader community, with parents potentially influenced by, or perhaps even resistant to how literacy is conceived and promoted in the policy. Ideally, schools should be producing policies that they are not afraid to share widely with all implicated or interested stakeholders, so such scrutiny and feedback will be part of the process of creation and revision of literacy policies, as I explore further in Chapter 5.

Scrutiny could even come from researchers such as myself (for example, Merga & Gardiner, 2018). While there are only a few researchers looking closely at WSLPs at this stage, recent research has used school-level literacy plans 'as a data source on school leaders' views on literacy education', as it is felt that such documents 'provide a glimpse into how the leadership teams who author them view literacy, how they view education in general, and how they approach educational leadership' (Thorbjørnsen, 2020, p. 1). As such, it is important to create a document that is truly reflective of how literacy is conceptualised and valued within your school, and which paints a realistic picture of its unique needs and students that you support.

I also feel that the WSLP is worth the perusal of future employees. Where a literacy instructive or supportive role is expected of a future employee, the WSLP could even be included as an attachment to consider during recruitment. We are experiencing teacher shortages in Australia (Wilson & Carabetta, 2022) and it may be desirable to facilitate early alignment between a school's values and expectations and those being brought to the role by a prospective employee. It could certainly save time and resourcing for both parties if the alignment is not there.

If I were a teacher weighing up employment prospects at two or more schools, I would definitely look at their WSLPs to get a feel for whether or not I would be a good fit within the schools. If the WSLPs were not available, this might be considered a red flag, perhaps suggesting that the school does not take a whole-school orientation toward literacy seriously enough to develop a policy to support its implementation. If the literacy policy communicated the impression that the school clearly had no confidence in their teacher's knowledge base, or no interest in supporting teachers to continue to develop their literacy support skills, that would also be a red flag for me. As I explore further in the subsequent chapter, what constitutes literacy and how literacy learning should be supported varies widely even between schools sharing a common curriculum, and with similar socio-economic and geographic contexts. As such, it would be prudent for job seekers who know that they will be expected to teach literacy as part of their role to refer to a school's literacy policy to confirm that the school's approach to literacy aligns with their own ethos.

Personally, I would want to work in a school culture that supported students' literacy engagement and did not primarily teach to the NAPLAN test, which is an unfortunate reality for some teachers (for example, Thompson, 2014). For instance, I would be looking for a school that created a supportive reading culture (Merga & Mason, 2019). While the job seeker cannot know the degree of fidelity a school has to their literacy policy (unless they have insider contacts), the WSLP makes it clear what (at least theoretically) a school does, and does not value.

CHAPTER 2

What is the 'literacy' in the policy?

Now that I have presented some brief background on the WSLP, the next step is to start to consider how literacy will be framed by the policy. There is a lack of available information on possible structures and components. Even in contexts where a school literacy or language policy is mandated, there may not be readily available guidance on what should be included and excluded to align with school needs, and how an underpinning understanding of literacy may shape these decisions.

For example, in Flanders, schools have considerable autonomy over the design and implementation of their literacy policy, and the Flemish Inspectorate only evaluates implementation during audits checks (Vanbuel, 2021). However, this level of autonomy, and lack of available clear guidelines for schools on policy implementation have obscured the true purpose of the literacy policy (Vanbuel, 2021). Arguably the most important aspect to decide on in relation to a literacy policy is what exactly this 'literacy' constitutes. Given the complex nature of literacy, this may be one of the hardest tasks.

The point of this chapter is to support you to decide how you can conceptualise literacy in your policy, and which 'literacies' you might include. Perhaps the one advantage of the breadth and complexity of literacy as a concept is that 'literacy, it seems, can mean whatever people want it to mean' (Roberts, 1995, p. 419). While this is not completely true in a schooling context where accountabilities and a need to meet curriculum requirements must surely guide how literacy is framed, there is certainly some degree of flexibility conferred by the somewhat nebulous, plural and constantly evolving nature of literacy.

In this chapter I provide a brief background to this literacy complexity and controversy, and the impact of high-stakes testing on how literacy is being framed both in schools and their policies. I then briefly touch on traditional literacy, multiliteracies and critical literacy, information and health literacies, disciplinary literacy, and literacies in other languages. It is crucial for me to clearly note here that these are *not* the only literacies that warrant consideration, however I just consider some key literacies to give you a feel for the breadth of the concept, and draw attention to some of the literacies beyond the traditional that you might wish to explicitly address in your policy. I also describe whole-school literacy here. Finally, I briefly consider some of the specific challenges to whole-school literacy, including those unique to primary or secondary schools.

Literacy complexity and controversy

No doubt you are well aware that defining and conceptualising literacy is very controversial. In 2019 (before the onset of the COVID-19 pandemic) I was at a literacy conference in Portugal, watching a German PhD student deliver a presentation on her project. A PhD student is a fledgling academic at the start of their career, absolutely vulnerable to the opinions of more established scholars, and while doctoral students need to be able to deal with constructive critical feedback (Merga et al., 2019), this feedback needs to be reasonable. In this case, the student was lambasted by a senior scholar for failing to provide a comprehensive definition of literacy as part of her conference presentation.

Actually, she *had* provided a definition that explained how she had conceptualised literacy for her purposes. It was sufficiently detailed given the restricted length of the oral presentation, and I pointed this out to the senior scholar to arrest his momentum in berating her. It was not the first time I have seen the complex nature of literacy be used as an opportunity to attack a vulnerable scholar without genuine justification.

Given the considerable attention given to literacy in the student's presentation, I suspected that the real problem was not that she had failed to define literacy. Rather, it was that what she privileged as literacy for her research purposes simply didn't align with what he privileged in his research. It is common for literacy researchers to seize onto an aspect of literacy, whether it be multi-literacies or writing or any of the other facets, and lose touch with the bigger picture of literacy as we become increasingly specialised in our knowledge around our area of focus. This is understandable, given that dealing with the full complexity of literacy is untenable.

As literacy is so complex a concept, literacy researchers tend to specialise in a subset of literacy, sometimes losing sight of how that fits into the bigger picture. Personally, I have spent a lot of my career exploring a range of these facets, including but not limited to reading engagement (Merga & Mat Roni, 2018a, 2018b), writing (Merga, Malpique et al., 2021), literacy environments (Merga, 2021b), literacy and wellbeing (Merga, 2022a), struggling literacy learners (Merga, 2020b), influence of technologies on reading frequency (Merga & Mat Roni, 2017), and initial teacher education and ongoing professional development in literacy instruction (Merga et al., 2020). However, I do not claim that these areas are the entirety of literacy; my own work barely scratches the surface. As literacy is so vast and complex a knowledge area, the reader will need to forgive the scanty sketch I provide in this chapter and do further reading beyond it if required.

It is also important to remember that the literacy priorities in prominence today will not be the same as those receiving the bulk of attention tomorrow. Some priorities are ephemeral and others are cyclical and bound to come back into fashion if we wait long enough. Education systems with the longest established traditions of teaching English literacy show an obsessive concern with literacy, and what is privileged and promoted as literacy has shifted continually (Goodwyn & Findlay, 2003).

However, some literacy controversies have persisted over time. Cambourne (2021) describes the 'Reading Wars' as having a lengthy history in reading education, beginning as competing pedagogical approaches, which were vigorously defended by advocates and attacked by adversaries within the professional community. These have the tendency to resurface regularly, gaining fuel from the media's fondness for polarising debate. These Reading

Wars have been long associated with vituperative arguments from academics and those with commercial interests in promoting a narrow understanding of reading. I feel that when it comes to determining 'what works' in the literacy space, theorists and academics have a lot to learn from teachers who are currently working in schools. More attention needs to be given to teachers' experiences and voices (Cambourne, 2021; Hammond & Macken-Horarik, 2001). We should spend more time listening to teachers, and less time fighting amongst ourselves.

This book is not going to weigh in on the controversies, though we should also consider the following:

- First, literacy is much more than reading. The debate itself between purely phonics, or a whole language approach to reading narrows the focus of literacy to reading, marginalising the attention given to the many other important literacy skills, such as writing skills.
- Second, most educators would argue that a wide range of literacy skills are important for developing students' literacy, so to devote time and energy to a distracting false dichotomy is pointless.
- Third, reading is actually a lot more complex than this argument would suggest, involving a diverse array of skills.

To this end, we can take a look at the complexity of skills underpinning the reading process according to Kim's (2020) direct and indirect effects model of reading (DIER):

> According to DIER, the reading process draws on a complex array of language, cognition, knowledge, and skills, including word reading, listening comprehension, text reading fluency, background knowledge (content knowledge and discourse knowledge [e.g., genre knowledge including text structure, register knowledge]), reading affect or socio-emotions (e.g., motivation, attitude, self-concept, self-efficacy, anxiety), higher order cognitions and regulation (e.g., inference, perspective taking, reasoning [see Note 1], monitoring, and setting goals), vocabulary, grammatical (morphosyntactic and syntactic) knowledge, phonology, morphology, orthography, and domain-general cognitions (e.g., working memory [see Baddeley, 2012] and attentional control [attentional control includes both cognitive or inhibitory control and behavioural control]. (pp. 469–470)

This model purely relates to the knowledge resources and capabilities that need to be fostered for students to read effectively, so it is not including all those needed for the development of the full breadth of functional literacy skills. This highlights how complex literacy is more broadly.

Similarly, in the domain of writing, skills in phonics form a key part of learning to spell, and they are part of a broader range of skills and strategies that students will need to draw on to spell effectively:

> It would be impossible to learn how to spell every word in the English language separately through memorisation, so children need to learn how the spelling system works and how to make generalisations, and this is best done when integrated with the teaching of phonological awareness, phonics, word study, vocabulary, writing and reading. It takes time to learn how to spell, but good spellers gradually develop automaticity or fluency in spelling high-frequency and known words, which allows them to dedicate their attention to the higher level cognitive processes involved in writing. (Oakley & Fellowes, 2016, p. 1)

As such, the skill of spelling is an excellent example of where a single approach to learning is unlikely to be successful. Phonics instruction alone will not teach children when to choose there, their or they're. However, phonics instruction remains an important part of learning to read and spell, as without the ability to recognise letter-sound correspondences, and how they may blend together, children will struggle when approaching unknown words as readers and writers (Konza, 2011). Even where researchers and policy makers stress the importance of single facets of literacy, schools typically know better than to exclusively privilege just one approach.

For example, primary school UK19 described how reading is taught within their school, including phonics as a valuable component along with other important facets, inclusive of, but not limited to engagement and creation of literature rich environments:

> 1. Whole Class Reading – develops listening skills, a love of literature and reading for pleasure. This is teacher led reading with children listening and responding to questions, predictions and vocabulary choices as appropriate to the level of the children. In all year groups this happens on a daily basis.

2. Shared Reading – immerses children in the pattern of story and features of text types. This happens in literacy sessions when introducing text and prior to writing. The teacher models as an expert reader and draws out the key elements of the content.
3. Guided Reading – targets children's reading skills. Guided reading takes place in small groups led by the teacher or teaching assistant using a levelled text. Progress records are completed at each reading session to monitor the pupil's progress (APP) and to set targets. A brief comment is also written in the child's Reading Record Book. Each group reads with an adult at least once a week.
4. Independent Reading – is encouraged in school and at home. Books are sent home with a Reading Record Book for communication with parents. Parents are encouraged to share in the development of reading skills by listening to their children read, discussing the story and to leave a comment in their children's Home School Book. Children are encouraged to choose books independently from the reading area to read or look at with their parents/carers. In KS1 particularly, children will work through a programme of sequenced books which will include books from the book banded reading schemes. However this may vary in order to encourage a wider range of reading material. In KS2 children may choose a library book to take home and these are changed regularly. Some children in KS2 continue through banded books to ensure the text is at the optimum level of difficulty and to further support their reading skills.
5. The Reading Environment – the print-rich environment encourages children to interact with displays, to follow instructions and signs, promoting functional language. Within the classroom the reading area is attractive and inviting, books are clearly accessible within labelled categories, by author or by genre. Themed displays are encouraged along with opportunities to write book reviews or make and use homemade books. Books are also displayed and promoted in the classroom and the whole learning environment of the school. Book and audio books along with story props and puppets enhance the reading environment.
6. Library – Children are timetabled to use the school library and to visit the local library at least once a year. Additional projects and events with [local] library are used to promote reading during the year.

7. Phonics – in Reception children continue to build on and develop early phonological awareness. Phonic knowledge is taught daily through 'Letters and Sounds'. This continues throughout KS1 and into KS2 where appropriate. Phonic knowledge is taught as a separate lesson although it is integrated into other lessons throughout the school day. Children are given a wide range of opportunities to use and apply their growing phonic knowledge and skills in reading and writing.

Schools are not typically buying into the dichotomous and limited view of reading and literacy promoted in the Reading Wars, instead drawing on a broader range of reading supportive strategies and resources.

Literacy and high-stakes testing

While schools' understanding of literacy does not seem to be as limited as that held by some researchers and policy makers, the reality is that many WSLPs show an understanding of literacy that is somewhat narrow. Schools often pursue a 'fixing model', whereby a literacy facet or skill is privileged for development over all others, and this is often related to scores on high-stakes testing. This approach is probably also responsive to a need to focus on a limited definition of literacy that is workable given its aforementioned complexity.

The influence of high-stakes testing on contemporary schooling is considerable, and it has a constraining impact on how literacy is taught within schools. In Australia as well as elsewhere, performance measurement has become a key means by which schools and educators are held accountable for the education they provide (Gewirtz et al., 2021). The force in action has been termed 'deliverology', and it can be defined as:

> a top-down approach to governance that focuses on improving public service delivery processes by identifying goals, and measures to assess progress towards them, that are designed to motivate and inform system improvements with respect to both excellence and equity and ensure that public money is well spent. (Gewirtz et al., 2021, pp. 504–505)

Deliverology in Australia is facilitated through NAPLAN testing, and research suggests that this testing regime strongly influences teaching practices. NAPLAN has resulted in a narrowing of teaching strategies and curriculum that is reflective of the facets of literacy that are assessed (Dulfer et al., 2012).

Recent research of te Riele et al. (2021) explored current literacy teaching in government schools, with a focus on understandings of literacy teaching and factors felt to influence it. They found that within schools, there was a tendency to collectively focus on a single element of literacy rather than a more balanced approach:

> Participants in three-quarters of the schools in our study reported having a single shared literacy focus, usually either reading or spelling. When asked how specific elements of literacy had become the priority, staff referred mainly to NAPLAN results or to 'results in general'. A teacher explained that on NAPLAN 'our spelling was down compared to our reading ... so we're going to have a whole school focus on spelling now' [PS_CT]. (te Riele et al. 2021, p. 4)

This was jarring for educators who had a curriculum-supported understanding of literacy skills as broader and interrelated, which makes the single focus approach seem risky indeed as the development of students' other literacy skills are comparatively neglected:

> This discrepancy was proving challenging for some staff, one specialist literacy teacher noting that:
>
> > When I first got here, there was a push for reading [to be] a major focus across the school ... but I've always seen literacy as very broad. You can't teach vocab without teaching reading, without teaching writing. It was very hard to ... grasp it at first – that it was just standing alone, reading – but I think that's the main focus in this school. [CS_LS] (te Riele et al. 2021, p. 4)

It is easier to demonstrate improvement if a single area of focus is seized upon and given whole-school attention. However, whether such a concentrated attention determined by high-stakes test scores is in the best interests of student literacy development is questionable.

It is also of concern that teaching to the test can divorce students from real world applications of reading comprehension. We do not learn reading comprehension skills for the sole purpose of sitting reading comprehension tests; we need these skills to communicate with, and understand a wide variety of texts we interact with in our daily lives. Some of these texts will impact on our ability to secure employment, interpret health information essential for our wellbeing, and make meaningful social connections with others. While direct instruction in reading comprehension can support improved equity performance, in isolation it does not lead to sustainable improvement as it lacks clear links to the world beyond school, and the diverse disciplinary purposes to which this knowledge can be applied (Luke et al., 2011). Therefore while teaching to the test does prepare students to sit tests (Reeves et al., 2018), literacy learning has to be much more than teaching to the test in order to serve our students.

Unfortunately, it appears that teaching to the test may consume a large share of student learning time, as noted in the context of the English learning area:

> At its most extreme, data from one participant indicated 20 weeks of English learning area time was handed over to NAPLAN practice in the lead-up to a NAPLAN sitting. If this scenario is repeated four times in a students' school life as preparation for NAPLAN in Years 3, 5, 7 and 9, that equates to 2 years of English learning area content and pedagogies being forsaken for NAPLAN practice. (Reeves et al., 2018, p. 30)

The potential negative impacts of dismissing or underestimating the amount of time dedicated to this narrowed curriculum are substantial, given the limited use of these very specific testing skills when compared with real world applications. While the Reeves et al. (2018) study is small, it is disturbing that a minority of teachers detailed practices aligning with ACARA's advice 'that "best preparation for NAPLAN is to continue focusing on teaching the curriculum"', with their data suggesting that the 'majority of the teacher respondents were caught in the fray, seemingly unable to enact ACARA's advice' (p. 30). Given the performance pressures on schools to improve literacy performance, and visibility of any gains and slumps through the publicly accessible data collected at school level, ACARA's advice is understandably difficult to follow. Indeed, as I explore with reference to real-world examples in the following chapter, it is not uncommon for the WSLPs of Australian schools to publish explicit literacy targets in their WSLP that are exclusively concerned with improving scores in high-stakes testing, with no literacy targets set for literacy areas beyond this narrowed scope.

It is also important to note that these approaches to the measurement of literacy skills do little to take into account individual students' unique backgrounds and circumstances (Lu & Cross, 2014). These tests highlight what knowledge and language is valued in Australia in ways that marginalise students who may lack proficiency in Standard Australian English. It is important to note that while Aboriginal and Torres Strait Islander students are over-represented as underperformers on high-stakes literacy assessments, these assessments are another way that Aboriginal and Torres Strait Islander dialects and 'non-standard and non-prestige English-lexified contact languages and English dialects' (Angelo, 2013, p. 92) are devalued within the Australian post-colonial schooling system. We know that 'language learning is not a neutral activity but is influenced by political, economic, and cultural factors working in the interests of power' (Fajardo, 2015, p. 44). Where Standard Australian English literacy proficiency is measured in Aboriginal and Torres Strait Islander students in high-stakes testing contexts, it is important to remember that these are students who have had this language imposed upon them; it is not the first language of their culture, or indeed their nation, given that Aboriginal and Torres Strait Islander peoples inhabited this continent for many thousands of years prior to colonisation and the introduction of the English language as lingua franca. I explore this point further in the subsequent section on literacies in diverse languages.

I will now move into discussion of some of the many kinds of literacies your policy might include. As aforementioned, this is not intended to be a fully comprehensive exposition; it would certainly require more than one chapter to cover the full expanse of literacies that offer benefit for students.

Traditional literacy

At the very least, schools are expected to develop their students' traditional literacy skills in reading, writing, speaking and listening. However, as aforementioned, NAPLAN testing does not even cover the breadth of traditional literacy, and this has led to narrowing of literacy skills taught. I found this reflected within the Australian WSLPs that I analysed, where there was often a lack of attention on key literacy skills such as handwriting.

Overall, in the Australian policies I analysed, there seemed to be the strongest focus on reading, followed by a lesser focus on writing, followed by limited focus on speaking and often no mention of listening skills at all, with some exceptions (for example, AU65). This can be reflective of mandated curricular priorities in some cases, but it is also likely to be reflective of the focus on high-stakes NAPLAN testing, which only measures a limited subset of reading and writing skills.

For example, here are the three improvement targets for English from one Strategic Plan:

- Close the gap between (Name) Primary School and the Australian Schools NAPLAN Reading mean score in Year 3, 5 and 7, 2011 to 2014 by at least equalling the Like Schools' mean.
- Close the gap between (Name) Primary School and the Australian Schools NAPLAN Writing, Grammar, Punctuation and Spelling mean score in Year 3, 5 and 7, 2011 to 2014 by at least equalling the Like Schools' mean.
- Improved levels of NAPLAN achievement through reduced percentages of students at or below National Minimum Standard for Reading, Writing, Grammar, Punctuation and Spelling, 2012 to 2014. (AU59)

As you can see, the targets for improvement are solely aligned with improvements in what is measured in high-stakes testing. There are no other targets listed.

Schools need to understandably be cautious when contemplating taking time dedicated to reading and writing skills that align with required accountabilities related to deliverology and reallocating it to neglected literacy domains of speaking and listening that do not attract the same degree of scrutiny. However, as I will touch on throughout the book, such a narrowed focus is problematic for students' acquisition of functional literacy skills for lifelong use both within schools and beyond.

Literacy skills are interrelated and paying scant attention to speaking and listening may limit student literacy learning. In addition to the benefits of building speaking and listening skills within their own domains, it is important to note that speaking and listening are also core skills that can enhance reading and writing. For example, as I have explored at length elsewhere (Merga, 2017a), listening to reading aloud can be extremely beneficial for building student vocabulary, enhancing skills and knowledge in reading and writing as well as listening and speaking. While explicit instruction in vocabulary occurs in schools, research suggests that most growth in vocabulary is the result of incidental exposure to language, with exposure to both oral and written language making a key contribution to this vocabulary development (Cunningham, 2005). Reading aloud to children when they are young 'sets in motion a causal spiral, in which print exposure stimulates language and reading development, which, in turn, stimulates the quantity of print exposure' (Mol & Bus, 2011, p. 285). As such, practices that involve listening such as reading aloud can influence literacy skills as well as reading engagement.

Despite these benefits of listening to language, research suggests that many children are not given regular exposure to such research supported practices as reading aloud in contemporary Australian schools (Ledger & Merga, 2018; Merga & Ledger, 2019) and homes (Merga & Ledger, 2018). Some policies did include strategies such as reading aloud. For example, AU70 defines this as follows:

> When an expert reader reads a difficult text to less experienced readers for the purposes of:
>
> - building a community of readers,
> - creating shared experiences amongst students,
> - exposing students to new ideas, story lines, characters and contexts,
> - exposing students to new vocabulary, text and language structures,
> - building a love of reading.

However, many policies made no mention of this strategy, or the relationship between the four traditional literacy areas.

Furthermore, students from diverse linguistic contexts may particularly need opportunities to build their speaking and listening skills in order to enhance their communicative competence. Anyone who has ever attempted to learn a new language will be well aware that having proficiency only in reading and writing, and lacking skills in speaking and listening, excludes you from a vast range of important interactions, from help-seeking behaviour in public, to making new friends. Therefore, while your policy may be understandably weighted toward what is being measured, some consideration of the importance of listening and speaking as valuable domains in their own right, and key supporting domains, should be given. Generally, UK policies paid far more attention to speaking and listening skill development, with UK1 describing support for students from diverse linguistic contexts:

> Pupils who are newly arrived, for whom English is not their home language, are given small group support with learning Standard English. Bilingual input from staff is given where appropriate. The appropriate ESB level is given to each child.
>
> English as an additional language: (refer to EAL Policy)
>
> 'Creating outstanding achievement for pupils with English as Additional Language'
>
> - High-quality support and a language enriched curriculum
>
> At (Name) Primary school, we ensure Newly Arrived children are assessed within two weeks and follow an effective induction programme. The teaching and learning within the school offers for all of our EAL learners a high-quality support programme and a language-rich curriculum. The school uses a range of strategies to enable all children to access the curriculum which allows children to make rapid progress. All teachers and support staff are regarded as teachers of English as an additional language and play an important role in supporting the children.

Given that many students in Australia also come from diverse linguistic contexts, Australia-based educators designing literacy policy could consider what is being more commonly done in the UK in order to create documents that can support these students.

Speaking and listening does garner some consideration in Australian documents. For instance, as part of the vision in their literacy plan, AU71 includes speaking and listening as a column of its own, alongside grammar and punctuation, reading and comprehension, writing and spelling, and visual literacy.

> Opportunities for speaking and listening are an integral part of our everyday lives. At (Name) State High School students are encouraged to participate in a variety of speaking and listening activities across all teaching and learning areas. Students will develop these skills further through:
>
> - Activities which value and encourage speaking and listening in their learning

- The acquisition of language and speaking skills which enables students to communicate ideas, ask questions and order thoughts
- Development which facilitates increased confidence in social and academic situations
- Communication which models our (School Name) Way and promotes positive relationships and improved self esteem

However, more schools need to take up the breadth of traditional literacy skills and knowledge and incorporate them in their literacy policies.

Multiliteracies and critical literacy

Beyond traditional literacy are many other literacies that can be included in literacy policies, and I will briefly outline why multiliteracies and related critical literacy warrant whole-school and cross-curricular consideration.

Multiliteracies have rich and extensive theoretical foundations which I will be unable to explore in expansive detail here (for a full overview, read the seminal work by Cazden et al., 1996). In brief, the New London Group describe embracing multiliteracies in response to the many communications forms and channels, with cultural and linguistic diversity warranting a far broader view of literacy than traditionally conveyed (Cazden et al., 1996). Multiliteracies normalise the use of widely diverse text types, overcoming 'the limitations of traditional approaches by emphasizing how negotiating the multiple linguistic and cultural differences in our society is central to the pragmatics of the working, civic, and private lives of students' (Cazden et al., 1996, p. 60). On a practical level, multiliteracies influence the kinds of texts students consume and produce, providing flexibility in students' capacity to represent themselves through making choices from a wide range of textual possibilities and modalities, 'whether verbally, through drama, through the lost arts of rhetoric and forensics, through graphic and plastic design, on-line or through traditional print' (Luke, 2003, p. 64).

As such, the definition of what constitutes a text to be consumed and created by students to support learning must be broad, and multimodal. This conceptualisation of text is supported by the AC. As previously mentioned, literacy sits as a general capability to be enacted across subject areas in the AC, and there is some consideration of multiliteracies within this curriculum in that there is explicit inclusion of multimodal texts in the description of literacy. It is noted that 'texts can be written, spoken or multimodal, and in print or digital/online forms', and 'multimodal texts combine language with other systems for communication, such as print text, visual images, soundtrack and spoken word as in film or computer presentation media' (ACARA, 2022d, p. 49).

One of a number of pedagogical approaches to multiliteracies is Critical Framing, the goal of which is to:

> help learners frame their growing mastery in practice (from Situated Practice) and conscious control and understanding (from Overt Instruction) in relation to the historical, social, cultural, political, ideological, and value-centered relations of particular systems of knowledge and social practice. Here, crucially, the teacher must help learners to denaturalize and make strange again what they have learned and mastered. (Cazden et al., 1996, p. 86)

The point of this approach is to give students the 'distance from what they have learned' so that they can 'constructively critique it, account for its cultural location, creatively extend and apply it, and eventually innovate on their own, within old communities and in new ones' (Cazden et al., 1996, p. 87). This ability to learn to identify our learned conditionings and understand the value-laden nature of text, to make visible that which has been rendered invisible, is also key to the multiliteracies approach.

In brief, for the purposes of a cross-curricular literacy policy, encouraging multi-modal approaches and texts, and raising student awareness of how forces such as selection of detail pervade both construction and reading of text, resonate with a multiliteracies approach. The New London group give an example of how multiliteracies viewpoints encourage critical awareness and can promote a more socially just way of interacting with the world, applying multiliteracies understanding in biology, demonstrating that this critical approach was never intended to be confined to the English subject area:

> ... imagine a student having to act and think like a biologist, and at the same time as a biologist with a vested interest in resisting the depiction of female things – from eggs to organisms – as 'passive'. The student now has to both juxtapose and

> integrate (not without tension) two different discourses, or social identities, or 'interests' that have historically been at odds. (Cazden et al., 1996, p. 87)

This critical questioning approach can be applied to many diverse curricular areas.

Critical literacy aligns with the multiliteracies approach in its recognition that literacy practices are also 'situated within specific social practices within specific discourses' (Gee, 2000, p. 189), and they reflect some of the underpinning principles of the AC. Using critical literacy approaches, students use a variety of modes of inscription 'to understand, analyze, critique, and transform their social, cultural, and political worlds', and critical literacy draws from diverse theoretical perspectives (Luke & Woods, 2009, p. 9). International critical literacy curricula focus on:

> social and cultural analysis and on how print and digital texts and discourses work, with a necessary and delicate tension between classroom emphasis on student and community cultural 'voice' and social analysis, as well as on explicit engagement with the technical features and social uses of written and multimodal texts. (Luke & Woods, 2009, p. 9)

This kind of critical consideration of issues around representation in relation to gender, race and class resonates with the AC General Capabilities beyond literacy. It also clearly relates to the general capabilities Critical and Creative Thinking; Personal and Social Capability; Ethical Understanding; and Intercultural Understanding (ACARA, 2022e). It can be contended that 'the "claimed" message of the Australian Curriculum is one that emphasises a functional approach to literacy, with less direct (but nevertheless clear) references to the importance of developing a critical perspective' (Lu & Cross, 2014, p. 44), however there is a greater overall emphasis on 'basic' literacy (p. 45), thus while critical literacy features in the AC, it is given relatively marginal consideration.

To briefly illustrate how critical literacy can be used in the classroom to trigger the transformation in viewpoints alluded to by the New London Group, we wrote an earlier paper that explores how social network comments can be drawn on as texts when investigating debates around racism in the Australian Football League (Merga & Booth, 2017).

We noted that:

> as educators, we often avoid directly challenging antisocial views in the classroom, particularly when powerful discourse communities support these views. However, developing a critical understanding of how texts can act to establish, maintain, and reenforce antisocial views can be undertaken as part of a widely accepted critical literacy approach to English. Using current texts with high accessibility and relevance cannot only enhance learner engagement through harnessing textual authenticity, it can also lead to perspective transformation that can have a lasting impact on an individual and broader social level. (Merga & Booth, 2017, p. 199)

Working closely with subject area experts within the school can help you to identify more than just key disciplinary literacies. It can also help you to identify where multiliteracies and critical literacies might be employed to support transformative learning experiences, and links can easily be made to other literacies, learning areas and general capabilities. For example, our analysis of the proliferation of racism in online discourse communities can also be used to build students' information literacy skills around online communication, and the implications of sharing hate speech in a public forum.

Information, digital and health literacies

Students need information literacy to critically source and appraise information in many diverse modes, and from many diverse sources. Simplistically, information literacy can be viewed as follows:

> Information Literacy encompasses knowledge of one's information concerns and needs, and the ability to identify, locate, evaluate, organize and effectively create, use and communicate information to address issues or problems at hand; it is a prerequisite for participating effectively in the Information Society, and is part of the basic human right of lifelong learning. (Information Literacy Meeting of Experts, 2003, p. 1)

It is easy to see how information literacy interrelates with diverse literacies. For example, without reading comprehension skills, it is virtually impossible to understand written information, and without critical literacy skills, it is difficult to evaluate the veracity of sources such as internet-sourced information about contentious issues. Therefore, like most literacies, it can be contended that information literacy can be viewed as 'a metaliteracy that supports multiple literacy types' (Mackey & Jacobson, 2011, p. 62). Where these information literacy skills are taught or drawn upon in a digital environment, *digital literacy* skills are needed to support information literacy skills. Acquiring, understanding and conveying information are cornerstones of information and related digital literacy, the utility of which continues to expand as young people are exposed to ever increasing sources of information, from traditional modes to emerging social media platforms such as TikTok (Merga, 2021e).

Digital literacy has recently become more visible in the AC. The General Capabilities underpinning the AC were subject to consultation and revised (ACARA, 2021b), with Digital Literacy replacing Information and Communication Technology (ICT) capability in version 9 of the AC (ACARA, 2022a). This was more than a shift in nomenclature, with the Digital Literacy capability having a greater emphasis on 'practicing digital safety and wellbeing' than the former ICT capability (ACARA, 2022a, para.1). However, ultimately information and related digital literacy remain a key facet of the Curriculum, expected to be applied and learned across the curriculum.

UK school literacy policies were far more likely than their Australian counterparts to include information literacy in the WSLP. For example, UK1 highlights the importance of library skills, specifying that 'all classes are timetabled to visit the school library on a weekly basis', and that in addition to using the library for reading and borrowing, 'children also access the library for research purposes, when appropriate, developing skills needed to locate and effectively use information'. Similarly, UK11 highlighted the importance of 'finding and using information':

> when listening to, watching and talking about texts with increasingly complex ideas, structures and specialist vocabulary. Children will develop critical literacy skills, including evaluating sources. They will show progression from finding and using information to recognising the difference between fact and opinion to identifying persuasive texts and evaluating sources independently.

This policy recognised the aforementioned relationship between critical literacy and information literacy.

It is also worth noting that in UK literacy policies, information literacy was often presented explicitly as a library skill, or in relation to libraries. This is unsurprising given that 'research and information literacy skills are taught and used in the library space, so that students can independently locate and effectively use information from a range of appropriate sources' (Merga, 2021a, p. 7). While Australian policies rarely made the connection between information literacy and school libraries, nonetheless, within Australian schools, teacher librarians are information literacy experts, and can work with the literacy leadership team to build information literacy across the curriculum, as it is part of their role to foster information literacy skills in both students and staff (ASLA, 2014b; Lance & Maniotes, 2020; Merga, 2020a).

Closely related to information and digital literacy is health literacy, and the fostering of student health literacy is crucial in the current environment. Health literacy relates to 'providing young people with access to current health information and teaching them the skills they need to individually source it and determine its credibility' (Merga, 2022a, p. 101). Given the pandemic conditions that we are living through, as well as the other health and wellbeing concerns that young people and their families may face, it should be considered an educational imperative, and given greater prominence in student learning.

In recent times, researchers have been able to quantify the impact of low health literacy on health outcomes. For example, research suggests that those with lower health literacy are more likely to be vaccine hesitant (Montagni et al., 2021), and 'the risk of being "anti-vaccination" or "hesitant", rather than "pro-vaccination", was higher among individuals reporting bad detection of fake news' (p. 695). To detect fake news and misinformation about health literacy, students will need a combination of critical, information, digital and health literacy skills which are supported by traditional literacy skills such as reading comprehension and vocabulary understandings.

Health literacy sits within the AC: Health and Physical Education as a key consideration:

> Health literacy is an individual's ability to access, understand, interrogate and use health information and services to promote their own and others' health and wellbeing. Consistent with a strengths-based approach, health literacy

> is a personal and community asset to be developed, evaluated, enriched and communicated. Health and Physical Education focuses on developing knowledge, understanding and skills related to 3 dimensions of health literacy – functional, interactive and critical. The curriculum promotes the progressive development of health literacy skills. First, students can access and apply information to respond to a health-related question. Then, they can independently apply new information to changing health circumstances. Finally, they can selectively access, analyse, evaluate and synthesise health information from a variety of sources to actively promote their own and others' health and wellbeing.
>
> When this proposition is considered as part of the planning process, classroom programs:
>
> - help students become critical consumers of health information, able to critique the reliability of published content from traditional and less-traditional sources
> - provide opportunities to access, critique and use relevant and meaningful health information and support networks
> - encourage students to apply their health knowledge and skills in a variety of complex and meaningful contexts. (ACARA, 2022f, para. 37)

As you can see from the ACARA excerpt, there is a real need for a diverse set of interrelated literacy skills to be able to have strong health literacy. Health literacy development is confined to the Health and Physical Education component of the curriculum, and therefore it is not situated as a general capability for consideration across the curriculum. However, given the growing need that young people be equipped with strong health literacy skills, ACARA may wish to rethink this positioning. Even if it is not expected to span the Curriculum, it is easy to see how students might consider activities such as the interpretation of health statistics and related quantitative data in mathematics, and health related issues are already covered in some science areas. Texts covered in the English classroom also provide opportunities to discuss health and wellbeing issues and how to source information to support students (for example, Eisenbach & Greathouse, 2020). Perhaps future revisions of the AC could at least meaningfully incorporate health literacy into the 'self-management' element of the Personal and Social capability (ACARA, 2022g).

Literacy learning beyond English: Content area and disciplinary literacy

This book has a clear focus on literacy as a whole-school responsibility, reflecting its positioning within the AC. Planning for building literacy in different subject areas supports students to develop their abilities to organise and express knowledge in textually appropriate ways that hold real world relevance (Fenwick, 2010):

> For example, students within the history classroom learn how to present logical and reasoned extended arguments, using primary and secondary sources to substantiate opinions and conclusions. Within science subjects, students learn how to write about inquiry approaches and use the technical, formal and impersonal language valued within the scientific community. A subject about work skills usually provides students with advice on letters of application and curriculum vitae. (p. 269)

Skills and knowledge in traditional literacies such as reading, writing, listening and speaking are valuable in other subject areas, as they will be the means by which learning is conveyed and demonstrated across the curriculum, though each subject area also has unique literacy needs (for example, Hand et al., 2003). While teaching to high-stakes tests might involve learning vocabulary out of context, vocabulary used in diverse subjects such as science and mathematics are the words needed to communicate within a subject area, making the learning more purposeful. Clearly, the application of discipline specific literacy skills can be essential for young people's ultimate success in their chosen professions beyond school.

It is important to distinguish between two key concepts at this stage, and I will be returning to these two concepts throughout the book. These are *content area literacy* and *disciplinary literacy*.

First, content area literacy has a focus on those transferrable literacy skills that are needed to comprehend and communicate across disciplines, such as reading comprehension used to understand texts in science or physical education. Content area literacy development can be supported across disciplines through *general strategy instruction*, involving the uncovering and teaching of 'strategies, routines, skills, language, and practices that can be applied universally to content area learning and are by definition generalizable to other domains' (Faggella-Luby et al., 2012, p. 69).

There is a wealth of research linking overarching, content area literacy skills with disciplinary attainment. For example, Sullivan and Brown (2015) found that childhood reading is substantially associated with progress in mathematics, and Neri and colleagues' (2021) recent research concludes:

> … our study complements previous research, demonstrating that students' reading comprehension and item word count as one linguistic feature affect science performance. Our results indicate that with increased reading comprehension and word count, students' science performance increases as well. Particularly good readers seem to be able to extract the substance of written text from more extensive tasks and utilize it to solve items correctly. To ensure that weak readers do not suffer from a lack of competence in one area in other domains, enhancing reading comprehension in schools should be seen as a task not only for language education but also for science education or even across all subjects. (pp. 56–57)

This argument for building content area literacy skills beyond the English subject area is more than a fashion; it is built on research findings that indicate that low content area literacy skills impede students' ability to demonstrate attainment across subject areas.

Consider this extract from a vignette by Weekes (2014) on how issues with literacy impact on student performance in subjects beyond English:

> It is my first day as a Music teacher in a secondary school in Sydney's Inner West. My Year 11 class is a diverse group from many cultural and linguistic backgrounds. None of my students have had individual lessons on an instrument. I ask them to write a review of a song by their favourite band and to refer to the concepts of music in their review. I am surprised when most students struggle with the task. Many seem unable to write a coherent sentence, even though they are 16 years old. I know that their writing has problems but I don't know how to fix it. (p. 1)

The lack of ability to 'write a coherent sentence' in the above vignette relates to issues with content area literacy, as they will influence student literacy performance across learning areas.

Second, disciplinary literacy is focused on students' use of literacy 'to engage in goals and practices that are *unique* [emphasis added] to each academic discipline' (International Literacy Association [ILA], 2017, p. 3).

Learning of disciplinary literacy involves discipline-specific strategies (Faggella-Luby et al., 2012), and this might include the teaching of skills and knowledge such as the protocols of scientific writing, or presenting mathematical formulae. Faggella-Luby and colleagues (2012) compare a discipline-specific strategy to a general strategy in the context of history to illustrate the difference between the two:

> ... a discipline-specific strategy might teach students historical reasoning to reconcile differences in primary sources; whereas a general strategy might teach students to compare and contrast differences between the two sources. An historical reasoning strategy would be appropriate only with social studies content; whereas the compare-contrast strategy could be generalized to any content. (p. 69)

Hannant and Jetnikoff (2017) describe a student struggling with these disciplinary literacy skills:

> Although Isaac knew he had to use scientific language, diagrams and a bibliography in his Science report, his assessment response indicated that he experienced difficulty applying this knowledge. Isaac critiqued his own report as lacking scientific language; he also included diagrams without referencing them in the written text and his bibliography was not formatted correctly. (p. 63)

The authors concluded that the students in this research would have benefited from 'an exemplar to enable them to conceptualise what the final product – a scientific report – looked like' (Hannant and Jetnikoff, 2017, p. 63). Given that just as the name suggests, disciplinary literacy is unique to a discipline, the provision of exemplars may be crucial to induct students into disciplinary norms, as it cannot be assumed that students have familiarity with these norms. Furthermore, other mechanisms such as the development of discipline specific vocabulary lists and citation style manuals may also be useful.

Both content area and disciplinary literacy skills are interrelated and important; across schooling years, students should build their literacy expertise while also acquiring disciplinary knowledge and skills (Billman & Pearson, 2013). Furthermore, students who lack functional literacy skills will be expected to struggle with disciplinary literacy skills, which is why researchers have contended that 'using discipline-specific strategy instruction exclusively as the pedagogical instrument to achieve college and career readiness for all adolescents is akin to building a house on sand' (Faggella-Luby et al., 2012, p. 81).

As such, in secondary learning contexts, it is not enough for teachers to be experts in their areas of disciplinary literacy – they must also be able to provide expert instruction and support in content area literacy through general strategy instruction in order to support their students' attainment within their learning area. Research suggests that instructors outside English employ strategies to support students' literacy learning, with teachers using 'their knowledge of their students' reading abilities for planning what their students would do before, during, and after each reading in order to meet reading purposes': 'for example, Mason, the AP U.S. History teacher, scaffolded analysis after each reading' (Townsend et al., 2022, p. 14).

Similarly, a teacher facilitating an environmental science lesson used a range of scaffolding strategies to support her students' reading comprehension and promote disciplinary literacy learning:

> When explaining her choice to focus on before reading activities, as well as read aloud to students and have them read collaboratively, Leah stated: 'many of them would've shut down really early in reading that article had I just given it to them and asked them to read it on their own.' Instead, to support students in meeting her reading purposes, she scaffolded students' understanding of important concepts before they read a text and then had them work together to analyse the text. (Townsend et al., 2022, p. 14)

Growth in traditional literacy skills should happen during disciplinary literacy learning; they are not exclusive experiences. For example, as reading skills such as reading comprehension improve, the capacity to read and comprehend complex disciplinary texts should also improve. However, from the lack of consideration of both disciplinary literacy and content area literacy in the WSLPs that I analysed, either not much is known in schools about how to promote literacy within and across the disciplines, or it is not considered important. I return to this consideration in Chapter 4.

In addition to articulating an expectation that literacy be taught in subjects beyond English, the AC further details what this can look like.

While I encourage you to familiarise yourself with the AC in this area, here are three examples from Health and Physical Education, Mathematics and Science.

Health and Physical Education

Health and Physical Education develops literacy by introducing specific terminology used in health and physical activity contexts. Students understand the language used to describe health status, products, information and services. They become critical consumers able to access, interpret, analyse, evaluate and challenge the changing knowledge base in health and physical education.

Students also learn to comprehend and compose texts related to Health and Physical Education. This includes learning to communicate effectively to different audiences for a variety of purposes. Students learn to express their ideas, evaluate others' viewpoints and express their emotions appropriately in different social and physical activity contexts.

Mathematics

Mathematics focuses on developing the skills and understandings necessary for students to communicate their thinking, reasoning and solutions to problems using appropriate mathematical language, notation and symbology within the context of given situations.

Students learn the vocabulary associated with mathematical concepts, skills, procedures and processes in number, algebra, space, measurement, statistics and probability. This vocabulary includes technical terminology and common words with specific meanings in a mathematical context. Students also learn that context affects the understanding of mathematical terminology, and that mathematical understandings are expressed using particular language forms and features. Students use their developing literacy skills to interpret and create a variety of texts that typically relate to mathematics. These range from calendars and maps to complex data displays and statistical reports. Students use literacy skills to understand and interpret contexts and problem situations, and formulate them into mathematical and statistical questions using the language features of mathematics and statistics. They pose and answer questions, discuss and collaborate in mathematical problem solving, and produce and justify solutions.

Science

In Science, students develop literacy capability as they explore and investigate their world. They comprehend and compose texts including those that give information; describe events and phenomena; recount experiments; present and evaluate data; give explanations; and present ideas, opinions and claims. They comprehend and compose multimodal texts such as charts, graphs, diagrams, pictures, maps, animations, models and visual media. Language structures and text structures are used to link information and ideas, give descriptions and explanations, formulate hypotheses and construct evidence-based arguments capable of expressing an informed position.

Scientific vocabulary is often technical and includes specific terms for concepts and features of the world, as well as terms that encapsulate an entire process in a single word, such as a 'photosynthesis'. Language is therefore essential in providing the link between the concept itself and student understanding, and assessing whether the student has understood the concept. (ACARA, 2022c, 'Key connections' section)

In addition to meeting curricular expectations and supporting students' academic achievement, there are pragmatic reasons for fostering certain diverse literacies that do more than secure success in the subject areas within school. As previously mentioned, fostering health literacy is crucial for promoting student wellbeing at all times, but particularly during the COVID-19 pandemic.

As the AC is broken up into subject areas, it can be easy to downplay the cross-curricular links and the importance of general capabilities such as Literacy, and to also side-line the overall purpose of school: to prepare students for their best outcomes beyond school. In the secondary school context, as you work with your subject area experts to build disciplinary literacies within the school, you will need to focus on the unique subject area needs (disciplinary literacy), but also the overarching student literacy needs for ongoing benefit will be valuable (content area literacy). As disciplinary experts enlighten you about what is needed in relation to literacy in their areas, you have the opportunity to further broaden their consideration of how the whole school can work more closely and strategically to support students' literacy learning, and to develop whole-school approaches to support content area literacy acquisition through a shared approach to general strategy instruction. In primary school, a single teacher will commonly be providing their class of students with education across most subject areas, so they will be able to consider both disciplinary literacy and content area literacy when planning and teaching, as long as they are given sufficient time, training and support to do so effectively.

Literacies in diverse languages

It is impossible to contend that language is neutral, and criticism of mandated school language is certainly not unique to the Australian context. For example, critique of the mandated school language policy in Flanders is focused on the 'strong yet implicit monolingual "language as structure" ideology that is inherent to the policy', which disadvantage multilingual students (Vanbuel, 2021, p. 4). A monolingual language focus in a literacy policy can likewise ignore the contextual relevance and importance of literacy in multiple languages, as well as often rich linguistic and literacy resources that students may bring with them from their diverse backgrounds.

The Australian Curriculum: English demonstrates a self-conscious balancing act in relation to linguistic privilege. The Australian Curriculum English focuses on Standard Australian English (SAE), with both AC version 8.4 and the more recent version 9 acknowledging that 'Australia is a linguistically and culturally diverse country' (ACARA, 2022c, para. 3).

However, it is SAE that is the privileged language, with both of the most recent versions of the AC noting that 'participation in many aspects of Australian life dependent on effective communication in Standard Australian English' (ACARA, n.d.-c, para. 2).

When we talk about literacy in the AC, we are typically talking about literacy relating to students' demonstration of knowledge and skills in SAE, unless referring to the Languages component of the curriculum. This is perhaps why the privileging of SAE is positioned in the previous ACARA quote alongside recognition of the contributions of Aboriginal and Torres Strait Islander peoples: it is clear that 'the idea of a standard language can be a form of gatekeeping to disadvantage certain groups' (Education Standards Authority NSW, n.d., para. 2), and the AC cannot ignore this. In Australia, we need to consider students' own linguistic and cultural identities and how they see themselves as SAE learners and avoid deficit language approaches which position SAE as superior and all other languages and dialects as inferior (for example, Steele, 2020), even though this is precisely what students' schooling experiences with the privileged SAE typically communicate.

While teaching Aboriginal and Torres Strait Islander students SAE is linked to their opportunities in post-colonial Australia, the languages of the original inhabitants of Australia are made peripheral in this focus, and non-standard varieties of English often used in students' home lives are not valued. For example, Eades (2015) describes switching between Standard Australian English and Aboriginal uses of English:

> The ability of some people to switch between two (or more) different cultures and different ways of communicating is also relevant to any discussion of the Aboriginal use of English. This bicultural (and bidialectal) ability is evident in the increasing number of Aboriginal professionals, including lawyers and magistrates, and can be likened to bilingual ability. Bicultural (and/or bilingual) ability develops from prolonged successful interaction with people from the second cultural (and/or linguistic) group. (p. 45)

As such, when considering literacies in languages other than SAE, educators need to consider other Englishes as well as what it means for students when the only language valued within their school environment is SAE. We need to value this bicultural and bidialectal ability and draw upon it to facilitate rich and relevant learning experiences for our students.

Despite the focus on SAE in the AC, in some rare instances, the literacy policies of some Australian schools already reflect the reality that literacy proficiency in local language is very important and culturally appropriate. For example, in its aims, AU19 included an aim 'to develop in children … competency in (local Australian indigenous language) reading and writing' with support from an Aboriginal Education Worker or member of the Aboriginal community, as well as listing supporting materials for learning this language. Regular daily reading requirements were to be in English or the local language, with both explicitly valued in the document.

Similarly, some UK documents also took a stance on the value of the languages other than English that students bring with them to their schools. For example, UK1 contends that 'all home languages are given status and treated with respect'. I suggest that greater consideration could be given to meaningfully reflecting the value of languages other than SAE, particularly when teaching students from diverse linguistic backgrounds. Not only will this enhance student learning, it can also play an important role in addressing pervasive social justice and educational equity issues.

Whole-school literacy and primary and secondary schools

Given what I have already covered in this book, it might seem obvious that any school with a WSLP should also have a whole-school approach to literacy learning, and supporting literacy learners.

However, many Australian school literacy policies do not situate literacy as a whole-school responsibility at all. I will cover this gap further in Chapter 4, but I have included this brief comment here so that whole-school literacy can sit in a chapter about conceptualisation of literacy, as it is clear that many schools are not seeing whole-school literacy as a priority, or not understanding what it is, though further research needs to be done to truly understand this phenomenon.

When considering which aspects of literacy will feature in a WSLP, different types of schools may face different barriers and have different priorities. First, a literacy policy cannot assume that all teachers are equally prepared to teach literacy, building content area literacy across the school. For example, primary school teachers who are early in their career may lack confidence and competence in supporting the acquisition of foundational literacy skills. In review of the small number of Australian studies that explore 'the extent of knowledge that preservice and/or newly graduated teachers have for the teaching of early reading skills', Meeks and colleagues (2020) concluded that:

> the findings from these studies would suggest that many primary preservice and/or newly graduated teachers have limited content and pedagogical knowledge for effective early/beginning reading instruction. In addition, self-ratings of preparedness to teach early reading ranged from not prepared to moderately prepared. (p. 162)

Pre-service and early career primary school teachers certainly do not hold a monopoly on feeling unprepared for supporting development of foundational literacy skills, and many secondary school teachers find themselves supporting students to acquire basic literacy skills. Our recent study of secondary English teachers found that two thirds of respondents did not feel that their initial teacher education prepared them to support struggling literacy learners in secondary English classrooms (Merga et al., 2020). As such, quality of initial teacher education to support foundational literacy skill development across learning areas could potentially be an issue at both primary and secondary school levels.

Furthermore, secondary schools may face unique barriers to positioning literacy as a whole-school priority. As aforementioned, secondary school teachers of subjects beyond English may be particularly resistant to having their teaching approaches directed by English educators, and they may feel that it undermines their 'professional security based on mastery of particular subject areas and familiar styles of presentation' (Beverton & Sewell, 2002, p. 24). May and Wright (2007) contended that a whole-school literacy approach may be particularly difficult to establish in the secondary context, given that 'the traditional organisation of secondary schools often specifically militates against whole school, cross-curricular initiatives such as these' (p. 370), which 'results in many subject-based teachers "resisting" the whole-school aims of a literacy policy, assuming these to be the "preserve" of the English department' (p. 374).

Any improvements in school literacy initiatives may also be harder to roll out in secondary contexts than in their primary counterparts, given that secondary schools are typically much larger, more complex, and labouring under greater bureaucratic constraints (May, 2007). Older research in the UK suggests that the vast majority of secondary teachers do agree that all secondary teachers have responsibility for improving students' literacy (Lewis & Wray, 1999); with appropriate support, it is likely that there is a will to boost student literacy across subject areas within the secondary schooling context. As I have already demonstrated in the previous section focusing on literacy learning beyond English, teachers in areas beyond English may already be drawing on literacy instructional strategies such as scaffolding to support content area and disciplinary literacy learning in their subject areas. However, this does not mean that teachers in areas beyond English are universally confident and well-versed in literacy instruction.

When rolling out a WSLP, the skills needed to support the enactment of this will must be considered, with professional development needs and the nature of the school needing to be taken into account, as I will explore further subsequently.

CHAPTER 3

Features of Australian school literacy policies

Now that we have considered which literacies we might want to include in the WSLP, the next stage is to identify how the policy might be structured in order to be of most use to its end users.

This is the largest chapter in the book as it draws upon analysis of Australian school literacy policies to illustrate key recurring features of these documents. I am going to keep my description of my collection of and analysis of these documents brief, as I assume that if you are reading this as a researcher with a desire to replicate my work or undertake a similar study, you will refer to my peer-reviewed journal articles in this area (Merga, 2021a; Merga & Gardiner, 2018). This book is for educators' practical use, so I provide a straightforward explanation rather than the more detailed expositions that are found in my journal articles. You can skip this section if you are not particularly interested in brief information on the collection and analysis of the informing WSLPs that appear in this book. The point of the activity was to collect a large body of whole-school literacy policy documents and analyse them in order to gain insights into possibilities for WSLP structures.

Collecting and analysing policies

First, I collected publicly available WSLPs or similar documents that were freely available online. To identify documents for inclusion, given the widely varying quality of these documents, I looked for documents that focused on how literacy was to be positioned and taught within a school.

Relevance and currency of these documents were important, so to be included, these documents needed to:

- be published or created since 2010
- be a recognisable document, not just be website content
- be focused on schooling years (not exclusively early childhood education)
- have a date of creation or publication, and
- be at least one page in length (Merga, 2021a).

In some cases I included documents with titles that did not directly relate to literacy where at least one full page of literacy policy or plan was part of this document. For example, a school improvement plan sometimes included a clearly recognisable literacy policy or plan as a key sub-component, often alongside other such documents, such as a numeracy policy, so this document could be included. To find the documents, I used a wide range of keywords and keyword combinations. I refer to these documents as WSLPs throughout for ease of discussion, even though many of the literacy planning and policy documents do not have a genuine whole-school focus.

Once a document met these criteria for inclusion they were added to the sample, and as mentioned in the introduction, I appointed an identifying code (AU1–83; UK1–83) so that even though any quotes from the documents would be anonymised, I kept a close record of where the material originated from to ensure that the original source could be located if required for auditing purposes.

While I primarily discuss Australian school literacy policies and plans here, as previously mentioned, I also collected and analysed the same number of UK documents and provide insights from these works, particularly in the following chapter. As previously noted, these are typically more comprehensive than their Australian counterparts and contain features that could be drawn upon by Australian educators to improve what is on offer here.

It is expected that the documents be different, given that they reflect different contexts, curriculum and statutory requirements. For example, as stated in literacy policy UK42:

> Statutory requirements for the teaching and learning of English are laid out in the National Curriculum in England: English Programmes of Study – Key Stages 1 and 2 (2013) and in the Communication and Language and Literacy sections of the Statutory Framework for the Early Years Foundation Stage (2017).

Despite these differences, there is much that can be drawn upon from UK documents when seeking to improve Australian offerings.

A total of eighty-three documents were collected from each context, and I needed a longer collection period to get eighty-three documents from Australia (November 2017 to August 2021) than the UK (September 2020 to August 2021), as there were far more documents available from the UK context. I stopped at eighty-three documents for each context as 'searches for Australian documents reached the point where no further documents could be sourced through the search mechanisms, with every applicable document included', and 'searches for UK document were curtailed at the same amount for the purpose of comparability of an equal number from both contexts' (Merga, 2021a, p. 4).

Table 1: Australian document characteristics

Characteristic	in sample (N= 83)
Year created	
2021	1
2020	10
2019	5
2018	13
2017	4
2016	10

Continued ⇛

Characteristic	in sample (N= 83)
Year created (continued)	
2015	11
2014	10
2013	6
2012	6
2011	4
2010	3
School location	
ACT	3
NSW	4
NT	2
QLD	8
SA	29
TAS	0
VIC	18
WA	19
School type	
Primary	63
Secondary	13
Combined	6
Special	1
Document length (pages)	
1-2	23
3-4	25
5-6	8
7-8	6
9-10	3
11+	18

*Document title**	
Literacy Policy	18
School Business, Site, Improvement or Operational Plan	12
Literacy or English Agreement	9
Literacy Plan	9
Whole-school Literacy or English Plan	7
Literacy and Numeracy Policy or Plan	7
Whole-school Literacy or English Agreement	6
English Policy	4
Continuity of Learning Plan: Literacy	2
Whole-school Literacy Policy	2
Literacy Programme	2
Literacy Unspecified	2
Language Policy	1
Whole-school Approach to Literacy	1
Literacy Curriculum Guide	1

*or very similar

Table 2: UK document characteristics

Characteristic	in sample (N= 83)
Year created	
2021	1
2020	8
2019	15
2018	15
2017	10
2016	14
2015	7
2014	5
2013	1
2012	4
2011	3

Continued ⇛

Characteristic	in sample (N= 83)
School location	
England	57
Northern Ireland	17
Scotland	5
Wales	4
*School type**	
Primary/Junior/Infant	44
Secondary	36
Combined	2
Special	1
Document length (pages)	
1-2	0
3-4	6
5-6	15
7-8	17
9-10	15
11+	30
*Document title***	
Literacy Policy	52
Whole-school Literacy Policy	9
Language and Literacy Policy	6
English Policy	4
English and Literacy Policy	4
Literacy and Numeracy Policy	3
English Language and Literacy Policy	1
Literacy Across Learning or the Curriculum Policy	2
Literacy and Oracy Policy	1
Literacy Strategy and Policy	1

*where UK schools were secondary apart from inclusion of Year 6 (e.g. UK63) they were classified as secondary rather than combined.
**or very similar

I then read through the documents many times to identify key recurring, common features that I could use to illustrate what a WSLP can look like. In this chapter I provide explanation of these recurring features, and the purpose of its inclusion is supported by examples taken from real but anonymised school literacy policies. This section of this chapter does not include every possible feature that can be included in a WSLP, just common features that I identified through my iterative analytical process which serve a key purpose.

These include the following fifteen features:

1. Information about the school
2. Definition of literacy
3. Rationale and goals
4. Explicit literacy targets
5. Implementation planning
6. Roles and responsibilities
7. Assessment of progress
8. Interventions, enrichment and accommodations for students with specific needs
9. Ongoing professional development for educators
10. Resources and the library
11. Links with policies
12. Defined roles for parents and external partners
13. Building capacity for parent-supported learning
14. Transition support
15. Policy evaluation and review planning

As you will see in the following chapter, following this fifteen point structure may not be enough to encompass all of the considerations needed for your school. I cover some of the noteworthy gaps in the subsequent chapter, and a comprehensive outline is presented in Chapter 6, with all of the key considerations rolled into a simple form for ease of use.

In this book, where quotes have been taken from freely available WSLPs sourced online, I do not intend to either highlight or target any particular school. To spotlight and judge individual schools is not my intention. Rather, excerpts are used so that readers can see something close to real world examples, and learn from the strengths and limitations of this material for ease of adaptation for their own purposes. Given how time and resource poor many schools are, it is simply not realistic to expect you to be able to create and write a WSLP without reference to what others have done.

To take steps toward preserving the anonymity of the schools associated with the freely available WSLP documents that I cite in this book, I have carefully edited the excerpts that I have included in order to remove any identifying details (such as unique names of schools, resources or programmes), and they may also be lightly edited where there were errors in spelling or grammar in the original work, or in order to condense content without distorting meaning. As such, excerpts are presented either verbatim or edited verbatim, with the original meaning preserved.

1. Information about the school

Context is a good place to start, and some WSLPs began with some useful background information about their school. These relevant details about their schools could be used to demonstrate that the plan is contextually and demographically responsive and engage stakeholders from the broader community. It can also be useful to revisit and revise this section as the school evolves over time to ensure that the WSLP continues to reflect its unique needs. Luke (2003) saw this information as key to the development of WSLPs, noting that they should include 'analyses of local community linguistic and cultural resources' as well as 'audits of teacher expertise and community involvement' (p. 78).

For example, a public primary school in Queensland (AU63) devotes the whole first page of the twenty-six in their document to describing their unique school profile. This profile includes historical and geographical information, information about school culture and priorities, and information about current performance on NAPLAN testing. It also details demographic information that may influence student learning needs:

> The local area has a growing population of around 7,237 people with high percentage of home ownership (78.2%). The median age of people has increased to 38 years. There are 2,071 families within (School) with the average number of children per family being 1.9. There is an increasing number of couple families without children (35%) and single parent households (11%). Some 30.6% of people are engaged with some form of self-education. 66.7% of the population identify as Australian born with a steady increase occurring in migrant heritage. There is a language other than English spoken in 17.2% of homes.
>
> Demand for student enrolment provides a fluctuating school enrolment of between 970 and 1,000 students catering for Preparatory to Year 6 primary education. An increasing 55% of students reside within the (School) State School Enrolment Catchment Area. The majority of out-of-catchment students reside to the north and north-west of (School) State School. 18% of enrolled students speak another language within the home. 1% of enrolled students identify as of Aboriginal or Torres Strait Islander heritage. 2% of enrolled students are formally identified as experiencing a low incidence (verified) disability and 25% of enrolled students are receiving professional learning support, extension or assistance. The student attendance rate is a steady 95% pa.
>
> Parents are equally well represented in all occupational groups from senior management and qualified professionals through trades and skilled office staff to machine operators, labourers and related workers. The school ICSEA (social-economic educational disadvantage rating) stands at 1,122 within Percentile 91 (1,000 considered to be average). The school continues to experience strong parent and community support. Parents expect, and staff aspire to deliver a more extensive educational programme than could be delivered, should this productive support not be afforded. There is a good working partnership and rapport between staff, parents and students resulting in high levels of 'goodwill' toward the school. Motivated and dedicated staff remain committed to (School) State School standards of excellence.
>
> In better managing student enrolment growth and trends, an Enrolment Management Policy applies. Enrolments from outside the School Enrolment Catchment Area are considered if Year Level enrolment capacity continues to exist. (AU63)

This snapshot gives a current overview of the school and its community.

Demographic details can focus on the specific literacy needs of the school community, and can also include comment on entry level literacy. For example, AU16 notes that 'there is a significant variation of literacy's [*sic*] brought to school with children ranging from very high literacy preparedness to those who have experienced limited literacy opportunities'. This information is obviously valuable due to its planning and practical implications, to meet the needs of students with widely varying preparedness upon entry into school.

Similarly, a school for children with hearing loss provides a clear context statement at the outset:

> (School) caters for primary, school-aged children with a significant hearing loss. The majority of students' hearing loss is in the severe to profound range requiring the students to use a combination of Cochlear Implants and Hearing Aids. All students utilise an FM , both at the (School), and also at their partner schools. All students who attend the (School) have a significant language delay. (School) has a philosophy of inclusion. Within the school, this means valuing all students, and involves adjusting curriculum, assessment practices, teaching styles to meet the needs of all students. Alongside this, the schools goal is to increase the students participation in regular mainstream education, and reduce their exclusion from the culture, curricula and communities of local schools. Students are enrolled into the (School) on the basis that they show the potential to be fully included into a regular school certainly by the end of Year 6 and earlier where possible. To this end, as a student's spoken language mastery increases, the students spend time accessing Primary School key learning areas at the partner school. Currently, we have seven Partner Schools, including DoE schools, Independent Schools, and Catholic Systemic School. (AU18)

While in the Australian context, these statements were most common in schools meeting the needs of students requiring significant teaching and learning adjustments, such statements are also valuable for *all* schools, and many WSLP did not include any contextual information about their school. Furthermore, a crucial component of information about the school could be details on historical and current literacy initiatives being enacted within the school (AU18). Not only is this useful as a baseline snapshot from which future interventions and change can build, it can also let current and future staff know what has been tried before (ideally with some indications on whether or not approaches have been successful and appropriate within the school community).

You can use this section to give a snapshot of the school's characteristics, including relevant geographic, socio-economic, cultural, linguistic and other factors that may influence literacy learning and student preparedness. You may also wish to note here any related details about historical and current literacy initiatives.

2. Definition of literacy

The previous chapter provides detail on how you might conceptualise literacy within your school in ways that are both responsive to curricular expectations and the real-world diverse needs of your students. Providing a clear working definition of literacy early in your policy helps educators within your school be on the same page across the school, providing an opportunity to establish shared understandings about literacy (Culican et al., 2001). Part of the role of the WSLP is to promote a shared professional language and agreed conceptualisations for talking about and teaching literacy, though this should not be read to infer that a single method or approach is desirable (Luke, 2003). While this level of agreement may be harder to achieve at a broader societal level, given the aforementioned complexities and controversies relating to literacy, it should be easier to manage at the micro level, within schools.

In addition, while a common language and framing of literacy is needed, policy need not be excessively didactic. There needs to be freedom for teachers to meet the needs of their classrooms, because just as schools will differ across a state, the needs of individual classrooms, and indeed, individual students, will differ within a school. Where WSLPs are too prescriptive, they run the risk of limiting the potential for teachers to meet their students' needs, as well as locking in approved practices and not permitting innovation and the incorporation of new approaches until the next iteration of the policy is created, which is clearly not desirable either.

No two teachers are likely to have an identical understanding of what literacy is, and being explicit about literacy is essential, particularly where teachers are still developing their literacy instructional skills. WSLPs can provide a working definition of literacy and/or language which does not assume that there is a static model of literacy that is tacit and understood throughout the school. Rather, the document makes how literacy is conceptualised within the school *explicit*. This conceptualisation is going to be responsive to myriad factors, so it is unlikely that a simple cut/paste from an externally produced curriculum document is going to be sufficient for your WSLP.

WSLPs typically broach the defining of literacy in very different ways. Some documents used a very simplistic and brief statement. For example, AU11 noted that 'literacy includes the capacity to read, understand and critically appreciate various forms of communication including spoken language, print, broadcast media and digital media' (AU11). Others used a more complex definition, often linked to the AC as in AU2.

Definition of literacy

Literacy is a wide ranging term which cannot be encapsulated fully within a single statement. Clearly, literacy is a means of cultivating each student's language capabilities to her potential. Through the development of literacy skills, we at (School) hope to provide our students with the:

- Ability to communicate through speaking, listening and writing.
- Ability to use the most appropriate text type when engaging in written work.
- Ability to receive, process and interpret information.
- Skills to locate information from a variety of sources, including written texts, visual texts, electronic media and information technology.
- Ability to follow oral instructions.
- Ability to express thoughts and ideas in a coherent and confident manner.
- Ability to function independently within a range of situations.
  Australian Curriculum, Assessment and Reporting Authority (ACARA), 2011

In the Australian Curriculum students become literate as they develop the skills to learn and communicate confidently at school and to become effective individuals, community members, workers and citizens.

These skills include listening, reading and viewing, writing, speaking and creating print, visual and digital materials accurately and purposefully within and across all learning areas. (AU2)

You will note that AU2 focuses on a very strongly AC linked conceptualisation of literacy.

Some UK policies provided definitions of literacy that considered how literacy might meet current and ongoing learner needs with consideration of social purposes of literacy given emphasis. For example, UK35 defined literacy as follows.

> Literacy is the ability to read and use written information and to write appropriately and legibly for a range of purposes, within a range of contexts and for a variety of audiences. It also involves the integration of speaking, listening and critical thinking with reading and writing and includes the knowledge that enables a speaker, writer and reader to recognise and use language appropriate to different social situations.
>
> In addition fundamental to [a] 21st century digital learner is the ability to read, understand and use information in multiple formats and platforms, including traditional print and on- screen material. Literacy permeates and develops learning in all areas of the curriculum, formal and informal, and all areas of social interaction and development. (UK35)

This policy also draws on literacy definitions from other sources around it framing of literacy, such as the PISA 2012 definition of literacy as 'understanding, using, reflecting on and engaging with written texts, in order to achieve one's goals, to develop one's knowledge and potential and to participate in society' (UK35).

You can also include facets of literacy covered in the previous chapter that are not foregrounded in the AC. There are somewhat limited examples of Australian WSLPs that do this, but there are UK examples that can be drawn upon. UK59 was one of the few literacy policies to mention critical literacy as part of their comprehensive imagining of literacy.

> **What is literacy?**
>
> **Reading/writing/speaking and listening:** to be literate is to be able to read, comprehend and react to ideas in texts and language. It means being able to use language to communicate both in spoken and written forms. Literacy is an intrinsic life skill. Functional literacy is not enough; reading ages must be aspirational and keeping pace with the demands of GCSE.

> **Non-verbal literacy:** to be literate is to be able to read and communicate in a variety of different kinds of languages and texts – visual as well as verbal.
>
> **Literacy as participation:** messages, ideas, feelings and identity are all mediated through language and texts of all kinds. To be literate is to be able to take control of these forms in order to participate as a member of society.
>
> **The four Cs of literacy**
>
> **Cultural literacy** – how language and texts operate in culture and society.
>
> **Critical literacy** – the ability to decode, interpret and respond to all kinds of language and text.
>
> **Creative literacy** – the ability to use language and texts of all kinds to communicate and organise ideas and feelings, to express identity and to influence others.
>
> **Competence** – the ability to control the forms, conventions and tools of communication including spelling, punctuation and grammar.

I should note that not all UK policies actually provided a working definition of literacy, however those that did often showed an attempt to frame literacy in thoughtful and comprehensive ways that extended beyond verbatim quoting of curriculum content.

In addition to an overarching conceptualisation of how literacy is being constructed and operationalised in the document, the literacy policy may also include sub-definitions of aspects of literacy. For example, as in AU8, it may explicitly define how the skill of writing is viewed within the policy.

> The act of writing consists of multiple processes, strategies and conventions that intertwine and overlap. Teachers need to be explicit in demonstrating and talking to students about what effective writers do. Teachers also need to provide opportunities for students to apply new understandings in their own authentic writing contexts. A successful writing program requires a daily block of time, with time allocated for explicit instruction on selected aspects of writing, time for students to write independently, and opportunities for students to receive and provide feedback.

It may also include definition of key terms, such as what constitutes a 'text' or 'literature' (AU13). Whether you opt for a brief and simplistic definition of literacy, or a more detailed exposition, you are setting important groundwork for how literacy is positioned within your school.

Some policies used the definition of literacy as an opportunity to emphasise conceptualisation of literacy as a whole-school responsibility, with a focus on content area literacy (as I have defined in the previous chapter). For example, UK43 defines literacy as follows:

> The term literacy covers speaking, listening, reading and writing.
>
> Students need to use these skills across the school in order to access the curriculum; therefore all staff share responsibility for literacy, whatever their subject, and must address together and as a priority the issues that literacy raises.
>
> Our regard for its importance extends from specific subject and support areas to cover the whole school environment, and also the vital communication between staff and students, and to our links with home, the local community and the world beyond.
>
> Relationships are at the heart of our ethos and these are built on effective communication.

As such, literacy is situated as a whole-school responsibility very early and unequivocally in this policy, which might be worth consideration.

Finally, I want to underscore that as with so many other areas within education, you have probably already noticed that the language employed when describing literacy is 'fuzzy', in that you may encounter numerous names and definitions of the same concept (Cuban, 1984). As long as the names and definitions you settle on can be easily substantiated, you have full power over the shared language you agree on for use in your WSLP.

> This section can be used to state how literacy is defined within your school and begin to detail a shared language that can be drawn upon to discuss literacy. This may also include consideration of how literacy supports students' attainment of social goals as well as academia and vocational. What is prioritised in this section can extend beyond what is foregrounded in the curriculum. This section can also situate literacy as a whole-school responsibility

3. Rationale and goals

The rationale of a WSLP goes beyond defining literacy. If the definition of literacy is concerned with *what* it is, the rationale and goals usually highlight why it is important. As such, they are also titled 'purpose' in some plans, or 'beliefs and understandings'.

The rationale and goals section often overlaps with the definition, and in some documents the definition and rationale and goals are intermingled rather than presented as separate. This is of course fine as long as the purpose of each section is considered, as these purposes are not the same; adequate depth of consideration needs to be given to articulating a rationale and goals in relation to the literacy needs of the school so that all stakeholders are striving toward the same outcomes. In this vein, Hill and Crevola (1999) argue that a key design element in the construction of a whole-school approach to literacy teaching is 'shared beliefs and understandings of both staff and students' (p. 6), including high expectations that all students can achieve significant literacy gains given adequate support and guidance from their teachers.

Like a definition, a rationale brings stakeholders to the same page, but in this case, we move beyond a definition by articulating the underpinning beliefs held within a school culture relating to literacy, and outlining shared overarching goals. For example, the rationale in AU23 is 'to improve the outcomes for students by adopting agreed whole school approaches to the teaching and learning of literacy'. Similarly, AU30 lists the following 'beliefs and understandings':

- High expectations and early intervention are essential.
- Literacy needs to be taught in context and across all key learning areas.
- Each day there should be 2 hours of explicit teaching devoted to literacy.
- Authentic assessment is a vital part of the teaching learning cycle and data needs to be collected to monitor and measure student progress.
- Staff should work together in collaborative teams to understand the data, determine targets and plan strategies, to ensure student outcomes are met.
- Teaching staff should work collaboratively together and share the resources and programs that are being utilised and implemented.
- The establishment of positive home-school relationships are essential.

- All classroom literacy programs should be informed by First Steps philosophies and beliefs, and strategies of automaticity.
- That students need to be catered for at the appropriate band level, not at year level, and that multi-level planning is essential.

It is interesting to see Hill and Crevola's (1999) high expectations articulated here. This section of a WSLP may also include an outline of the structure of the document with related guidance on how to read it. For example, AU8 states that 'the Literacy Plan is laid out in sections, each interacting with those that follow'. This prepares the reader to look for a development of ideas that are structurally interrelated.

The rationale will typically stress the importance of literacy being seen as a whole-school priority. AU50 uses the rationale to create an argument for the importance that literacy be viewed as such:

> At (Name of primary) School, literacy is everyone's business. High expectations in literacy lead to successful life pathways and maximise opportunities for students. We envision a future where every graduate student is literate. In order to achieve this, all learners are provided with effective learning opportunities based on their needs, abilities and aspirations. A consistent, coherent and focused whole school approach promotes and sustains high quality literacy teaching and learning.
>
> While much of the explicit teaching of literacy occurs in the English learning area, it is strengthened, made specific and extended in other learning areas as students engage in a range of learning activities with significant literacy demands. These literacy-rich situations are a part of learning in all curriculum areas. ACARA Literacy Continuum, v 6.0, 2013

AU50 also outlines an overall approach:

> Our site supports an effective whole school approach to literacy development and improvement through being:
>
> - Coherent – we all agree on how to support literacy improvement for all learners
> - Consistent – we use common language, approaches and methods to enact the agreement
> - Effective – we continuously review, refine and improve our approach in response to data and emerging needs.

While in some policies the rationale and goals were separated, it was common for there to be considerable overlap. As such, a rationale often incorporated a statement of general goals or aims to be achieved. These are still quite general at this stage of the WSLP, and are not linked to concrete targets as they are in the subsequent section. Goals are aspirational, but unlike the explicit literacy targets that are responsive to them, there is no associated accountability. Lewis and Wray (2001) note that one of the 'major factors of effective schools and effective teaching of literacy' is 'shared goals within the school/classroom community' (p. 47).

As a further example of how the goals can state what the policy seeks to achieve in very general terms, AU7 lists a range of goals as 'aims' that it values without explicit related targets:

Aims:

- To provide the opportunity for all children to develop their capacity and extend their ability in all language modes: listening, speaking, reading, viewing and writing.
- To encourage students to explore the meaning of texts, including multimodal, and to comprehend how meaning is conveyed.
- To provide a range of texts for listening to, reading and viewing, developing accuracy, fluency and an understanding of purpose.
- To create purposeful opportunities for students to speak, write, create and reflect on increasingly complex and sophisticated texts.
- To appreciate, enjoy and use the English language in all its variations.
- To develop an awareness of the English language's richness and power to evoke feelings, convey information, form ideas, facilitate interaction with others, entertain and persuade.
- To understand how Standard Australian English works in its spoken and written forms and, in combination with non-linguistic forms of communication, to create meaning.
- To develop interest and skills for inquiring into the aesthetic aspects of texts and develop an informed appreciation of literature.
- To use explicit teaching to enable students to become competent at critically reading, viewing, writing, speaking and listening.

- To empower students to apply their knowledge and skills in a variety of situations.
- To use an Inquiry approach when teaching English and to develop literacy strategies when teaching Inquiry skills.

The above is a good example of where literacy policies borrow closely from existing external documentation.

This brings me to a point about how to ethically incorporate existing external documentation into WSLPs. I am not going to suggest that it is necessary to re-invent the wheel and reword everything taken from external documents such as the AC, but without *correct attribution*, verbatim cut and paste of AC content is problematic. While including direct quotes or paraphrasing from existing external documentation is a good way to show alignment with curriculum expectations, attribution should be acknowledged to:

- avoid plagiarism;
- make visible that the literacy policy is reflective of current AC expectations, which may be lost without explicit attribution; and
- identify the version of the AC in the citation so that this material can be updated as the AC evolves through further versions.

This final point is due to the fact that AC is not a fixed document. I experienced the implications of this first hand while I was writing this book. AC v.9 came out (ACARA, 2022b) and 8.4 was superseded, sending me scrambling to update all of the applicable references in this book. New versions of the AC are released quite often (ACARA, n.d.-d), so where the AC is being quoted verbatim, a reference is needed so that the version being quoted can be updated in subsequent revisions of the WSLP.

You can use this section to articulate the shared understandings the school holds around the importance of literacy principles and policy, and the related general literacy goals of the school. You may also begin to make links between these beliefs and practice in a broad sense to foreshadow that these beliefs are not merely aspirational. Where you draw on content from other published sources, it is a good idea to provide correct attribution.

4. Explicit literacy targets

Following the previous sections that conceptualise literacy and articulate shared understandings and goals, concrete literacy targets were often set in literacy policies. Unlike the more aspirational content prior, these are explicitly defined literacy targets to be attained, with concrete performance-related changes to be observed. Hill and Crevola (1999) argue for the value of 'detailed information about the kinds of content to be covered and the stage of schooling in which the material is to be covered', as well as development of 'performance standards and associated targets' (p. 6).

In many cases, explicit literacy targets related exclusively to improved performance in high-stakes testing, and I have already discussed why this is problematic in Chapters 1 and 2, and in the following chapter I will discuss the importance of literacy measures beyond test achievement.

AU14 demonstrates how explicit literacy targets were often expressed in relation to NAPLAN testing. In relation to writing, 'targets identified from critical analysis of student performance data' were exclusively 'the NAPLAN data for 2008 Year 5 Cohort, in Year 7 (2010), will see Value Adding so that 85% (27 out of 32) of the cohort have made Moderate to Very High Progress in Reading according to Student Achievement Information System data' (AU14). Here, student performance and improvement in writing is entirely conflated with NAPLAN scores.

The level of self-consciousness and awareness of external accountability was often clear in these documents. In Australia, student performance on high-stakes NAPLAN testing is publicly accessible on the My School website, which allows for comparison with similar schools.

> In summary, the My School website provides profile information on each school's:
>
> - educational outcomes – including the results of NAPLAN testing and an indication of students' improvement as they progress through school, participation in vocational education and training courses and school-based apprenticeships and traineeships, senior secondary outcomes and, for jurisdictions with available data, post-school destinations
> - student population – including the level of socio-educational advantage (SEA) of the school student body, the proportion of students with an

Indigenous background, and students with a language background other than English, as well as student attendance rates
- capacity or capability – including the type of school, the year range, student and staff numbers, school financial information, and location. (ACARA, 2014, p. 2)

AU28 had the following three 'whole school literacy targets', and their reliance on My School data was clear:

- Increase the % of students in the stable cohort achieving high and very high progress in NAPLAN reading and writing as they progress from Year 3 (2015) to Year 5 (2017).
- In 2015, 2016 and 2017, maintain a positive comparison to schools with similar students (as reported on My School website) in relation to student gain Year 3 – 5 (stable cohort) in reading and writing
- In 2015, 2016 and 2017, maintain % of students achieving in the top 20% above that of All Australian Schools in Years 3 and 5 reading, writing, spelling and grammar and punctuation.

This document is not subtle; these targets are clearly all about comparison with other schools and external visibility of literacy attainment. However, it is concerning that the narrow conception of literacy covered in NAPLAN tests is the sole focus of whole-school literacy improvement in this document.

This fixation on explicit literacy targets solely associated with high-stakes testing performance is not surprising given that schools must be responsive to the compliance models of policy within which they exist (Luke, 2003). Recent research also suggests that improvements in performance against high-stakes test scores can be a source of great pride within schools.

> Many participants took great pride in their school improvement agenda being driven by data, evident in the prevalence of 'data walls' in the schools we visited. These data walls displayed mainly standardised test results for every student, as well as benchmarking results and teacher ratings (on a scale from A–E) against the Australian Curriculum [e.g. PS_AR16]. Frequently, the walls were referred to as valuable visualisation tools and participants reported that having a data wall had 'made a massive difference [because] you need to see the results to know what you're doing is working' [PS_CT]. (te Riele et al., 2021, p. 6)

The reality of contemporary schools is that their achievement is judged quantitatively in light of high-stakes test scores. As noted by Dulfer, Polesel and Rice (2012), in Australia, 'NAPLAN is viewed by the teaching profession as "high stakes testing"', and their research suggests that teachers perceive that 'NAPLAN performance may negatively impact on the public's view of their schools, their enrolments and students' movements' (p. 31). I could write another whole book on the issues and limitations of such testing regimes, but in the current lived reality, schools must nonetheless be responsive to them as they exert a powerful influence on them.

Thus while I challenge schools to diversify and present literacy targets that extend beyond NAPLAN score improvements, I do not suggest that schools must exclude them, as to do so would be to ignore the lived reality of contemporary schools. However, I also have concerns about how improvement as determined from quantitative data generated by high-stakes testing is being interpreted within schools, and the data literacy and analysis issues with deeming improvement across cohorts. If your school is going to be heavily reliant on NAPLAN improvements to demonstrate meeting of literacy targets, you will need to have at least one staff member with strong data literacy skills to avoid claiming improvement where there is high likelihood that improvement is an anomaly, or a result of other factors.

Of course, there are also numerous issues with determining student literacy levels based on a single test, which include but are not limited to the following considerations:

> - Due to time limits, tests can usually only test a small amount of the knowledge or skills in any given area. Test designers make choices about what to include, so the balance of items in a test may suit one student better than another. This can lead to a stronger result for the first student and a weaker result for the second;
> - Individual students vary in how they perform on a test on any given day due to different factors: how interested they are in doing the test, noise or distractions at the time of the test, or how well they slept;
> - Tests work well for measuring some knowledge and skills, but are not as good for measuring other things we may see as important goals of schooling, such as enthusiasm for learning or social skills.
>
> (Rice, 2014, para. 5)

Some schools are already writing school literacy policies that include targets related to literacy improvement beyond NAPLAN. For example, AU23 includes 'literacy aspirational targets' and explicitly contends that 'these targets are set at school based level and *not set against NAPLAN National Targets*' (my emphasis); 'they are based on research evidence and negotiation with staff, and will be monitored annually.' It is worth noting here that this is the policy of a very small (less than thirty students), very remote school with students from the early years of schooling to Year 10, with 100 per cent of students from Aboriginal and Torres Strait Islander backgrounds and no students identified as coming from English speaking backgrounds.

Instead of NAPLAN targets, this whole-school literacy plan (AU23) targets growth in areas such as 'sight words', where 'students will have measurable gains in word recognition', and 'letter names, sounds and phonemes', where 'students will have measurable gains in phonemic awareness'. Rather than focusing on improving high-stakes testing scores, this school is being responsive to the needs of its community, focusing instead on specific skills it has presumably highlighted are needed by its EAL/D students.

It is also important to note that literacy targets should not just be concerned with changes in student literacy scores and skills, and some policies considered a greater breadth of targets that will also be associated with improved student attainment, such as through the professional development of teachers. For example, AU27 set the target to 'build a literacy improvement cycle' by providing 'high quality professional development that supports teachers in producing improved literacy outcomes'. 'Strategies' included:

- PD to all staff including explicit criteria for identifying and supporting literacy development in all learning areas
- Literacy map developed in each curriculum area
- Inclusion and explicit addressing of the Australian Curriculum Literacy Capabilities in all curriculum areas
- Receive feedback from students from one class per semester
- Discussion of feedback with line manager. (AU27)

'Measurements or evidence' included:

- Inclusion of literacy components in unit plans in all curriculum areas
- 100% participation in some form of PD directly related to literacy

- Common use of language terminology across all learning areas
- Teachers supported by leaders and executive
- PLC formed drawing on teachers' specialist skills in Literacy
- Collect, analyse and incorporate feedback on students'
- Inclusion of literacy components in unit plans. (AU27)

The full form of the acronym PLC was not explained anywhere in the document, but I have still selected this example because it is a useful snapshot of how literacy related targets that are not directly concerned with student performance may be articulated and measured.

You can use this section of your WSLP to state explicitly defined literacy targets to be attained, and the concrete related changes to be observed so that the reader knows what success will look like. While it is understandable given accountabilities schools must grapple with that some of these targets may relate to improved performance in high-stakes testing, this should not be the extent of literacy targets. Literacy learning and high-stakes testing cannot be unproblematically conflated. Literacy targets and related changes may include targets that extend beyond student performance, to encompass facets such as educators' professional development

5. Implementation planning

Once you know what you want to achieve, the next step is to make clear how you will actually achieve it.

Implementation planning for literacy improvement in the documents I analysed provided clarity around how explicit literacy targets were going to be reached on a practical level. In the more detailed and lengthy policies, this was easily the largest component, and could run over several pages, but as you can probably guess just from looking at the typical length of Australian schools' literacy policies (Table 1), many did not include any implementation planning at all. As such, it is fair to say that these documents remain purely aspirational, and are unlikely to have much practical value.

Some documents included detailed planning for implementation, stating specific practices and procedures which could be linked to specific periods of the year. For example, a WSLP might state expected literacy activity implementation per term across the year and/or per skill (for example, AU14). In this vein, AU38 first identifies as Element 1 a need for 'effective and evidence-based teaching of literacy and numeracy'. For each of four literacy elements, it then includes a table of indicators and strategies, proposes a timeframe and delegates responsibility. One indicator is 'Teachers plan and implement a structured sequence of lessons focused on the explicit teaching of early writing skills'. The related strategies are 'K–2 teachers attend professional learning focused on early writing skills'. The time frame is March/April 2016, and the responsibilities are listed as K–2 teachers. As you can see, this planning is explicit, with responsible parties identified.

In other cases, implementation planning was less detailed, appearing as a list of practices or strategies to be employed without associated timeframes. For example, AU31 lists 'agreed high impact teaching practices':

> TARGETED DIFFERENTIATED TEACHING: Teachers will build on what each individual learner knows and use this information to identify and scaffolds future learning needs; use data to inform stretch and enrichment priorities; and track and monitor progress and efficacy using specific measures.
>
> LOGICAL AND INTENTIONAL SEQUENCING OF THE LEARNING: Teachers will: build connections in learning using well sequenced, manageable and intentional steps; vary the steps according to student needs; support students to develop their own learning goals; and support the gradual expansion of skills and knowledge in each child,
>
> CLEAR LEARNING INTENTIONS: Staff will develop and communicate clear learning intentions for a sequence of learning. Students will know what is expected. Goals are challenging and specific, success criteria are explicit and transparent and learners understand what success means. Students experience clear transitions between lessons and predictable routines.
>
> EXPLICIT TEACHING: Teaching practice will show students what they need to do to be successful and how through: clear learning intentions and instructions; correcting misconceptions; promoting cognitive strategies; teaching sequentially; and allowing practice time. Learning is scaffolded to support gradual release.

MULTIPLE APPROACHES: Teachers use a variety of approaches to instruction; use effective questioning, design multiple exposures and representations and include collaborative learning.

ONGOING FEEDBACK: Teachers will provide timely advice and actionable feedback for all students using differentiated methods. Feedback and assessment are formative and may include peer, small group and individual feedback.

This content from AU31 is so general that it falls short as implementation planning. While this WSLP states that the practices that are going to be used to achieve the desired literacy goals, there are no associated ways to deem if the practices are being successfully implement and/or if they are achieving the desired goals.

AU43 took a user friendly approach to implementation planning that will also be useful when the time comes for revision and evaluation of the document. It organises implementation planning under four headings, and it provides a brief explanation of how these headings are expected to function as per Table 3.

Table 3: Explanation of heading for implementation planning (AU43)

Priorities	Targets	Strategies	Evaluation Measures
These are the agreed 'big picture' results that have been identified through analysis of data	Agreed, specific targets that clearly indicate what improved outcomes learners will achieve or demonstrate	The key actions that staff – teachers, SSOs, leaders – commit to do, so that learners are supported at classroom level to achieve the Targets	The processes, data and timelines to be used to monitor / measure / evaluate progress towards achievement of the Targets (how will we know?)

This level of clarity is useful, and it will certainly support the efforts of their current and future literacy teams to maintain and extend implementation planning with a shared and clear understanding of how this should be devised.

You do not need to stick to four categories if you would prefer for your plan to be more detailed. One example from AU48's implementation planning is included in Table 4 to show how implementation planning might look when a greater breadth of elements are incorporated.

Table 4: Example of implementation planning (AU48)

Priority	Strategies/ Action	Timeline/ Responsibility	Evaluation Measures	Baseline Data Target/s	Student Outcome
Develop whole-school continuum maps around functional grammar and language features to be covered at each year level.	Develop whole-school continuum maps around functional grammar and language features to be covered at each year level.	Literacy Coordinator Literacy Team EAL/D Team	No whole-school agreements are currently in place for what is to be taught and covered at particular year levels in terms of functional grammar and language features.	Improved competence and understanding of all teachers.	Improved understanding of functional grammar and language features at each year level.

As such, there is no standard group of headings to use in implementation planning, though there seems to be a common overall approach.

It should be noted that the targets and student outcomes in the example from AU48 are still very general, and therefore perhaps not specific enough to meet the evaluation measures required by AU43. It is not clear how 'improved competence and understanding of all teachers' and 'improved understanding of functional grammar and language features at each year level', will be determined. In revisions of this policy, if a more specific set of targets is felt to be beneficial, changes could be made. As such, while at a glance AU48 seems to have more comprehensive planning, it falls short of the rigour of the evaluation measures proposed by AU43, which cover 'the processes, data and timelines to be used to monitor / measure / evaluate progress towards achievement of the Targets (how will we know?)'. I will address goal setting in further detail in Chapter 5 in relation to the value of setting clear short-, mid- and long-term goals.

In this section you can state explicit literacy related targets and specify how these will be reached on a practical level. There are many ways to do this, but you may wish to detail priorities, targets, strategies and evaluation measures to determine success of implementation. Evaluation measures should be sufficiently detailed to determine if progress has been made.

6. Roles and responsibilities

One of the key purposes of a WSLP is to promote responsibility for literacy across the school and its community. Roles and responsibilities were sometimes allocated in relation to implementation planning, as per the previous section, however overall literacy-related roles were often described in a separate section. It was interesting to note the differences in how responsibilities were allocated and described across the documents.

Documents often included explicit roles to be performed by internal stakeholders, and this was often included within implementation planning. Sometimes the responsible parties were literally named, such as in AU37: 'Reading Support Teacher, (name of teacher), to support whole-school approaches in Reading in Early Years'. However, it was more typical for responsibilities to be associated with roles rather than persons.

For example, AU22 includes clearly articulated roles for the Literacy Leader, Literacy Coaches, Curriculum Area Team (CAT) Leaders, classroom teachers, library staff, parents, and students. It states:

> The Literacy Leader is responsible for:
>
> - Managing the Literacy Program across the college
> - Developing a support program for students with additional literacy needs
> - Managing the collection, use and distribution of literacy data and developing protocols for the use of this data
> - Coordinating the analysis of literacy diagnostic assessment for the whole school, year, class and individual levels
> - Establishing and resourcing classrooms that support literacy
> - Supervising the Literacy Coaches program
> - Organising Professional Learning sessions for all staff to develop consistent literacy practices. (AU22)

As such, responsibilities could be absent, briefly noted, or noted in comprehensive detail.

UK policies provide exemplars of a far more comprehensive consideration of responsibilities of key stakeholders throughout the school than what is typically seen in Australian documents. For example, UK2 includes the following.

Roles and responsibilities

English Faculty: provide pupils with the knowledge, skills and understanding they need to read, write and speak and listen effectively. The English Faculty should support staff in developing their understanding of teaching the above skills explicitly.

Deputy Headteacher: Teaching and Learning to support departments in the implementation of strategies and empower departments to learn from each others' practice by sharing ideas.

Teachers across the curriculum: provide a consistent approach to pupils in the development of language, since speaking, listening, writing and reading are, to varying degrees, integral to all lessons. Teachers should also mark for literacy using (online testing of grammar and punctuation) guidance and federation codes and the yellow literacy stickers to promote high quality writing. They should also ensure that pupils have opportunities to draft and improve work, using the (name) writing model to develop written skills.

Teaching and Learning Action Research Groups: lead and give a high profile to literacy, and keep this focus at the forefront when discussing teaching pedagogy.

Parents: should encourage their children to read at home and write with accuracy.

Pupils: understand what strategies are being used in lessons, take increasing responsibility for recognising their own literacy needs, make improvements using such strategies and commit to reading widely outside of school. Pupils are to use green pen in all subjects to develop an understanding of common errors in their work and how to improve their literacy standards across all subjects regularly.

Governors: governors may meet with staff and pupils (for example, at link visits) and report progress and issues to the governing body.

SENCO: the SENCO (Special Educational Needs Coordinator) and Teaching Assistants will identify pupils and intervene, where necessary, with those pupils in need of additional literacy support.

Librarian: the library is pivotal in supporting the development of literacy and provides a secure supportive working environment to develop project or research work. The school librarian should:

- provide appropriate resources to support the curriculum

- provide appropriate resources to support homework and other curriculum tasks
- support staff in teaching pupils how to research independently from a range of sources
- help promote reading for pleasure across the school
- provide facilities and support to encourage independent reading and writing

> Each academic year, key staff will identify and implement new approaches through INSET and the wider CPD programme. (UK2)

As you can see, this is comprehensive coverage of expectations, and it may be useful for you to adopt a similar approach if you wish to allocate staff across the school as literacy instructors with specific and sometimes unique roles to play in improving students' literacy outcomes. This kind of detail promotes accountability and helps the different members of the team to understand the role that the other members may play, which may not otherwise be visible to them. For example, as previously mentioned, there may be poor understanding of the literacy educator role played by the school library professional by classroom teacher colleagues and leadership beyond the library (Merga, 2019a). Improving understanding of each other's roles may also potentially strengthen opportunities to collaborate to build student literacy.

To this end, some literacy policies stressed the importance of staff collaboration around literacy learning, and it is important that the work of support workers known as education, classroom or teaching assistants not be forgotten in your policy (for example, UK32). This inclusion of emphasis on collaboration can stress the importance of strong collaborative relationships between educators and their support staff, and it may also illustrate how the school works to upskill support staff in their literacy support capacity through a collaborative approach.

In general, UK policies were more likely to consider the role of support staff than Australian policies. For example, UK37 included a whole one-page appendix on the 'role of the classroom assistant'. This greater interest in support staff in WSLPs produced in the UK context may be reflective of the fact that more than a quarter of the education workforce in the UK are teaching assistants, though the numbers of education support staff are also increasing in Australia, the US, Greece and Finland (Chambers, 2015). Inclusion within WSLPs may be increasingly relevant as numbers of Australian support staff grow, and their influence on student learning may likewise be expected to burgeon.

Research suggests that once teaching assistants (TAs) are employed in Australian schools, typically to meet the needs of students requiring significant teaching and learning adjustments, 'they become frustrated and marginalised due to role confusion between TAs and teachers, their limited knowledge and skills, lack of clearly defined duty statements, lack of planning time with teachers and restricted access to appropriate training' (Butt, 2016, p. 64). Thus clarifying their role, and the role of others can do much to support these support staff to understand their workload expectations, and how these might intersect with, or support the roles of others within the school. The WSLP could also consider how to provide ongoing professional learning for these staff that aligns with the literacy needs of the school.

Finally, perhaps the most important reason to have a separate section on roles and responsibilities in a WSLP is the vital communication of expectations that teachers in secondary schools in subject areas beyond English have clear responsibilities related to the teaching of literacy. UK28 includes this:

- Take responsibility for the teaching and development of literacy skills, including reading, writing, communication and their application in the curriculum
- To ensure that students make progress relative to starting points in literacy
- To ensure that there is explicit teaching of spelling, punctuation and grammar in lessons in line with exam specifications to maximise achievement
- To ensure that teaching of all aspects of literacy is evident in planning and assessment
- To ensure that all staff in the curriculum area are marking work and giving feedback in accordance with the School Literacy Marking Policy
- To ensure that all staff in the curriculum area record the spelling of key words and record the correct spelling of previously incorrectly spelled words.

Clearly stating these responsibilities can raise staff awareness of their important role in student literacy learning, and literacy related instructional expectations.

> You may wish to clearly allocate roles and responsibilities in relation to implementation planning and literacy learning. In secondary schools, highlighting that the instruction of literacy is a whole-school responsibility beyond subject English can be articulated here. The importance of collaboration between educators and support staff can be stressed here.

7. Assessment of progress

Explanation of assessment of student progress in literacy is typically included in WSLPs. This is important because assessment is essential for monitoring progress towards meeting the defined targets featured in implementation planning, and for determining gaps that need to be addressed in current and future teaching and learning (Hill & Crevola, 1999).

For example, AU12 notes that 'we follow the School's Assessment Schedule, which is reviewed each year'. This includes the following:

- Ongoing teacher assessments including anecdotal notes, work samples, learning portfolios, Student Observation Survey, PM Benchmark reading (running records and comprehension), (name of brand) spelling tests, (name of brand) word lists, (name of brand) reading and spelling, writing assessments etc.
- Centralised testing e.g. (mandatory national high-stakes testing), (names of assessment products).
- Student reflection and self-assessment.
- Ensure that assessment and monitoring occurs continuously for all students and that
- Individual Learning Plans are created and regularly reviewed for all students.
- Use a variety of assessment and evaluation strategies. Refer to yearly assessment schedules.
- Identify and provide additional assistance to students who require it.

- Planning for additional assistance will be consistent and supportive of all students who have individual literacy learning needs.
- All students to have an Individual Learning Plan which is to be reviewed regularly. (AU12)

This policy avoids a narrow conceptualisation of assessment, instead using a comprehensive and diverse range of assessments to determine changes in student literacy achievement, though of course, states and territories will also need to be responsive to current and emerging assessment requirements that are externally mandated.

Ideally, you should include assessment types that are educative, and that extend beyond formal assessment to include such items as student reflection and self-assessment as in AU12. While student self-assessment can encompass a very broad range of practices, generally self-assessment is viewed as students' monitoring their own processes and products to make changes that enhance learning and performance, and there is a positive relationship between self-assessment and student learning (Andrade, 2019). Ideally, as I also explore in the following chapter, assessment of progress should not be reduced to quantitative scores on tests. Assessment types such as student self-assessment have the potential to offer meaningful educational gains. In contrast, student completion of assessments such as NAPLAN are not typically seen to improve student learning (Thompson, 2014).

Other policies provided detailed information on assessing specific skills. For example, AU32 included comprehensive planning for the assessment of spelling:

> LEVEL A SCREEN TEST
> Foundation students are screen tested once Level A is completed within a 10 week program. The results are graphed and parent teacher interviews are held to discuss the results. These results indicate whether the child is ready for formal learning by assessing, visual skills, auditory skills, gross motor skills, fine motor skills and laterality & dominance.
>
> PLACEMENT TESTING
> The test is used to place students into the program at their approximate achievement level. The test is arranged in order from the most difficult (Level T) to the easiest level (Level C). Testing should begin at the point that the tester believes

> is beyond the ability of the best achieving student in the class/group. Testing is completed backward working from unknown to known to ensure the student finishes the test having achieved rather than failed. As each student completes two consecutive groups (rows) correctly collect the student's paper and record the level reached. Then allow them to read silently. The tests will have been collected in achievement order, chose four lowest common denominator points from the tests to group the students into four manageable teaching groups. It is advisable to retest and reassign groups after approximately 3–6 months. (AU32)

If you want to include this kind of detail, it could also be incorporated as an appendix rather than the body of the literacy policy.

> In this section you can include explanation of how student progress in literacy will be assessed, ideally including a range of assessment activities, as I explore further in the next chapter.

8. Interventions, enrichment and accommodations for students with specific needs

Documents should include accommodations and interventions for students with specific needs, and this is needed because even with the best instruction, many students will need extra time, resourcing and support to reach functional literacy (Hill & Crevola, 1999). In many Australian documents, while struggling students are mentioned, there is little consideration of specific issues impeding literacy, and how they are to be addressed at a whole-school level.

For example, in relation to intervention, AU15 notes that 'students whose literacy development does not keep pace with site / regional / state targets become part of the school's intervention program and may also be referred for further assessment'. Similarly, under the heading 'Identification, Planning and Intervention', AU17 notes:

> … quality educational programs, including enrichment and support, will be provided to meet the needs of all students including:
>
> - Students at Educational Risk, inclusive of gifted and talented students
> - Students with learning difficulties
> - Students with ESL and/or indigenous backgrounds.

The document then details 'targeted programs to support learning' for these students, as well as providing information about students requiring academic extension and enrichment in literacy. It also notes that in relation to Students at Educational Risk, 'guidelines are followed to ensure transparent and effective processes are implemented to identify, support and monitor students at risk of not making expected progress in literacy', and 'collaborative team processes are developed to coordinate support personnel', with relevant personnel positions explicitly listed.

A few policies provided more comprehensive insight into school-based intervention and enrichment, such as the strategies listed below in effect at AU67:

- Personalised Learning & Intervention Program (PLIP Reading): This involves individual support for 1/2 hour each day with a trained teacher aide developing skills in reading, fluency and comprehension.
- PLIP Writing: Targeted students work in small groups with trained teachers focussing on developing effective writing strategies, spelling, vocabulary and editing skills.
- Learning Support: Our Learning Support Teacher works as an extension to classrooms providing support to student identified as being at risk.
- Lunchtime programs: These 'clubs' cater for students who demonstrate a talent in areas such as, dance, chess, visual art, sport and media.
- Homework Centre: This program provides support for our indigenous students through assistance with homework and related topics.
- Gifted and Talented Committee: These members are currently working towards developing a plan of action to enhance teachers' knowledge and understanding in effectively identifying and catering for the needs of these students. This involves enrichment programs both in and out of the classroom setting.

Some UK policies provided considerably more detail on literacy intervention programmes. For example, UK38 includes two full pages and lists eight interventions. I am not endorsing any particular approaches to intervention here, but here is an example of where a policy has detailed how a specific programme will be rolled out within the school.

> (name of programme) (year levels where implemented)
>
> This is a 10 week programme carried out in terms 1, 2 and 3. It involves 2 pupils at a time, who are of average ability and need reinforcement in reading. The (name of reading test) is administered at the beginning and at the end of the programme to monitor progress made. It is administered by a classroom assistant/s who have been trained in (name of programme). (UK38)

As you can see, this included:

- the name of the programme
- year levels where it may be implemented
- brief summary of the nature of the programme and what is involved
- mechanism for assessment of success of the programme
- responsible parties within the school for implementing the programme.

If you are intending to include interventions in your policy, providing this basic information could be useful, rather than just mentioning the intervention, though I would suggest also including brief comment on how students will be identified for participation in the programme.

Australian WSLPs are particularly light on how they will identify struggling literacy learners, but this is valuable information that should be included. What was really lacking from these policies in general was a *whole-school* approach to meeting the needs of struggling students, which was not actually surprising given the findings from my aforementioned recent research into how secondary schools support struggling literacy learners. This found that leadership support for the positioning of literacy as a whole-school responsibility was perceived to be lacking in many schools (Merga, Mat Roni & Malpique, 2021a). To help you to fill this gap, in the next chapter I address issues with screening and identifying struggling students, and interventions.

> In this section you can include accommodations and interventions for students with specific needs, including strategies for early intervention whether you are in a primary or secondary schooling context. Content on intervention programmes can include the name of the programme,

year levels where it may be implemented, a summary of the nature of the programme and what is involved, mechanisms of assessment of success of the programme, responsible parties within the school for implementing the programme, and how students will be identified for inclusion in the programme.

9. Ongoing professional development for educators

A recurring feature of WSLPs was an articulated expectation of ongoing professional development for staff to attend as individuals or teams (Hill & Crevola, 1999). This is important as even experienced teachers may need more training to support evolving student literacy needs (Merga et al., 2020).

Australian WSLPs sometimes reflected the Australian Professional Standards for Teachers (APST; AITSL, 2011) in their discussion of professional learning. For example, AU1 aligns their Primary School English Operational Plan with the APSTs, and in relation to Standard 6 (Engage in professional learning) the document records the following desired outcomes for professional learning through 'Curriculum Leader coaching and in-class support' and an outcome to 'Build capacity in staff through Professional Learning Communities, coaching conversations and peer observations'.

Similarly, AU81 seeks to 'build the capacity of our staff' with a 'Focus on: Professional Knowledge; Professional Practice; Professional Engagement'. This is again aligned with the APSTs, though with breadth beyond Standard 6, with the document expounding the school's belief that 'Staff have the knowledge and skills to assess their students' literacy needs and plan, explicitly teach, and review their strategies. – Reference APST: Standards 1, 2, 3, 5 and 6'. Related implementation planning involved 'literacy staff development course including: High gain strategies (within Literacy agreement); Data use: analysis / strategies / implementation, differentiation in the classroom'.

While the expectation of professional development being an ongoing commitment was articulated in WSLPs, the details were often lacking. However, in some cases, specific accountabilities could be associated with professional development activities, such as in the case of AU77.

Professional Development

Literacy and Numeracy teaching strategies will remain a priority when planning professional development during the life of this plan. The new focus each year will be on building the capability of staff and to train beginning and new teachers.

Professional Development is delivered through a differentiated approach, which is timely and relevant, designed to meet the needs of all staff. Student Professional Development Days and Twilight Sessions, and Pop-Up Professional Development sessions, Staff and Faculty Meetings, Leadership planning days and Professional Learning Communities.

This improvement plan will be delivered to staff through targeted professional development and resourced further through resources and visuals displayed in both classrooms, student diary and through the (Name) State High School website. Resources are also shared with parents through the (Name) State High School Website, Parent Program and newsletter. Heads of Department, Teaching and Learning Mentors and expert teaching teams provide systemic support to teachers through professional development, observation and mentoring opportunities.

School wide access to targeted resources will provide the opportunity for all teachers and teacher aides to develop a common skill set. (AU77)

This example is more useful, but I suggest that given the importance of ongoing professional development for staff in literacy, tailored and specific professional development planning following a similar approach to the previously described implementation planning might be better. Given how busy schools and educators are, where there is too much ambiguity or flexibility around the delivery of professional development, it could easily fall by the wayside. In the following chapter I provide further details about an approach you can take.

> In this section your policy should specify how it will enable ongoing professional development in literacy, with a targeted focus on student needs and teacher knowledge gaps. Further details are provided in the following chapter.

10. Resources and the library

A variety of literacy resources were listed to be drawn upon to achieve the policies' aims, and this addition to a WSLP is valuable as resources form a key part of the feasibility of a school policy (Allen et al., 2021).

Policies listed a range of commercial educational products which also revealed the extent to which schools invest in such products for literacy improvement. I do not name these products for reasons I explore in greater detail in Chapter 7.

Resources also included infrastructure, staffing, materials, information technology and a range of other material items used to promote literacy within the school. For example, AU10 includes a detailed list of assessment instruments that the school uses to measure student achievement in language. Resourcing should also consider facilitation of ongoing professional development for the key human resource, the educators within the school.

UK documents typically went into more detail around resourcing than Australian documents, with UK37 noting:

> Children have access to a wide range of age and developmentally appropriate resources which meet the diverse range of children's interests and abilities. The variety of resources available includes:
>
> - a wide range of fiction, non-fiction, play scripts and poetry books to suit children of differing abilities and interests
> - Interactive whiteboards and a range of ICT/media resources (see ICT policy)
> - a variety of appropriate games and activities which will be integrated into day-to-day
> - teaching and learning (commercially/teacher produced)
> - a range of writing tools , e.g. dry-wipe boards, chalks, markers, pencils, etc.

In some cases, particularly in UK documents, resources were included as appendices appearing at the end of the policy. For example, UK22 attached phonics resources, advice for parents seeking to support reading in the home, guidance to support parents to aid students in reading aloud in the home, parent literature on the importance of reading with children, lists of common exception words, a weekly reading timetable, year level appropriate reading and writing targets, guidance on reading (decoding) and writing as appendices.

Some schools also generated their own literacy support resources (for example, AU70). For instance, AU77 includes mention of a 'Writing Genre Booklet' designed to support a 'Whole School Approach to Literacy':

> Students will be supported in writing through the writing genre booklet. This will provide exemplars for all writing genres specific to the 7–12 curriculum. This will be completed through an audit of all writing genres and samples produced by the expert teaching team in all faculty areas. The booklet will be made available to students and community as an online resource.

I explore the use of exemplars further in the 'enacting whole-school literacy' section of the next chapter. In some cases, reading resources could even be student-generated, with AU73 using I-charts, which 'are designed at the start of the year to establish effective classroom routines and behaviours (e.g. Read to Self, Independent practise expectations). These are created with the students and remain posted for easy reference.'

It is important that resourcing be responsive to current research relating to best literacy outcomes for students. For example, as I have explored extensively elsewhere, books, and fiction books in particular, remain a resource associated with literacy benefit. The reading of many other text types does not have the same volume of research support for literacy benefit, though they may offer other kinds of educative benefits (Jerrim et al., 2020; OECD, 2010). Paper books are also still typically preferred by young Australians over eBooks at this stage (Merga, 2014e; Merga & Mat Roni, 2017; Rutherford et al., 2018).

As such, while barely mentioned, the availability of books and a library within schools remains important, and literature resourcing can be a key component of literacy resourcing. For example, UK36 lists the following under reading 'resourcing'.

> It is our intention to provide as wide a variety of book materials as possible, within the financial restraints imposed on us. This will be kept regularly under review. The school does not rely solely upon one scheme as it is felt this may

> limit pupils' learning experiences. Examples of schemes and resources can be found in the appendix.
>
> It is our aim that each class will have a varied collection of fiction and non-fiction. We will carefully consider the balance of fiction and non-fiction.
>
> The pupils will be taught necessary book skills. They will be encouraged to compare fiction and non-fiction and to recognise that factual information may be gleaned from reading fiction.
>
> We recognise the need for pupils to read at different levels and will seek to facilitate this in our organisation of book material.
>
> We intend to build up a collection of texts other than books, including telephone directories, catalogues, recipe books, timetables, brochures, comics etc.
>
> We will continue to encourage children to visit both the public library and the library vans. We will endeavour to display books in an attractive manner in class libraries and at times topic display areas.

Here the emphasis was on facilitating student access to literature, including reference to access to literature in class libraries, the public library and through library vans, and elsewhere in the document there is also mention of strong use of the school library service.

The school library was included but underrepresented as a literacy and literature resource in Australian WSLPs. As per my previous research, while libraries (in general) were mentioned in just over a third of Australian policies, they are far more likely to feature in those of their UK counterparts (Merga, 2021a). Where there is a school library, and it is a useful literacy resource as will almost certainly be the case, it should be situated as such within the school's literacy policy.

As I explained at a recent keynote (Merga, 2021c), inclusion of the school library in the WSLP signifies the following:

- **Esteem indictor**
  Shows that school libraries and their staff are valued, and this is important given that school libraries in Australia are more likely to be facing budget cuts than increases (Softlink, 2021), and morale of school library professionals is low, which may impact on staff availability and attrition (Merga, 2019a; 2019b).

- **Student outcomes**
  Recognises that school libraries can have a positive influence on student literacy outcomes, reflective of the literature (for example, Lance & Kachel, 2018).
- **Marketing**
  Aligns with growing expectations that school library professionals more effectively 'market' what is on offer in their libraries in relation to student literacy attainment (Aharony, 2009).
- **Insurance policy**
  Protects the professional role. A key issue facing library professionals in Australia is deprofessionalisation, with unqualified staff in school library leadership roles (Dix et al., 2020; Merga, 2022a), so school library professionals' concerns about being replaced by a less qualified and therefore cheaper counterpart are reasonable. Linking school library professionals with literacy can also help to prevent deprofessionalisation in school libraries by recognising the contribution of qualified staff to student literacy gains (Lance & Kachel, 2018).

Some Australian policies did explicitly mention the role of the teacher librarian within the school library as key to promoting literacy. For example, AU77 links the teacher librarian to the promotion of reading and writing, and opportunities for student exposure to rich and interesting activities associated with literacy and literature.

> **Whole School Focus on Reading and Writing:**
> **Resource Centre**
> Whole school reading and writing is promoted by the Teacher Librarian targeting reading improvement. This includes facilitating the Premier's Reading Challenge, Guest Author Workshops, Attendance at Brisbane Writers Festival and promotion of the Resource Centre literature collection.

Similarly, AU22 designated literacy related roles and responsibilities for library staff, noting that 'the library plays a key role in supporting student literacy development by … maintaining a vibrant reading area', 'supporting student learning', 'promoting reading across the school', and 'supporting the teaching of research skills' (AU22).

More detail on the value and purpose of the library resource was found in UK documents such as UK34, which noted:

> The library is pivotal in supporting the whole school development of students' literacy. The librarian will work with the English Faculty in order to promote all aspects of literacy. It is a central space which is open to members of the school community for lessons, reading and research (including the use of ICT). The library will support the development of literacy in the following ways:
>
> 4.1 Act as a working English classroom for fortnightly Literacy Lessons – during these, Year 7 and 8 students will follow a specific scheme of literacy work and complete Reading Logs (see Appendix 2).
>
> 4.2 Work with faculties to promote the use of the library to research and complete homework.
>
> 4.3 Encourage reading for pleasure through fortnightly library lessons.
>
> 4.4 Ensure Year 7 students understand how to use the library.
>
> 4.5 Provide reading lists for KS3 and KS4.
>
> 4.6 Work with the English faculty to promote the Book Buzz initiative to foster independent reading.
>
> 4.7 Offer enrichment through reading groups with a focus on national and local competitions.

While libraries often do much more than this to support students' literacy attainment (for example, Merga, 2019a, 2019c, 2020b, 2021a), at least some of their literacy supportive role should feature in the WSLP so that this resource continues to be maintained and available into the future amongst the competing demands on resourcing faced by schools.

This section of your policy can list a range of required resources that your school will need to draw upon to meet the literacy learning needs of your school community. In some cases it may be appropriate to add these as appendices to the policy. Where possible, consideration of resourcing should include consideration of how to support and make the most of the school library and staff.

11. Links with other policies

Australian school literacy policies may make explicit links to internal and external policies and documents. These links serve a range of purposes, demonstrating the school's alignment of strategies to best-practice documentation. For example, AITSL's aforementioned APSTs were linked to professional development within the school (for example, AU81).

Ideally, linking should be to policies that need to be drawn upon concurrently to make best use of the WSLP. For example, under 'Links', AU44 includes that 'other policies which are connected to this policy' are detailed as '(School) Oral Language Policy 2014', '(School) English as an Additional Language Policy 2014', and '(School) Assessment and Reporting Policy 2015'. Hyperlink use was common; for example, policies might provide hyperlinks to relevant school, state, national or international policy resources, or other school-level policies (for example, AU14, AU77). In other instances, relevant policies were included as attachments or appendices, and in some cases reference lists were provided (for example, AU53).

UK policies included similar links. For example, UK21 states:

> This policy should be read in conjunction with the following school policies:
>
> - Assessment and Record Keeping
> - Marking policy
> - Special Educational Needs Policy
> - Computing Policy
> - Equal Opportunities Policy
> - Health and Safety Policy
> - Homework policy.

Your school may have similar policies to be read in parallel with your WSLP, and you may wish to provide a similar list, though as you can see, when the list is presented removed from relevant and related sections of the WSLP, the links are not clear, and the policy relies on the reader's ability to make the connection themselves. In the case of a WSLP which is intended to meet the needs of diverse stakeholders with varying degrees of background in literacy and knowledge of related policies, this may not be advisable. It may be more desirable to include reference to external policies within related or relevant sections, even if this is just added as a footnote or ideally a hyperlink (depending on the nature of the document).

As I explored in reference to rationale and goals previously, some WSLPs plagiarised external content without compunction, and in relation to other policies, it should be noted that some WSLPs leaned very heavily on this external documentation, pasting in large amounts of externally-produced content, and including very little of their own interpretation and application. As such, these inclusions did not appear very useful, as they contributed nothing new, and were not thoughtfully targeted to the needs of the school. Making links with policies in relevant sections within the WSLP supplants the need to paste in poorly contextualised chunks of external policies, and they enable schools to link to evidence for further professional reading, demonstrate responsiveness to accountability requirements, and show that their WSLP is reflective of current internal and external positioning on student learning.

> In this part of your policy you can include appendices, links or hyperlinks to relevant internal and external policies that can enhance understanding and use of the school literacy policy, while demonstrating that the policy is responsive to both internally and externally imposed requirements. Avoid pasting in poorly contextualised chunks of externally produced policies. Ideally, hyperlinks to external policies should appear in relevant sections so that the WSLP is not reliant on reader expertise to make connections between WSLP content and external policies.

12. Defined roles for parents and external partners

By this point you have already considered who you are writing your WSLP for, and it is likely that parents and other external partners may be part of the intended audience. Schools typically recognise the importance of literacy partnerships with parents and the broader community, so defining roles for parents and external partners provides important information to support educators' efforts to build and sustain these relationships.

Parents can be valuable literacy partners. There is a wealth of research linking parental support for child literacy within the home to favourable literacy outcomes, through practices such as reading aloud (Duursma et al., 2008; Hutton et al., 2015). Home literacy encouragement can also result in the fostering of positive attitudes toward literacy practices such as reading (Merga, 2014b, 2017b).

As such, it was not surprising that some policies included clearly defined roles for key external stakeholders such as parents and members of the broader community. For example, in relation to communication of student progress to parents, AU9 actions this, promoting 'inclusive home/school partnerships by communicating to parents through student portfolios, School Reports, IEP Meetings, Parent Information Workshops and Newsletter Updates'. This quote is primarily concerned about the school's responsibility for meeting the needs of external stakeholders. Other documents list specific roles and responsibilities for parents, with parents at AU11 expected to 'encourage reading for pleasure, encourage students to borrow from the library, support and encourage the completion of homework set by the teachers, and read to and with their children'.

UK documents were typically more comprehensive on parental roles and responsibilities. For example, UK14 included the following:

Homework and the Role of Parents

We see parents as important partners in the process of developing children's literacy skills. They have an important influence on children's language before they come to school. They provide valuable support at home in helping children to become confident readers and writers. They offer a useful audience for children in their development as speakers and listeners, readers and writers as the children move through the school.

We therefore encourage parents to play their full part in their children's education by:

- Involving parents in the school's reading programme from the moment their child starts school.
- Providing parents with age-specific guidance through information evenings as their children move through school so that they can continue to offer appropriate support.
- Giving parents termly topic overviews of the curriculum areas in English that each year group will be studying.
- Sending homework home in accordance with the school's Homework Policy and encouraging parental support.

This kind of whole-school directive on engaging parent support for student learning at home should also be shared with parents, so that they can see that they are a valued part of their child's literacy learning team. Our research has found that there can sometimes be ambiguity around the parental role in supporting literacy at home, particularly once young people can read independently, so suggested roles and responsibilities for parents can help to provide clarity around the ongoing benefit of literacy supportive practices enacted within the home (Merga, 2017a; Merga & Ledger, 2018), as I explore further in the subsequent section in this chapter.

As part of generating roles for parents as external partners, understanding their capacity as supports and their views toward literacy can be a valuable starting point. To this end, AU40 conducted 'school community audits' in order to explore 'links between home and school literacy practices and school literacy achievements', and uncover the values of the 'school parent community'. They discovered the following.

> For parents, the most important aspects of literacy are:
>
> - Information and communication (including communication of thoughts)
> - Being conversant with all modern forms of literacy, including reading, writing and listening and computers
> - Understanding
> - Being able to obtain and use information
> - Being able to assist our children
> - Freedom of access to all areas of opportunity
> - Functional needs e.g. forms, recipes
> - Pleasure/recreational e.g. novels. (AU40)

Interestingly, this school also surveyed its students to determine what they viewed the most important aspects of literacy to be. They also investigated parental conceptualisation of functional literacy, noting:

> Parents believe that to operate effectively within our community, their children need to:
>
> 1. Read, write and understand (reading for meaning)
> 2. Know what is going on in the community (use of newsletters)

3. Have a broader perspective on what and how the community is driven.
4. Understanding community needs and behavioural needs of others.
5. Respect others; observation of rules, laws and help others
6. (Have) comprehensive understanding of all aspects of literacy … to succeed in the workforce.
7. (Be) able to communication effectively. (AU40)

By identifying parental beliefs, understanding of their child's needs and parental literacy priorities, this approach to engaging external stakeholders may be more effective than an approach which does not draw on the perspectives of the target group of stakeholders. It is also worth noting that this document dedicated two of its twenty-six pages to tabular planning for 'strategic community partnerships', further demonstrating a valuing of partnerships. Here is one example in Table 5.

Table 5: Partnership building example (AU40)

Current practice	Goal	How	Who
Links with (Name) District High School (and other High Schools)	Increase links in curriculum and general areas.	Liaise with secondary staff to support transition and provide continuity for Year 8 students – access Middle Schooling funding.	Principal Classroom teachers Parents

Links with community were also forged in order to reduce student disadvantage. For example, UK32 including multiple links with the community and its local library, including but not limited to the following.

- Links with Neighbourhood renewal are strengthening each year. The school principal is a member of the education sub group committee for the (Name of Neighbourhood Renewal group). She has helped formulate the educational bid which seeks to allocate funds to educational initiatives in the hope of reducing underachievement among pupils from very deprived wards within (area). The afterschool Literacy support programme offered to Primary 4 the talking partners and reading partnership programmes.

- (School) and (local library) staff are working closely to encourage families with no internet connection to use the library's ICT provision to access 'Mathletics, 'Bug Club' 'Lexia,' 'Accelerated Reader' and the 'Parents' section on our website. This is working well for a small group of parents who live in housing close to the library.
- We also make use of the library for 'story time' etc and promote its summer time reading challenge in an effort to encourage pupils to use the public library. In the 2016/17 school year pupils from Primary 4 and Primary 6 took part in a library project whereby they learned about the function and layout of the local library.

Making visible these valuable community connections to reduce student disadvantage is important, as not only does it raise awareness of these connections, it also highlights their value so that they can be further developed and preserved into the future. In Chapter 5 I extend this consideration further, exploring how you can facilitate stakeholder support and buy-in from parents and the broader community.

> Your policy can include clearly defined roles for parents and external partners, as well as planning for meaningful communication with these stakeholders to further build these relationships. Collecting data from these partners on their capacity as external supports and their views toward literacy may be a useful starting point. Community connections aimed at reducing disadvantage for vulnerable students should be forged and highlighted.

13. Building capacity for parent-supported learning

Strengthening communication between the school and home around literacy learning and the role that parents can play is important (Culican, 2001). As previously mentioned, school literacy policies detail defined roles for parents and external partners, but in order to enact these roles, these stakeholders may need training and support.

Australian school literacy policies give attention to building capacity for parent-supported literacy learning. For example, AU1 details the following strategies and activities:

- Reading workshops for parents – PP & Year 1 'Listening to your child read', Year 3 (educational product)

- Opportunities for parents to be invited into classes to participate in Literacy activities.
- Student access to (educational product) and (educational product) to support reading at home.
- Parent/Caregiver meetings to set goals for improvement or extension for SAER/GATE students.
- Teachers and parents actively promote and encourage students to take part in the Holiday Reading Challenges.
- Facebook and website information to engage the family in literacy development of their child.

Similarly, AU3 described a programme run by the school's Literacy Coordinator 'to assist parents to support their child's literacy development at home and those parents working in the classroom during Literacy sessions'.

Some of these policies tended to assume that parents had the necessary resources and skills to act as effective literacy supports within the home, so it was good to see AU1 recognising that parents who have never been read to themselves may need a workshop and support to share this activity with their own children. Our earlier research suggests that programmes that support parents' capacity to foster literacy learning within the home can be crucial for many reasons, not the least of which is that it cannot be taken for granted that parents have been read to as children, and therefore have had exposure to what literacy learning support within the home might look like. In our study of parents reading to their primary school aged children, we found that a quarter of respondents had not been read to as children, though many of these parents were now reading with children of their own (Merga & Ledger, 2018). We also found that parents can also gain from these read aloud opportunities, as 'most parents enjoyed reading aloud to their children, with learning opportunity, enjoyment, and interpersonal connection the key motivations behind this enjoyment' (Merga & Ledger, 2018, p. 185).

UK policies such as UK5 also understood the importance of building capacity in parents:

> Through the government initiative 'Getting Ready to Learn' our parents, within the early years, are provided with reading workshops which outline the

importance of reading, the need for frequent reading sessions and ideas to develop a love and passion for reading. Children should have opportunities to read aloud when at home through the use of internet apps, online books, novels and stories. Literacy scheme books can be sent home for homework where and when appropriate.

What is missing from policies is planning to build parent capacity to be ongoing supports of students' literacy engagement *beyond* primary school. This is a concerning gap, given that research suggests that there may be a decline in some literacy supportive behaviours and attitudes in older children. For example, young people's attitudes toward reading decline significantly as they move beyond the early years of primary school (Clark & Teravainen-Goff, 2020; Darmawan, 2020; Parsons et al., 2018). Given the many literacy related benefits of sustaining literacy practices such as reading for pleasure beyond the early years of independent reading skill acquisition, we need to avoid communicating to young people that expectations that they read for pleasure end with learning to read (Merga, 2018). Research suggests that students may perceive *expired expectations* that they read for pleasure, which leads to them deeming this an activity that no longer holds importance for them (Merga, 2014b). Encouraging children to read beyond early childhood may become an *orphaned responsibility*, with neither parents or teachers performing the role (Merga, 2017c).

Parents can play an important role in supporting engaged reading beyond primary school (Merga, 2014b), and schools can communicate parents research-supported strategies for enacting this role. It would also be good to see greater consideration of strategies for involving parents who may need extra support to assist their child's literacy learning in the home; in many cases this is not due to a lack of a will to be involved, but rather linguistic, cultural or socio-economic barriers, or negative personal experiences with schooling.

Both primary and secondary school literacy policies should include planning to build parental capacity to foster literacy learning and engagement within the home, and to increase engagement of parents both in the early years and beyond.

14. Transition support

As students move through the years of schooling, they can hit speedbumps during transition periods that impact on their literacy learning. It is vital that student learning achievements and needs are effectively communicated from year to year so that future educators can pick up the baton from earlier teachers and support continuity in learning.

There has been ongoing interest in the impact of key education transition periods on student learning, though more broadly transition can be seen as a constant beyond those key periods, whereby 'transition becomes something that happens in real time; from one part of a literacy lesson to another and as students shift from one institutional year level to another' (Garoni et al., 2021, p. 71). Such micro transitions are indeed an ongoing occurrence, and your WSLP may wish to consider mitigating any negative impacts from transitions, including but also perhaps extending beyond the key transition periods of early childhood education to primary school, and primary to secondary school.

Some Australian policies mentioned these transitions, and the consideration was focused on the sharing of student assessment data for diagnostic purposes, in what AU70 deems the 'transition handover document'. For example, primary school AU40 considers smoothing their students' transition beyond their school by liaising 'with secondary staff to support transition' using specially allocated funding, and by providing 'necessary literacy test data to secondary school'. Similarly, AU67 notes that 'collecting and analysing meaningful data over time is integral to school-wide accountability, as well as assisting transitions between the years'. AU58 also gives consideration to communication of literacy between year levels:

> At (name of) Primary School, as students move through year levels and from one teacher to the next, a Student Data Record is completed ready for their next teacher. Student Data Folders provide teachers with an overview of results from diagnostic assessments to help inform planning and identify possible students for intervention programs.

This is accompanied by specified agreed literacy targets, supporting teachers to identify students falling below agreed norms.

One primary school (AU74) sought to strengthen external partnerships between 'home, school and community' through 'Literacy / Numeracy Instructional Leader's involvement in school kindergarten transition program'. The expected outcomes were as follows:

> Transition programs reviewed to identify opportunities to enhance student literacy and numeracy development in line with relevant objectives from the Early Years Learning Framework & the related document 'Playbased Approaches to Literacy & Numeracy'
>
> Literacy Numeracy Training Officer will provide feedback and Professional Learning specific to enhancing opportunities for integration literacy and numeracy. (AU74)

These were underpinned by the following two performance measures:

- 100% of Literacy / Numeracy Instructional Leaders will contribute to transition programs through planning, consultation &/or modelling and demonstration within the transition environment
- Extended transition to school programs exist. (AU74)

The school also allocated responsibilities for achieving these actions, and how they will be developed and enhanced, supporting the transition of young students beyond the early childhood phase of learning.

Similarly, transition was a focus of UK policy documents. For example, UK11 provided the following detailed consideration:

> **Nursery/Primary/Secondary Transition**
>
> Many children have experienced pre reading, early reading games and writing activities at home and/or through the nursery. Staff liaise pre-school staff to allow children build on these experiences in Primary 1. The reading and writing frameworks allow staff to work together to identify the progress the children have made from Primary 1 to Primary 7. As children move from one class to another, staff discuss their progress in literacy and plan for any additional support required. A written record of learning is passed to the next teacher as part of the transferral of information process. P7 children are given opportunities to visit the secondary school and staff visit the children at primary school. Effective communication at transition stages is essential to ensure progression in knowledge and skills which

> takes account of prior learning and makes effective use of the knowledge of each child as a learner. Joint planning, including Learning Community planning, takes place to enable literacy to meet the central principles and practices of Curriculum for Excellence. Transfer of information takes place in line with (name of) Council guidelines. (UK11)

Again, the focus is on identification of, and communication around student progress and planning for support, as well as smoothing the experience for students making leaps between phases of schooling.

The policy for secondary school UK28 similarly includes consideration of transition, but also notes specific implications around benchmark attainment that trigger additional support for students, and this is explicitly labelled within their policy as a 'whole school' responsibility:

- We work closely with our partner primaries to ensure a smooth transition from year 6; Pupils who are below the 'expected standard' mark of 100 at KS2 SATs and pupils below the National Average mark [105 in 2018] will commence a structured 'reading recovery' scheme on entry to Y7. SATs scores are cross-referenced with reading age on entry.
- Should pupils still be below their chronological reading age at the end of Y7, this programme should continue into Y8 and beyond if necessary.

As such, transition points can be useful opportunities to detect students who have fallen through the cracks in literacy learning, triggering supportive remedial strategies to prevent them from falling further behind their peers.

> You can draw from Australian and UK policies when considering how students can be supported to make large (for example, from primary to secondary school) and smaller (for example, from year to year within school) key transitions, and ensure that staff are adequately prepared to support these shifts, and that communication around student learning needs is clear to enable continuity of support. You may also wish to build in diagnostic opportunities to deliver targeted support for struggling literacy learners at and beyond the point of transition.

15. Policy evaluation and review planning

Once you have a WSLP, you need to maintain it, and schools should comprehensively review and update policy documents as required (Allen et al., 2021). Given the constant internal and external changes that schools need to be responsive to, no literacy policy can be expected to retain optimal usefulness over time.

In addition to the ongoing need to be responsive to any revisions to the informing literacy curriculum and learning environment, schools must grapple with a wide range of changes, many of which cannot be accurately projected, such as the impacts of future coronavirus variants on schooling interruption and delivery. Even if these external factors were to magically become no longer tumultuous, the needs of the student body do not remain static over time.

As such, policy evaluation planning is a key feature of the WSLP, and some documents included planning for policy review and evaluation. For example, AU11 stipulated a timeframe for review as well as providing brief mention of evaluation criteria, noting that 'this policy will be reviewed as part of the school's three-year review cycle', and that 'a variety of formal and informal evaluation strategies will be used to assess student learning. AusVELS results and NAPLAN results will be used to assess the adequacy of the school policy and program'. While it is great to see commitment to policy evaluation, reference to results from standardised testing should not be the only data employed to determine the efficacy of a policy, as I explore further herein.

While it was quite common for planning for policy evaluation and revision to be undertaken every three years, there was no one uniform standard point for policy evaluation. AU22 proposed more frequent review, noting that 'as part of an ongoing evaluation process the Literacy Leader will review the effectiveness of the Literacy Policy at the conclusion of each year. Improvements to the processes and procedures will be adapted when required'. This document also detailed the consultative process for review as part of evaluation planning, in chronological order, with responsibilities clearly given:

- Literacy Leader and Campus Principal review current policy
- Campus Meeting and CAT meetings: Feedback and input from staff about draft Literacy policy
- EDPOL notified of Literacy policy review
- School Council: Literacy Policy presented to school council to be ratified.
- College Meeting: Final Literacy Policy presented to staff. (AU22)

An even shorter initial review period was proposed in AU49, which stated that 'this policy will be reviewed in six months' time to ensure adequacy and completeness', and that 'this policy will also be reviewed as part of the school's three-year review cycle.' For a newly launched policy, this short initial review period may be desirable, with the first six months an opportunity to pilot the WSLP before subjecting it to fine-tuning if indicated through real world application of the policy.

Many WSLPs stated a specific date for review (for example, AU51). While this may be ideal for ensuring that the review actually happens amongst the competing demands for time and resourcing within schools and staffing, given the current climate, gauging an appropriate evaluation and review period that is realistic and achievable while allowing the school to be sufficiently responsive to change may be challenging. On one hand, it is important to allow the policy to be employed unadulterated for a sufficient period to determine its utility. On the other, if too long a period is allowed to lapse before evaluation and review, there is a risk of declining policy relevance.

Very few Australian policies described any kind of process of evaluation and review beyond stating that it would happen. AU77 attached accountability to their plan by labelling their small subsection on evaluation 'Evaluating and Communicating Impact', noting that 'The Literacy and Numeracy Committee will evaluate the effectiveness of the plan. This process is guided by the Inquiry Model and Standards of Evidence (DOE 2017). The Literacy and Numeracy Committee reports to staff through the Leadership Committee.'

Despite the lack of attention given to the process for evaluation in Australian WSLPs, it is useful to briefly detail what the evaluation process will entail, and who will be responsible for it; indeed, this information is needed to determine when evaluation and review will be feasible, partly based on the logistics involved in this process.

Policy evaluation and review can involve multiple stakeholders. For example, UK65 envisions evaluation of policy impact as being generated by multiple perspectives within the school community:

> The impact of the literacy policy will be reviewed by:
>
> - Analysis of reading age data (whole school, case studies and nurture group)

- Analysis of AP progress and achievement data (English, including nurture group)
- Student voice
- Staff voice
- Parent feedback.

This is a good example of where policy efficacy is not just determined by quantitative shifts in achievement data. Qualitative data in the form of the perspectives of students, staff and parents can also be drawn upon.

Evaluation of the success of your policy in relation to high-stakes testing performance needs to come with a caveat. Many factors influence student achievement, so making assumptions about causation, such as contending that the WSLP led to an improvement in NAPLAN performance, so the policy has been a success, cannot usually be justified (Rice, 2014). You can usually claim correlation but not causation, and in schools, the variables impacting on student learning are constantly shifting.

Similarly, if there is a strong research base for the strategies you employed in your WSLP, but improvements on testing results were not perceived, this does not necessarily mean that your strategies were not beneficial. For example, drops in performance can be as much attributed to the test being undertaken during a period where a number of students were recovering from COVID and experiencing lingering cognitive effects, or the strategy you employed might need more time to take effect. You will need to consider potential mitigating and enhancing factors that may have been at play.

As a final note, I recognise that there will always be a conflict of interest where a school evaluates its own policy, and where the evaluators are the literacy team that created the policy, this may be problematic. On one hand, this team will be most familiar with the WSLP and most closely acquainted with its successes and limitations. On the other, as with most instances of self-evaluation within schools, there will be 'inevitable tensions between rigour and depth on the one hand and a natural desire not to undermine the confidence of parents and superiors on the other' (OECD, n.d., p. 6). While in the final chapter of this book I argue that you do not need an external consultant to develop a WSLP, in some cases, you might wish to consider involving an external party for the purposes of evaluation, as I discuss further in this section.

> Your policy should state a definite time period for policy evaluation and review, and who will be responsible for this process. Your WSLP should also at least briefly detail what policy evaluation and review will involve within your school so that the evaluation process can be adequately resourced. Perspectives of diverse stakeholders can be drawn upon to evaluate policy impact and efficacy. The success or failure of a policy should not be solely related to student performance on NAPLAN testing.

CHAPTER 4

Gaps to consider

The fifteen features detailed in the previous chapter are useful facets of current Australian literacy policies, but even as you read through them, you probably noticed that there are gaps and issues that might warrant consideration in your WSLP.

Perhaps the most jarring realisation I had while analysing the Australian WSLPs was that many of these policies did a poor job of supporting the enaction of whole-school literacy, with many failing to set literacy targets beyond seeking gains on high-stakes testing. Consideration of motivation and engagement in literacy learning is often completely absent. There is a lack of tailored and specific professional development planning, and on a related note, there is little consideration of the importance of literacy-supportive school cultures. Many school literacy policies fail to materially plan support for their most vulnerable students, with little detail on screening and identifying struggling students and planning for interventions across the school. Policies typically feature a narrow understanding of literacy, and basic skills such as handwriting were often not mentioned at all. Given that many of the documents analysed were written pre-pandemic, it is understandable that there is little evidence of consideration of the impact of the pandemic on student literacy, and how to mitigate its affects, but this will need to change from this point on. Few documents made reference to any rigorous evidence base.

To address these gaps, I present another fifteen features for your consideration, some of which were rarely touched upon in Australian WSLP, and some of which were not mentioned at all:

1. Identifying responsible parties for planning and implementation and their role
2. A role for every teacher
3. Enacting whole-school literacy
4. Literacy measures beyond test achievement
5. Literacy motivation and engagement
6. Literacy and reading culture
7. Tailored and specific professional development planning
8. Identifying struggling students
9. Support for struggling literacy learners
10. The plurality of literacies
11. Pandemic responsiveness
12. Research evidence base
13. Handwriting and typing
14. Uniform feedback mechanisms
15. Literacy for ages and stages.

Many of the gaps explored here became apparent in analysing the UK documents after their Australian counterparts. As noted in the previous chapter, the UK documents were typically far more comprehensive, and this is not just reflected in their greater average length.

As a side note, do not feel overwhelmed. I know that I keep presenting new things to consider for inclusion in the WSLP, and you may be wondering how to bring all of this information together into a comprehensive whole. Based on the gaps identified in this chapter, the framework emerging from the previous chapter, and considerations I provide around practicalities of WSLP planning and implementation in the next chapter, in Chapter 6 I provide guidance in the form of a possible structure that the literacy team can use to plan a literacy policy that is both comprehensive and practical. As I explain further in this section, this structure is not expected to be concrete, rather one approach that can be tailored to your school's needs.

1. Identifying responsible parties

There are many reasons to do this, and one of them is to get credit for the work you do on the WSLP. It will be easier to include your WSLP in a promotion application, or when applying for a new role, if your name is actually on it.

You also need to give credit where credit is due. Your literacy policy could include mention of the literacy team responsible for designing it, stating the names of leaders and members of the team responsible for the creation and revision of the literacy policy. This may be an extant literacy committee.

Few Australian policies identify responsible parties for planning and implementation and specify their role in relation to the WSLP. Some documents list the literacy policy planning team under 'responsibility' (for example, AU13), and this confers both immediate and ongoing accountability as well as recognition of important roles that should be considered in the workload of these individuals.

Beyond the team, some documents also include greater breadth than a simple listing of the literacy team responsible for the policy. For example, AU18 lists the individuals and organisations that 'have been identified as key stakeholders to promote and implement the literacy plan', naming the 'Literacy Committee Members', but also broader school representatives ('Principal, Information Technology Department, Special Learning Needs Department, English Department, Library, Media Officer'), related 'professional organisations' and listing 'community bodies' including philanthropic organisations, the local public library and newspaper. In this secondary school, it is interesting to note that staff in subject areas beyond English are not seen as key stakeholders, ignoring the importance of disciplinary literacy and the use of literacy skills beyond subject English.

Similarly, AU77 uses its Literacy and Numeracy Improvement Plan to provide detail on the role, purpose and composition of their Literacy and Numeracy Committee:

> The role of the Literacy and Numeracy Committee is to plan, implement, review and reflect on the use of these strategies school wide.
>
> The committee will propose initiatives for approval by the Leadership Committee for approval. Heads of Department through their Faculty Improvement Plans will identify how initiatives will be implemented in each curriculum area to meet the proposed guidelines. Faculty accountability rests with HoDs.
>
> The Literacy and Numeracy Committee, chaired by the Literacy Teaching and Learning Mentor will assist and guide Heads of Department to implement and evaluate the effectiveness of the improvement plan.

This example avoids naming specific individuals and/or their titles. While this reduces both individual accountability and credit, where there is ongoing staff fluctuation in a school, keeping responsibility allocations at title level rather than individual level may be appropriate.

However, I do feel that in most cases, it is appropriate to explicitly name the literacy team members responsible for leading the literacy policy initiative. Acknowledgement of the literacy policy team is important recognition for the time and effort that you and your team have invested in developing this document. Being able to add this role to your resume may be of use to further your career, and your role in the leadership of this document is important evidence of your capacity for literacy leadership.

While all staff will contribute in some way, a literacy policy team is typically headed up by a clearly identifiable individual dedicated to working on the WSLP. If you are leading the WSLP in your school, this is you. This person may be given a range of titles. It may be appropriate to clearly define their role within the policy, so that the rest of the school knows how the literacy co-ordinator can support them. This detail was rarely seen in Australian WSLPs.

For example, we can look to UK3 which provides a defined scope for the role of Literacy Co-ordinator in their school language and literacy policy that you may find useful to draw upon:

Role of the Literacy Co-ordinator

The Literacy Co-ordinator is responsible, in consultation with the principal, teachers and parents, for improving the standards of teaching and learning in Literacy through:

- monitoring and evaluating
- pupil progress
- provision of literacy (including intervention and support programmes)
- the quality of the learning environment
- the deployment and provision of support staff
- ensuring that children are progressing through the colour bands at an appropriate rate
- audits and requisitions reading/writing resources
- team teaching
- joint planning
- monitoring children's work
- monitoring teachers' plans
- in class observations
- taking the lead in policy development
- auditing and supporting colleagues in their CPD
- purchasing and organising resources
- keeping up to date with recent Literacy developments
- ensuring channels of communication are open and active with all relevant outside agencies …

While in tone, this example may seem to be primarily focused on accountability and measurement, you might want to develop a scope that is a little more balanced, with focus more equally on the role of the literacy leader as a key instigator in the support of whole-school literacy improvement.

Your policy can recognise and name the literacy team responsible for its creation and revision. It may also detail individual responsibilities for design, implementation and evaluation of the WSLP. It may particularly define the role of the leader of the literacy team, so that everyone understands how the literacy leader can support their efforts to promote literacy across the school

2. A role for every teacher

As I have mentioned in the 'roles and responsibilities' section of the previous chapter, defining roles and responsibilities of key parties within the school can be a key part of the literacy policy. However, in general, Australian documents do a poor job of defining the role of the largest group of educators within the school, the classroom teachers.

Teachers need to know their roles and responsibilities in relation to the WSLP. While some scant consideration was given to this in Australian documents, coverage was far more clear and comprehensive in UK documents. For example, secondary school UK8 includes the following, which takes up a whole page of the fifteen-page policy:

Teachers

All teaching staff should:

- ensure that they are familiar with the specific literacy demands of their subject and ensure sufficient coverage of these skills in their lesson planning;
- aim to raise the level of attainment for all young people through high quality teaching for every child, early intervention and additional support for actual, or potential, underachievement;
- deliver the agreed initiatives and use identified strategies in order to teach speaking and listening, reading and writing skills;
- report on a pupil's standard of literacy at the Parents' Evening, as appropriate;
- liaise with the LITCO (Literacy Coordinator), SENCO and Learning Support Teacher to access guidance when required to support individual pupils;
- undertake robust tracking and monitoring of a pupil's progress through effective use of data – such as Cognitive Ability Test assessments, internal assessments or diagnostic testing carried out by the Learning Support Teacher;
- involve pupils in target setting and evaluation to improve standards;

- be responsible for meeting a pupil's needs when barriers to learning are impeding progress;
- implement procedures to ensure early intervention when barriers to learning are detected;
- provide a literacy based learning environment, modelling high expectations of literacy i.e. through the use of displays.

This policy also provides roles and responsibilities for the SENCO, Curriculum Leader, Literacy Co-ordinator, Senior Management Team, Board of Governors, Librarian, parents/carers and students, however the greatest detail and attention is given to the mainstream classroom teachers. This secondary school firmly establishes literacy as a whole-school responsibility of all educators by providing more detail around educator roles and responsibilities than is typical, and this could have a beneficial impact on how literacy is positioned within the school.

> Giving extra attention to defining the roles and responsibilities of the classroom teachers in relation to the policy can provide clarity for the largest group of educator stakeholders within the school, and can highlight that literacy is the responsibility of every educator

3. Enacting whole-school literacy

While research suggests that there is good conceptual understanding of what constitutes whole-school literacy in schools, the concept is often not actualised effectively, and implementing WSLPs can be challenging and contentious (May & Wright, 2007). From the early days of the LAC movement, translation from theory to practice within schools was slow (May & Wright, 2007), and while the positioning of literacy as a whole-school responsibility is now a key feature of the AC, this does not guarantee that a whole-school approach is comprehensively adopted.

There may be many barriers to universal enaction of whole-school literacy approaches, including insufficient initial teacher education preparing teachers to enact this role. Recent research from Scotland suggests that secondary student teachers from a range of subject areas may hold generally positive views of their ability to teach literacy, with 82 per cent of student teachers preparing to teach STEM subjects having confidence to provide literacy learning experiences. However, this research did not explore if this confidence translated into effective practice, and this still leaves nearly one in five STEM bound teachers lacking this confidence (Campbell et al., 2020).

Many Australian educators may also lack confidence in the complex range of skills and knowledge required for literacy instruction. On reviewing the Australian literature in this area, Fenwick (2010) notes that for most teachers in Australia, 'literacy and language teaching has not been part of their education and many feel that they do not have the knowledge and skills required to teach literacy and language explicitly' (p. 269), though more and recent research is needed to capture the factors that inhibit and enable teachers to enact whole-school literacy. Given the aforementioned perceived lack of leadership support in some cases for whole-school approaches to literacy issues such as supporting struggling learners (Merga, Mat Roni & Malpique, 2021a), if teachers lack confidence in their abilities, or have gaps in the skills and knowledge needed to teach literacy across the curriculum, there may be barriers present at multiple strata within a school.

It was clear from the policies I analysed that there are issues with enaction of *whole-school* literacy directed by a WSLP in our schools. This was an interesting finding given that my sample was solely comprised of literacy policy adopters. Schools without such a policy may be even less likely to have a whole-school approach to literacy.

Many of the Australian policies I analysed detailed an aspirational approach toward enacting whole-school literacy, without careful planning for how this will actually be supported. While not entirely absent from the policies I analysed, actual details and close consideration of enacting whole-school literacy that clearly extended responsibility across all subject areas was surprisingly infrequent. It might be contended that this was tacitly articulated in whole-school implementation plans, but where responsibilities and expectations are not explicitly extended beyond subject English and the teachers of other subjects, I do not believe it is realistic to assume that a whole-school approach to literacy that encompasses every educator and every subject can be reasonably surmised, despite the fact that the national AC positions literacy as a cross-curricular priority as I have previously outlined.

For example, AU22 notes that 'every teacher is a teacher of literacy', including a nod to disciplinary literacy in noting expectations that 'all subjects have specific vocabulary and text conventions that need to be specifically taught by subject teachers. All teachers need to reinforce comprehension strategies'. This document also includes roles and expectations for Curriculum Area Team (CAT) Leaders, who are:

> responsible for identifying the literacy demands of their subject areas and helping class teachers to plan to address this through the curriculum. This involves working with the literacy support team to identify these expectations and implement effective classroom strategies. CAT leaders, with the support of the Literacy Leader and coaches who will analyse the college literacy data to identify trends in student skill development, will coordinate the development of curriculum units for a whole year level and additions and modifications to curriculum units for groups of students that target the literacy gaps and misunderstandings of students in their CAT area. (AU22)

Whether at primary or secondary school level, all subjects should include literacy teaching and learning relating to both content area and disciplinary literacy, and in secondary school, where students typically have different teachers for each subject, this extends the responsibility to instructors beyond the subject English. This needs to be explicitly stated in the policy, as in many cases, subject area teachers beyond English may not see literacy instruction as part of their role, even when it intersects with their disciplinary literacies and influences student performance in their subject.

As I mentioned in the previous chapter, literacy is a general capability in the AC, and:

> this recognition gives credence to the role that literacy has always played in other areas; for instance, a child who fails a math test based on word problems may fail due to poor reading comprehension rather than low numeracy skills. This is one of the reasons that literacy skills are not just about performance in the English classroom or even in writing. Literacy skills are absolutely foundational, gateway skills to achievement across the subjects. (Merga, 2018, p. 8)

Research also suggests that building discipline-relevant literacy skills can enable students to demonstrate their learning across the curriculum, with a study finding that 'the systematic integration of all four literacy components, speaking, listening, reading, and writing, in content area instruction improves both content knowledge acquisition and writing organization and development' (Evans, 2018, pp. 109–110).

In general, the UK documents had a higher expectation that a whole-school approach be *meaningfully* adopted. For example, UK13 lists whole-school strategies for supporting literacy that span across multiple pages in the sixteen-page document. It includes a range of strategies, activities and events, such as the development of 'writing frames' which 'support pupils in the writing process', noting that 'subjects should adapt and/or withdraw these as pupils gain in confidence and develop planning and writing skills'. It also describes use of 'literature across the curriculum':

> As part of the literacy initiative, some subject areas have developed the use of literature, where appropriate, into their Schemes of Learning for the following reasons:
>
> - To extend and support subject learning
> - To add engage pupils
> - To offer a human dimension to the appreciation of the subject
> - To extend pupils' moral and emotional understanding
> - To offer different perspectives on people and culture
> - To extend the use of language through the subject context. (UK13)

This provides purpose and clarity for use of literature in subject areas beyond English that also resonate with a broad range of the AC's General Capabilities. Similarly, UK16 details expectations for all subject teachers in both reading and writing. The reading expectations are as follows.

> - Ensure that students read, or listen to appropriate text in all subjects every week;
> - Explicitly outline what types of reading they require from students in their subject area, such as skimming and scanning, information retrieval or reading for inference and understanding;
> - Model reading for understanding in their subject area;
> - Explicitly guide students to use their text books effectively, these may include dictionaries, thesauruses or other subject specific texts;
> - Give access to complex texts using a range of strategies to enable students to understand;

- All students will have the opportunity to practise common assessment rubrics and will be given guidance in understanding these. (UK16)

UK2 refers to *schemes* of work which Australian readers might better understand as curriculum plans or overviews, overarching documents that inform the daily lesson plans (Independent Teacher Workload Review Group, 2016), and it is also worth noting that such planning documents may be subject to inspection by the UK Office for Standards in Education, Children's Services and Skills (Ofsted; Rowley, 2019). UK2 requires that clear planning for literacy aligned with the four traditional domains be adopted in every appropriate subject:

> All schemes of work should include specific literacy objectives (where appropriate for the subject). These objectives should focus on reading, writing and speaking and listening. Activities that utilise reading, writing and speaking and listening skills should be built into schemes of work in order to provide a variety of opportunities focused on literacy. (UK2)

Specific planning for literacy learning across the curriculum was also featured in policies (for example, UK60). For instance, UK20 included examples of 'Embedding Literacy across the Curriculum' as per Table 6.

Table 6: Embedding Literacy across the Curriculum (UK20)

Subject area	Examples
Maths	Teaching mathematical vocabulary and technical terms, by asking students to read and interpret problems to identify the mathematical content, and by encouraging them to explain, argue and present their conclusions to others.
Spanish	Learning new vocabulary by making links to words they are familiar with; speaking and listening tasks in the classroom.
Humanities	Extended writing; research; debates supported by factual information, encouraging students to explain, argue and present their conclusions to others.
ICT	Keywords embedded into lessons; opportunities to learn new vocabulary; 'reading' and interpreting coding languages.
Performing Arts	Speaking and listening opportunities in role play; formulating responses (spoken and written) to music, movement and theatre; research.

Continued ⇛

Subject area	Examples
Art, Design & Technology	'Reading' visual work and formulating spoken and written responses; research; annotating and labelling own and others' work.
PE	Learning of new vocabulary and key terms; spelling by making cross curricular links, e.g. to Science; formulating responses to movement; communication in team sports.
Science	Learning and spelling of key terms; debates and presentations around controversial issues, encouraging students to explain, argue and present their conclusions to others.

Similarly, UK42 included a more detailed account of how literacy learning will look in diverse subject areas. Here is their statement on literacy learning in mathematics:

> English contributes significantly to the teaching of mathematics in our school. Children in the Foundation Stage develop their understanding of number, pattern, shape and space by talking about these areas with adults and other children. Children in KS1 are immersed in stories and rhymes that rely on counting and sequencing. Children in KS2 are encouraged to read and interpret problems in order to identify the mathematics involved. They communicate mathematically through the developing use of precise mathematical language. Mastery skills can be acquired by a child's ability to reason and justify their understanding of mathematical concepts. Every class teacher strives to achieve this by supporting children's developing explanations. (UK42)

In this vein, UK59 included information on what literacy learning can look like across the curriculum, with literacy learning in physical education (PE) potentially involving students looking at 'different sports company logos and discuss the sporting or physical qualities suggested by their shapes, colours and symbols', then using 'these ideas to frame reflection on physical activity and attitudes in the lessons'.

Planning for literacy learning across the curriculum will involve close consideration of how specific literacy objectives are integral to, and can further learning across subject areas. In secondary schools, close liaison with teachers of subject areas beyond English can aid the literacy team in identifying these objectives, drawing on their subject area expertise and giving these teachers a sense of ownership and responsibility over defining students' literacy needs in their area.

Another interesting feature that emerged in analysis of UK documents was content from UK29 on 'the structures and language features of some important types of non-fiction texts'. Spanning across two full pages of the twenty-eight in this document, this material included purpose, text structure and language features of six types of non-fiction texts: recount, report, explanation, instructions, persuasion and discussion. For example, here is the material on the report:

> **Report**
> **Purpose:** to describe the way things are
> **Text structure**
>
> - an opening, general classification, e.g. Sparrows are birds.
> - more technical classification (optional), e.g. Their Latin name is ...
> - a description of the phenomena, including some or all of its: qualities, e.g. Birds have feathers.
>   Parts and their function, e.g. The beak is ...
>   habits/behaviour or uses, e.g. They nest in ...
>
> **Language features of report**
>
> - written in the present tense, e.g. they nest
> - non-chronological
> - focus on generic participants (birds not a particular bird) (UK29)

These kinds of supplementary materials can support staff across subject areas to guide students to understand acceptable purpose, structure and language features on a general level, which can then be tailored more specifically as required in order to meet unique subject area needs. You may also want to consider attaching exemplars of discipline specific texts (such as scientific reports) to the WSLP as appendices or hyperlinks to where these documents might be hosted on the school's intranet. You may wish to include a range of exemplars for different year groups. For example, the expected content and complexity for a Year 8 scientific report would be expected to differ from that of a Year 10 equivalent. As mentioned in Chapter 3 in the section on 'resources and the library', there was some mention of exemplars in

Australian WSLPs, with AU77 including reference to a 'writing genre booklet' that aimed to 'provide exemplars for all writing genres specific to the 7–12 curriculum'.

Finally, some WSLPs (typically in the UK) identified agreed, whole-school literacy approaches to be revised over time to be responsive to evolving literacy needs. For example, UK45 included the following whole-school literacy priorities to be focused on over a two year period:

> All teachers will focus their contribution on different aspects of the following whole school priority areas for the development of reading, writing and speaking and listening skills according to according to curriculum content:
>
> - Improving writing skills in use of appropriate vocabulary, sentence and paragraph construction and accuracy of spelling and punctuation.
> - Encouraging pupils to become more independent as learners through reading as research, using text books, library books, newspapers and the Internet.
> - Encouraging pupils to become more effective readers by setting appropriate reading tasks and promoting reading for pleasure.
> - Encouraging all pupils to take an active role in speaking and listening activities by supporting and rewarding participation.
> - Ensuring regular and sustained participation by using focused questioning.
> - Developing the use of individual, paired, small group and whole group activities within lessons to encourage varied skill development.
> - Use ICT as a tool to improve literacy. (UK45)

This range of targeted priorities can also bring all teachers onto the same page and unite them in implementation of common literacy practices for common purposes. Unlike narrowing of the curriculum to help students score better on high-stakes testing previously discussed in this book, the range of agreed approaches presented in UK45 considers a broader scope of literacy, inclusive of such diverse considerations as motivation and fostering autonomous learning dispositions.

> Your policy should go beyond the aspirational recognition of the importance of whole-school literacy and actually plan for implementation of this orientation. This might include whole-school

initiatives such as a consistent approach to delivering feedback on literacy. It could also include specific literacy objectives that are appropriate to each subject and responsive to the disciplinary literacies explored within them, as well as materials on purpose, text structure and language features of common texts produced in subject areas beyond English. A broad scope of whole-school priorities and a related timeline may also be set.

4. Literacy measures beyond test achievement

Most types of assessments are very limited as student learning opportunities, and weighing the pig does not make it fatter. Unfortunately, 'tied narrowly to test scores in low-order math and reading skills, school effectiveness research and programs ignore many skills, habits, and attitudes' beyond assessments (Cuban, 1984, p. 5).

Measurement of student literacy is typically situated in policies as assessment of literacy skill gains in areas such as reading comprehension, writing proficiency and vocabulary acquisition, and this is reflective of a broader preoccupation with assessment within the educational culture of Australia that has persisted over time (Hammond & Macken-Horarik, 2001). The issues facing student literacy today are broad and varied, and Luke (2003) noted that 'a simple test driven basic skills regime will not solve these complex problems':

> One would no more judge the sum total efforts, needs, successes and failures of a school system by a single high stakes test result than we would purchase a vehicle on the basis of horsepower numbers or choose a food solely on the basis of one of the many pieces of data conveyed on the labels. (p. 75)

Schools wishing to take the pulse of their success in literacy instruction should employ measures inclusive of, but also extending beyond NAPLAN, though this can be challenging given that NAPLAN scores are given more credibility as indicators of student learning than teacher's judgement based on a broader range of indicators, and observed over a greater length of time:

> The constant collection of data pertaining to students' learning, and the subsequent disregard of teachers' professional judgment in evaluating students'

> learning, reflects broader socio-political and cultural-discursive conditions that increasingly validate more material-economic forms of data that can be readily presented in a physical form to justify claims of learning to colleagues, school administrators and parents. (Daliri-Ngametua et al., 2021, p. 14)

Many WSLPs relied solely on shifts in high-stakes testing performance as measures of literacy improvement. As I have previously noted, 'while literacy has always been important for academic achievement, for better or for worse, increasing emphasis on international literacy testing and benchmarking has increased the visibility of current literacy levels' (Merga, 2018, p. 24). This should not lead to the conflation of student achievement and performance on high-stakes tests.

Some Australian WSLPs did give some cursory recognition to the fact that student effort and motivation influence their achievement. For example, AU63 included '98% of students achieve a C or above rating in Effort' and '90% of students achieve an A–B rating in Effort' as school targets, along with targets for improvement in testing, though there is no information about how 'Effort' will be supported or measured.

When literacy skills are discussed and developed in a manner closely tied to testing, this may have deleterious consequences. There are indications that students may see reading as something done for the purposes of testing, rather than a worthwhile or enjoyable activity. My previous research has touched upon this concern:

> When I asked both tweens and teens about how their teachers felt about reading books, reading was often seen as something done to facilitate testing. For example, teen student Craig explained that reading was part of 'the grading thing,' as 'we have to do that, we get marked on that, so we have to read a few books, you know, if we want to get good marks for that.' The pressure to meet testing requirements is related to high-stakes testing such as NAPLAN, but it is also related to gaining or maintaining a position in an academic extension program, with Craig describing a 'threat' to perform to meet the grading requirements. (Merga, 2018, p. 118)

In a similar vein, many teachers are not seen as avid readers (Merga, 2016b), and they do not necessarily enjoy reading (Nathanson et al., 2008; Vansteelandt et al., 2017). Even secondary English teachers who value reading may struggle to maintain strong reading practices that enable them to model keen reading (Sroka, 2021). However it may be the emphasis on literacy for the purposes of testing that prevents young people from seeing their teachers as role models in finding pleasure from literacy activities such as reading for pleasure.

> While many teachers were successful in communicating that reading was important, fewer successfully communicated that it is enjoyable. For example, while Fiona did not know if her teacher liked reading, she did agree that her teacher thought that reading was generally important, 'because they're teachers, and they want you to read'. Lucian did not know if his teacher liked reading, though he felt that his teacher viewed reading as important, 'because we're reading quite a lot this term and we've all had reading tests'. Similarly, though Veronica was not sure if her teacher liked reading, she felt that her teacher regarded reading as important, as 'we do reading comprehension things, we do reading tests, and like, we did one the other day and we did English'. (Merga, 2016b, p. 262)

When literacy is positioned as something done purely for the purposes of testing, students absorb this, and it influences their perceptions of the value of literacy activities. Privileging a breadth of literacy measures inclusive of, but also extending beyond test achievement, may be crucial if we want our students to be lifelong and engaged literacy learners. In the next section, I will explain why pleasure even matters, and why literacy engagement needs to be factored into literacy planning far more than it currently is.

Furthermore, when we are looking to see gains in students' literacy performance, simply relying on test results is easier than taking the time to interrogate the issue more closely. One of the UK school literacy policies, UK44, included details on how it investigated strengths and weaknesses in students' writing, with data collected from both teachers and students.

> A survey was conducted in 2014 within school which focussed on the different text types that student's produce and the strengths and weaknesses which students exhibit in their writing. It highlighted that a range of text types were already promoted across different subjects. When discussing the different text types that students produce, teachers highlighted a number of common barriers to effective writing which included: an inability to structure an argument; difficulty in synthesising material; and inability to write concisely and difficulties in

> evaluative writing. A sort survey amongst students corroborated these findings, revealing that many struggled with writing introductions and conclusions; structuring analytical and evaluative writing; and that they desired more essay writing guidance through the use of topic sentences. (UK44)

The school did not stop there, with further investigation highlighting that more could be done to promote literacy more holistically (beyond writing) within subject areas, and to devise and implement common language and approaches.

> Further investigation showed that a number of mnemonics and visual images are currently being used within school by different departments to remind students about internal structure with paragraphing (although topic sentences were not routinely taught or referred to outside of English lessons). While staff knew the mnemonics that they used within their department, there was a lack of knowledge about how other departments used them to structure writing. Consequently teachers are less able to make students aware of how to transfer their literacy skills from one subject to another.
>
> Further research conducted by the Literacy Working Party in 2015 highlighted how many members of staff focus on literacy within writing and have not yet fully considered the role of speaking and listening in the development of literacy skills.
>
> Inspection of existing practice within school has highlighted the need to ensure that teachers use a common language when promoting literacy skills within their teaching, marking and classroom display. It has also emphasised a need to broaden our whole school approach to literacy to one that draws upon and reinforces the links between reading, writing and speaking and listening. (UK44)

Similarly, UK60 was keenly engaged in 'involving pupils in evaluating learning', noting that 'gathering pupils' views and opinions' is 'a regular feature of school life'.

> We believe that pupils are the stakeholders most likely to be affected by decisions, and are invited to contribute unique viewpoints as to how decisions are working on the ground.
>
> The views and ideas of our children are sought, whenever possible, when planning, developing and reviewing policies and procedures that might affect them. Some of these are:

- Consulting through pupil bodies – e.g. school council representatives;
- Group or class discussions;
- Circle time;
- Questionnaires or surveys;
- Focus groups or workshops;
- Initiatives such as learning detectives/roving reporters.

> We believe for learning to be effective, children need to be actively involved in this process, so that they are motivated, engaged and able to develop as independent learners. We encourage pupil participation is something which all pupils experience at the classroom level. Whole-school approaches to pupil participation through learning are encouraged by adopting and developing strategies such as Assessment for Learning, by involving pupils in deciding what and how they learn, in evaluating their learning, and planning for improvement. (UK60)

As such, literacy measures beyond test achievement can include whole-school captures of teacher- and student-perceived gaps in literacy knowledge, as well as consistency and breadth of literacy learning opportunities across the school. However, it can also give students a sense of agency over their learning, and encourages a metacognitive orientation where students think about their thinking, learning and progress. Rather than being constantly externally measured and on the receiving end of learning, students have the chance to inform their educators and shape the learning and assessment process.

Furthermore, it can be argued that where data are being collected through exercises such as audits or surveys to 'highlight existing shared practice and areas for development' (for example, use of *uniform feedback mechanisms* for the marking of spelling, which I explore further in this titled section), these kinds of activities can have 'both an information gathering and a consciousness-raising impact, both of which can have an important role in developing a shared vision and goals within the school community', and 'unity of purpose is associated with improved educational outcomes' (Lewis & Wray, 2001, p. 48).

It is not sufficient to measure changes in student literacy performance solely on cohort results in high-stakes NAPLAN testing. This promotes a narrow view of literacy and an overreliance on a flawed measure (see previous chapters). Students may begin to conflate literacy with assessment, potentially influencing student motivation to engage in literacy strengthening practices such as recreational reading. Literacy measures beyond test achievement may also relate to collecting feedback from teachers and students on gaps in literacy knowledge, and data on whole-school literacy implementation.

5. Literacy motivation and engagement

We have raised previous concerns about the lack of attention WSLPs pay to the role of engagement in literacy learning (Merga & Gardiner, 2018). By engagement, I refer to positive attitudes towards literacy practices, and frequency of undertaking them, which influence, and are influenced by student literacy skill attainment (Merga, 2022a).

We cannot exclude engagement from consideration in a WSLP, because motivation to engage in literacy practices is important for learning. As noted by Boomer (1992), 'before teaching can proceed the students must be motivated in some way' (p. 9), and there are a range of theories from the domain of educational psychology that explore how motivation can play an essential role in learning. These theories seek to account for the impact of various intrinsic and extrinsic factors on literacy-related engagement, such as the Matthewson and McKenna models (see McKenna et al., 1995) and expectancy value theory (see Wigfield & Eccles, 2000).

While engagement always matters for learning, as children move through the years of schooling, and struggling literacy learners experience successive failures, engagement becomes increasingly important. Engaging students in learning is essential for effective literacy education, and 'if students are alienated rather than engaged in learning, then it is likely that they are similarly alienated in developing the literacy knowledge, skills and capabilities required for meaningful participation in academic, social and community life' (Culican et al., 2001, p. 4).

My recent research looking at teachers' experiences with struggling literacy learners in mainstream secondary classrooms found that 'students' attitudes and level of engagement in literacy learning constituted an intrinsic barrier that was often perceived as shaped by extrinsic factors' (Merga, 2020b, p. 386). Teachers described 'low levels of engagement as "years of educational disengagement and avoidance", and a "history of failure, lack of motivation"' (p. 386). Only 20 per cent of secondary teachers working with struggling literacy learners in mainstream Australian English classrooms agreed that their struggling students held positive attitudes toward literacy learning (Merga, 2020b). If we want to develop a literacy policy that meaningfully supports the learning of disengaged students, we cannot continue to downplay or ignore the relationship between engagement and learning.

UK policies were more likely to note the connection between literacy learning and engagement than Australian documents. For example, in its rationale, UK16 notes that 'improving literacy and learning can have an impact on students' self-esteem, motivation, behaviour and attainment. It allows students to learn independently and is empowering'. This inclusion in the rationale is also supported by further references to building student engagement, such as in the school's aim to 'encourage the enjoyment of books and reading so that the students develop a life-long enjoyment of text'. UK34 also includes a statement on the capacity of literacy to empower students:

> To be literate is to gain a voice and to participate meaningfully and assertively in decisions that affect one's life. To be literate is to gain self-confidence. To be literate is to become self-assertive ... Literacy enables people to read their own world and to write their own history ... Literacy provides access to written knowledge – and knowledge is power. In a nutshell, literacy empowers. (UK34)

As such, literacy is linked with building of personal capacity, and individual agency.

The Australian literacy policies I analysed typically showed a poor understanding of the relationship between literacy engagement and learning, and the benefits for struggling learners. For example, AU15 lists the 'components of a balanced literacy program', stating:

> At each level of schooling, the focus is on the continued development, broadening and strengthening of each element of literacy, as listed below, for individual students:
>
> - oral language
> - phonological awareness
> - letter – sound knowledge

- high frequency sight words
- comprehension
- vocabulary
- fluency
- handwriting.

While this skills focus concentrates on valuable facets of literacy, fostering and maintaining engagement in literacy activities such as reading is not included here, or in the related section on 'teaching practice', and this is a characteristic shared by many Australian policies (for example, AU69).

Consideration of engagement cannot be omitted from, or be positioned as peripheral to the literacy policy. Boomer (1992) contended that 'if teachers set out to teach according to a planned curriculum, without engaging the interests of the students, the quality of learning will suffer', and 'student interest involves student investment and personal commitment' (p. 13). Engagement must be closely considered and planned for. I have addressed this subject at length in relation to reading engagement in my previous works (for example, Merga, 2018).

There are many interventions that can be adopted in order to enhance students' literacy engagement. I explore the building of a whole-school reading culture in the subsequent section, but in relation to influencing students' attitudes toward reading, many factors have research support (Merga, 2022a). Just as schools plan activities and strategies to promote literacy learning across the school, they should also consider whole-school interventions to enhance students' literacy engagement.

This can involve paying attention to students' perceptions of literacy, and themselves as literacy learners. For example, UK primary school policy UK32 is an expansive document eighty-four pages in length which dedicates the second and third pages purely to student feedback about their feelings toward literacy activities.

> Literacy in (School) is designed to foster a love in each child for reading, speaking and writing. Our children are aware of the work which teachers do to make it exciting, innovative and active. We asked the children in KS1 and KS2 how they felt about literacy in (School).

This suggests that not only is engagement a priority for this school, but that they are determined that teachers focus on teaching literacy in ways that will optimise engagement, and look to student feedback to ensure their success. Here is a brief sample of some of the many comments that are captured from students and presented in a prominent early position in this policy:

- I like reading new books because they are interesting and I can find out new information.
- I like to work with a partner when I am writing because we are both thinking together and we can work quickly.
- I like listening to new stories and writing about what I think will happen next.
- I liked writing my food poem. I had to plan for it first and then write verses with rhyming words.
- I like reading lots of different types of books – story books, history books, funny books and information books.
- I love doing story writing because we can come up with very good ideas to write good stories.
- I love doing plays and acting out stories we are reading in class.
- I enjoyed tasting pancakes to describe how they taste and smell and then writing a poem all about it. (UK32)

UK32 really stood out as a literacy policy that valued student engagement, but also student feedback and experiences. While no doubt there has been purposeful curation in the choices of student feedback provided in this policy, what has been included suggests that students are exposed to multiple points of entry for enjoyable experiences with literacy, whether they be pancake related or related to acquisition of new knowledge.

> School literacy policies need to recognise the relationship between student engagement and student achievement. They should plan to adopt research-supported strategies to foster literacy engagement. Student attitudes toward literacy activities can be gauged and improvement in engagement should be a priority in parallel with improvement in performance.

6. Literacy and reading culture

For many students, the most effective literacy interventions are those that enable them to build their literacy skills through practice. For example, for students who already have the ability to read independently, and who have functional reading comprehension skills, research supports the contention that 'there is no question that the act of reading itself builds vocabulary, automaticity, reading proficiency, and general knowledge', and that 'this in turn suggests that many students who show signs of difficulty with reading might simply have a "reading volume deficit"' (Spichtig et al., 2022, p. 13).

To increase reading volume, students need opportunities for sustained reading for pleasure during class time, and they need to be motivated to read. This is where the building of a reading-supportive school culture is so valuable. While a supportive whole-school reading culture has been defined in varying ways, it can be deemed a school environment which provides availability, opportunity, encouragement and support for reading (Daniels & Steres, 2011). Building such a culture requires the planning and implementation of strategies to motivate students to read (Loh et al., 2017). Therefore if schools wish to create these reading supportive cultures, the intent and execution must be considered in the WSLP, and school leadership support must ideally be gained (Merga & Mason, 2019).

While rare, some Australian documents detailed intent to develop a whole-school reading or literacy supportive culture. For example, in the section on developing a reading culture, AU22 included the following:

> Opportunities for independent reading will be created within class time. The English program at Years 7 to 9 will devote at least one period a week of class time for independent reading practise during which reading skills are explicitly taught. All subject areas have a responsibility to promote wider reading around their subject area and to reinforce these comprehension strategies. The Campus Libraries play a particular role in promoting a reading culture across the college. (AU22)

AU50 positions 'promoting a love of reading' on the first page of their six-page Whole Site Literacy Agreement, demonstrating that it is a key literacy priority for their school. The mention is also far from cursory, with detailed information on how a reading culture is being built within their school 'for enjoyment and learning'.

This includes

- Displays of new and interesting books, giving students a voice in book selection and purchasing books with the specific aim of engaging our students
- Whole school events such as Children's Book Week
- Supporting and encouraging participation in the Premier's Reading Challenge, Lucky Book Club
- Acknowledgement of reading success, in either achievement and/or effort, at assemblies or through awards
- Special reading events such as the Book Week Pyjama read-along
- Reading to and with (name of school) preschool children on a weekly roster basis
- Inviting, encouraging and acknowledging parents who listen to students read in the classroom
- Acknowledging time spent reading at home
- Conducting parent workshops to increase parent knowledge and understanding of how they can support literacy development at home.

In the classroom we promote a love of reading by

- Reading aloud to learners every day, modelling what good readers do
- Providing time to read for enjoyment
- Providing time for learners to share thoughts and ideas about books and participate in discussions about books
- Encouraging learners to promote books they have read to their classmates
- Engaging with buddy classes and preschool students focused on reading. (AU50)

In a similar vein, UK12 devotes half a page of its seventeen-page policy to description and images of what a 'reading area' should look like.

> At (School), we promote the importance of Reading for Pleasure. We believe in the importance of teaching our children to love and value books and to treat them with respect. Each classroom should have a designated 'reading area' in which the class reading books are displayed. This area should be/have:
>
> - Inviting and attractive to the children e.g. drapes, cushions, pretty lights, posters, plants, soft toys etc.

- Well organised. Books should be labelled clearly e.g. non-fiction, stories from around the world, poetry books, myths and legends, books by particular authors.
- Perhaps an author focus, a pin-board for children to pin recommendations, or a place for displaying book reviews.
- Books displayed in different ways e.g. some facing outwards, some on shelves, some in boxes, some on stands.

As such, some schools are already using their policies to describe their intent and planning to develop whole-school reading-supportive cultures, though many fall behind in this area or only give cursory consideration (as detailed in Merga & Gardiner, 2018). WSLP attention on developing a whole-school reading culture may include implications for resourcing, pedagogy, environments, and may include a range of other factors and practices.

> WSLPs are important opportunities for articulating intent to develop whole-school reading supportive cultures, as well as to detail steps to create and sustain this literacy-supportive culture.

7. Tailored and specific professional development planning

While professional development was mentioned in some Australian documents, it was rarely carefully considered in relation to improving student literacy learning. While there is a surprising lack of research that explores the influence of teacher knowledge on student learning outcomes (Guerriero, 2014), given that a key purpose of teachers' professional development is to transform new knowledge into practice to benefit students' learning (Avalos, 2011), this is an important area that deserves greater consideration.

It is also important to note that many Australian teachers in secondary schools are teaching in areas outside their field of expertise (Weldon, 2016), so it cannot be assumed that even staff acting as secondary English teachers have in-depth knowledge of how to foster students' literacy learning. As such, many of your teachers may need literacy training across the range of subjects.

When planning for professional development, it is worth considering how to tailor learning experiences so that they are more useful for educators.

> Professional learning opportunities for teachers have traditionally been offered through time-limited, short-term professional development courses. While these 'events' are frequently reported to lack relevance and value, be disconnected from teachers' previous learning, offer little follow-up and fail to promote opportunities for implementation of the new learning gained, they continue to persist as the dominant approach to teacher professional learning. (Keay et al., 2019, p. 125)

Where professional development is being planned to improve student literacy, it needs clear relevance and value. This will involve the planners talking to their educators and using needs analysis tools such as surveys to ensure that the learning planned meets the real-world needs of their teachers. Ideally connections should be made with teachers' previous learning, and rather than professional learning being a one-off or episodic affair, there ideally needs to be some continuity, with follow-up and opportunities to continue to extend learning through further self-paced activities. Opportunities for practical implementation of the new learning gained should be highlighted at the outset and at additional points along the learning journey, given that teachers typically prefer pragmatic and practical professional development such as 'shared practice, mentoring, observation of colleagues, and collaborative lesson development' (Jones & Lee, 2014, p. 245), with more abstract, theoretical approaches seen as lacking in value (Merga et al., 2020).

The professional development needs of your school community in relation to whole-school literacy are going to change over time, which is why it is unlikely that the professional development planned for within the WSLP will hold currency at evaluation and review. For example, at a US elementary school that was active in professional development of their staff as part of a school wide literacy reform, teachers' needs did not remain static; 'two years ago, staff development was focused on comprehension instruction during read alouds and during guided reading' and 'last year, the focus was teaching writing', while 'next year, staff development will focus on the word study portion of the literacy diet' (Walpole et al., 2004, p. 281). While professional development needs in this case were deemed somewhat foreseeable, enabling projected future planning, it is important to conduct regular needs analysis in this area as these targets may shift due to unpredictable issues emerging within the school population. For example, an unanticipated change in the local area of the school that sees an influx of refugees from non-English speaking backgrounds may trigger a need for professional development in supporting EAL/D learners across the curriculum.

The importance of thoughtful inclusion of professional development in the WSLP is a key theme featured in the literature on the creation and enactment of WSLPs (as reviewed in te Riele et al., 2021), however I argue that it is not sufficient to just mention that the intent is there. While consideration of professional development needs featured in WSLPs, the consideration was often cursory, and your school may benefit from professional development planning that is intentional and specific. For example, as noted by Alford and Windeyer (2014):

> in 2011, the recently formed Australian Curriculum, Reporting and Assessment Authority (ACARA) made it explicit that *all* [emphasis added] teachers will be required to provide pedagogy that responds to the language learning needs of students whose first language is not English, regardless of whether these teachers have had formal language teacher training. (p. 76)

If your school has a number of students who fall into the EAL/D category, but only some of your teachers have expertise in teaching English as an additional language or dialect, planning to meet this gap in professional learning to meet both student and curricular expectations would be prudent, with relevance and value that should be immediately apparent. In secondary school contexts, this will mean ensuring that teachers of subjects other than English (or Language Arts in the US) understand how to foster English language skills within their disciplines. For example, as noted by Tiegert and Lieder (2021) in the context of art education, 'it is important not to assume that the language, literacies, and content of the arts are organically accessible to CLD (culturally and linguistically diverse) students' (p. 429); 'art teachers need to be prepared to purposefully offer these students full and equal access to the art curriculum' (p. 429). To unlock the curriculum across subject areas, students from EAL/D backgrounds need to have strong English literacy skills, and how this will be facilitated needs to be built into the policy document.

While simply stating that professional development will be provided in the policy does allow for wriggle room to target emerging literacy issues, in many cases where student needs and issues are already well-known or foreseeable, tailored and specific planning should be possible and ideal. Literacy policy documents could benefit from stating professional development-related targets and specifying how these will be reached on a practical level. As with literacy-related targets, there are many ways to do this, but you may wish to detail professional learning priorities, targets, specific strategies and evaluation measures to determine success of implementation.

Furthermore, it could be prudent to build in ongoing professional development in secondary schools for teachers in subject areas other than English. For example, in UK60 it is noted:

> the third aim of the (name of school) Literacy Policy is 'To support and empower staff to effectively teach literacy skills in their subject'. In order to facilitate this, every half term the Literacy Across the Curriculum (LAC) Bulletin is circulated to all teaching staff. The LAC Bulletin provides CPD, guidance and Learning and Teaching ideas to help teaching staff effectively embed literacy teaching into their practice. Previous editions of the LAC Bulletin can be found here (hyperlink included).

This means that beyond using the literacy policy as a one-off opportunity to articulate how literacy learning should occur beyond subject English (and this is actually also included in the policy through a table that provides 'examples of how literacy is being embedded across the curriculum'), ongoing guidance will also be provided.

> It is unlikely to be sufficient to briefly note that facilitating professional development is a feature of the WSLP. Student needs and gaps in teacher's professional learning need to be identified, with commitment to ongoing review to identify emerging areas needing focus. Tailored and specific planning for ongoing professional learning that is responsive to current and evolving school needs can be detailed. Ongoing provision for professional development in literacy for secondary school teachers in subject areas other than English may be beneficial. Professional development should be practical rather than theoretical in its orientation.

8. Identifying struggling students

To meet the needs of students struggling with literacy, we need to know who they are, and what their needs are. It was concerning that so few Australian WSLPs articulated strategies and plans for screening students for specific learning disorders such as dyslexia, both in primary school contexts and beyond.

Early identification is important. Research suggests that timely identification of dyslexia is challenging and 'the closer assessments are to school entry the more accurate predictions become' (Thompson et al., 2015). Unfortunately, while early identification and intervention are beneficial for students with dyslexia, many children are not identified in the early years of schooling, with some not receiving support until they have substantially fallen behind their peers at school (Sanfilippo et. al., 2020). Unlike in the UK, in Australia 'there are no nationally recognized definitions of dyslexia or criteria that allow students with dyslexia to receive special education assistance at school', and 'to receive assistance in school, students must be assessed by an educational psychologist and receive a formal dyslexia diagnosis' (Sadusky, 2021, p. 472). While diagnosis can then enable schools to put into place resources and adjustments for these students, lack of an agreed system for identifying students with dyslexia in schools means that students can complete formal schooling without ever being identified and thus given appropriate support (Sadusky, 2021). Indeed, students who minimise the visibility of their struggles with good behaviour and compensatory strategies may be most likely to fail to be identified (MacCullagh, 2014), limiting their capacity to reach their full potential during schooling and beyond.

As such, processes for screening and identifying struggling students should take place at both primary and secondary schools to ensure that older students who have slipped through the cracks receive the support they need in order to attain functional literacy by the end of formal schooling.

Strategies for identifying students with specific learning disorders and difficulties that can impact upon literacy learning are needed in primary school, but given that many students enter secondary school while experiencing these issues, these strategies must also be present in this context. Our recent research found that 'less than two thirds (60.96%) of teachers agreed that their secondary school has effective strategies to identify students with specific learning disorders and difficulties (for example, dyslexia) that can impact upon literacy learning' (Merga, Mat Roni & Malpique, 2021a, p. 542). We need *all* schools to be able to identify the needs of struggling literacy learners beyond the early years, and every teacher can be part of this process. By including identification of struggling students in the WSLP, it becomes a whole-school responsibility.

UK policies provide examples of what this can look like to inform WSLPs developed in the Australian context. For example, in a Northern Irish primary school context, UK3 details addressing 'underachievement as soon as it emerges by identifying underachievement through ... teacher and classroom assistants' observation' as well as a range of listed diagnostic tools, with the dual focus on observation and assessment being a common feature of UK policies more broadly (for example, UK17). The UK3 policy then notes that the 'class teacher decides on the appropriate form of support', with a range of possible approaches listed. The policy also lists mechanisms to 'address continuing underachievement with support from other staff in the school' as well as to 'address continuing underachievement with support from outside the school'.

Similarly, UK11 takes a proactive approach to identifying struggling literacy learners.

> In literacy and language, an electronic tracking sheet is used to quickly show where difficulties are experienced, and any support required by the child is put in place immediately; progress is monitored by the class teacher and if not quickly resolved then this is reported to the headteacher who will consult on appropriate action to be taken. Educators meet each term with the headteacher to evaluate Curriculum Planning and children's progress. Children requiring support or extension are identified and appropriate interventions are planned. Staged Intervention is put in place in consultation with the parent and child. The Learning Support Teacher may undertake more detailed assessments with children who are experiencing difficulties e.g. the dyslexia screener and portfolio.

This identification involves careful monitoring of student achievement at classroom level, and further referral to additional internal supports for 'more detailed assessment' if required.

School literacy policies should plan for a whole-school approach to identifying struggling literacy learners to identify their issues and needs, and provide them with support. This should include processes for identification as well as responsible parties, particularly where further specialist help may be needed. Commitment to identifying struggling literacy learners needs to feature across the curriculum, and span both primary and secondary years of schooling.

9. Support for struggling literacy learners

Given that a whole-school approach to literacy should support all struggling literacy learners, their needs must be featured in WSLPs. The unfortunate reality is that most children who struggle with foundational literacy skills such as learning to read do not catch up with their higher achieving peers, but in fact, fall further and further behind (Walpole et al., 2004). It was surprising to find that in addition to failing to note how struggling literacy learners will be identified, many Australian WSLPs do not include mention of how to meet the needs of struggling literacy learners. This inclusion has pragmatic implications for teachers' practice: for example, 'a whole-school, co-ordinated approach to meeting the needs of students with dyslexia' can ensure that 'there is consistency among teachers in setting homework, marking work, and making assessment arrangements' (Long et al., 2007, p. 133).

Learning difficulties such as dyslexia do not only impact on students in the English classroom. Their impacts are felt in every subject where students are required to read and write. This is why whole-school approaches to supporting these students should be outlined in literacy policies where schools have applicable students. Furthermore, as noted by Burden and Burdett (2005), 'if mainstream schools are to become truly "dyslexia friendly"', whole-school literacy policies will need to also consider the emotional and motivational experiences of struggling literacy learners, in order to 'foster strong feelings of self-worth and self-determination in all pupils – generating, in effect, a truly inclusive ethos' (p. 103). Therefore, policies need to consider both the pragmatic requirements for interventions for skill development, but also the psychosocial aspects to support student wellbeing.

As I have previously mentioned, improving literacy skills can in some cases just be a matter of providing opportunity for practice, enabling the development of skills in key literacy areas. However, this is not going to be sufficient where fundamental skills are lacking. For example, as noted by Spichtig et al. (2022):

> simply increasing reading volume may not be helpful to students who typically read rapidly but with poor comprehension. Such students are more likely to benefit from instruction that promotes decoding and automatic word recognition, develops comprehension skills, teaches comprehension monitoring strategies, and incorporates strategies to motivate engagement such as utilizing texts tailored to each student's ability level and interests. (p. 13)

In addition, strategies such as reading aloud to students well beyond the early years of schooling can have a powerful effect in scaffolding and developing skills in struggling adolescent learners, supporting their learning without withdrawing them from the mainstream learning context for remedial assistance (Westbrook et al., 2019).

It is not enough to plan to meet the needs of students with diagnosed learning disorders or difficulties that impact upon their literacy learning. There is a wide diversity of reasons that struggling literacy learners fall behind. Most teachers are working with students experiencing diverse barriers to literacy learning at both group and individual levels, and many of these students do not have a diagnosed learning difficulty or EAL/D status (Merga, 2020b).

Reasons for falling behind may be complex and include both learner based and contextual issues (Walpole et al., 2004), but in reality, there is often more than one issue at play, at group and individual level (Merga, 2020b). For example, in my recent research a mainstream secondary English teacher listed some of the issues they were accommodating within their classroom that were felt to impact upon student literacy learning.

> EAL/D, Intellectual impairment, Speech language impairment, low attendance, multiple primary schools, ADD, ODD, ADHD, dyslexia, inability to sound out words, low comprehension, poor verbal expression, difficulty understanding verbal and/or written instructions, bullying, disengagement, difficulty spelling,

> limited vocabulary, gaps in education, health issues (e.g. spent significant time in hospital), low stamina for writing and reading, illegible handwriting, low expectations of themselves due to failing every semester for YEARS, lack of early intervention, working at different year levels significantly below the grade they're in. (Merga, 2020b, p. 380)

As such, strategies to improve student literacy may extend far beyond adjustments to pedagogy. For instance, where a key underlying issue in low literacy relates to high absenteeism, obviously no adjustments to pedagogy are going to make a difference for these students if they are not at school to be exposed to them. Any interventions included in school literacy policies must consider the breadth of issues faced by the students within the school, and the implications of collocations of these issues (for example, dyslexia and low attendance).

Furthermore, just as students become accustomed to failure, teacher expectations of struggling literacy learners may also decline, to the detriment of the student. Crevola and Hill (1998) provided professional development for teachers in schools adopting a 'whole-school approach to prevention and intervention in early literacy' (p. 133). The initial sessions 'revealed that the teachers held certain beliefs regarding the learning capabilities of the students within their schools', and that 'teacher, parent, and student expectations were all contentious' (Crevola & Hill, 1998, p. 146):

> It was obvious during these initial sessions that teachers had unwittingly lowered their expectations to match their beliefs regarding the level of the children in these educationally disadvantaged schools. The challenge that faced this group of teachers was accepting that all students were ready to learn and that their role was to create appropriate instructional experiences for each individual so that learning could take place at the point of need. (Crevola & Hill, 1998, p. 146)

As such, interventions to support struggling literacy learners may involve changing teacher beliefs and behaviours as well as their teaching approaches. Students struggling with functional literacy skills may not be exposed to higher order learning of skills and knowledge in critical literacy, and 'too often literacy programs, and practising teachers, take on a deficit model of literacy in which the assumptions made about low socioeconomic and marginalised students are that they can only handle basic literacy practices and skills' (Gutierrez et al., 2021, p. 54).

Where struggling literacy learners were included in Australian WSLPs, a statement around how supporting these students was a whole-school responsibility was often lacking, and further details on how this would look were also missing. For example, AU20 notes that 'students who are at risk of achieving below expected achievement standards (but not funded) will have a Personal Learning Plan (PLP) to monitor goals and targets for literacy development', but there is no articulation of how these students' needs will be met across the school, and no indication that this was even an expectation. It should be noted that AU20 was a four-page literacy policy produced for a remote school which takes students from the early years to the end of Year 12. Many of its students come from culturally and linguistically diverse backgrounds, and therefore, it could be contended that a far more comprehensive policy is needed to support these students.

Where interventions were included in Australian WSLPs, it was often related to intervention programmes that involved withdrawal of students, rather than strategies to support students within mainstream learning contexts. For example, AU68's only mention of dyslexia or dyslexic students is in relation to 'small group reading intervention groups for students diagnosed with Dyslexia with a teacher trained in the (commercial) Program'. This brevity could be because this primary school's entire Whole-school Literacy Agreement was a single page in length, but this serves as an illustrative example of why such brief documents may not be fit for purpose. Ideally, WSLPs could include 'regular small group literacy interventions' as such initiatives when delivered 'by subject staff given "moderate training" is more effective than in-class support' for 'raising reading ages' (Beverton & Sewell, 2002, p. 25). As such, teachers in subjects beyond English can and should be involved in literacy intervention once they are given sufficient training and support to be effective.

In contrast to their Australian counterparts, some UK documents identified key areas of focus and articulated a whole-school approach for supporting students facing a particular issue. For example, UK10 details 'Key Priorities Agreed for 2015–2016' for supporting EAL/D students:

> Each department will provide literacy interventions to support the progress in literacy of EAL students by:
>
> - Providing key vocabulary and definitions

- Supporting the spelling of key vocabulary
- Providing sentence stems and writing scaffolds where appropriate
- Using text modelling to support and develop the literacy footprint of EAL students
- Providing opportunities for role play and talking the text out loud to support
- understanding of register and different text types.

Similarly, UK52 provided a short list of key priorities for the same time frame, as well as a commitment to review:

- The use of the specific reading strategies of skimming, scanning, reading for meaning and reading for enjoyment.
- The modelling of writing by all teachers.
- The use of connective mats and vocabulary pyramids by all teachers
- The extending and embedding of strategies for teaching EAL/D pupils across the curriculum.
- Review of school priorities will take place: annually.

In this way, supporting students with EAL/D status is positioned as a whole-school responsibility, with a united whole-school approach taking the ambiguity out of whose role it is to support these students, and how this support should be delivered.

Specific strategies and resources for the support of struggling literacy learners were typically more detailed in UK documents than in those from Australian schools. For example, primary school UK17 describes some of the issues faced by students within the school, detailing external supports that may be drawn upon, and mentioning the Individual Education Plan as a key mechanism for logging student information and support initiatives:

> A small number of children throughout this school have difficulties in relation to language and literacy skills. These include speech problems, specific language difficulties, poor language experience and auditory problems. These pupils once identified, are referred for suitable outside agency support – e.g. Speech Therapy, Peripatetic Hearing Service Support and pupil need is recorded in an Individual Education Plan. All teachers in this school have responsibility for identifying and providing for pupils deemed to be gifted, underachieving, or with special

> educational needs within their classes. Diagnostic tests (e.g., PM bench marking/ Running Records) will be used appropriately to aid understanding of specific areas of difficulty, and to inform remediation.

Again, *all* teachers are explicitly implicated in this work.

In some cases, specific content was added to policies to support teachers perhaps not accustomed to helping students with literacy issues to support struggling students. For example, UK75 includes a one-page table in its seven-page document with support strategies for four commonly occurring writing issues that may be displayed by struggling literacy learners. These problems were:

> 1. Slow handwriting/tires easily. This can be due, in part, to Dyspraxia. Also it may be 'learned helplessness' in response to pressure. The logic goes, 'If I write slowly I won't have to do as much and perhaps someone will do it for me.'
> 2. Inefficient grip – may shake hand, massage fingers etc.
> 3. Poorly formed/shaped letters despite adequate practice
> 4. Poor page layout – may write down the middle of the page or over to the right. (UK75)

Guidance around the fourth problem ('Poor page layout') was detailed as follows.

> - Dyslexic and dyspraxic learners may share a lack of awareness of the importance of the left hand margin as the place to start writing.
> - Drawing bold margins on both sides of a page seems to help.
> - Persistent reminders to write down the left hand margin and to get close to the right hand margin seem to help, providing the main preoccupation is with learner's self-esteem.
> - Aim to 'accentuate the positive', using the language of success wherever possible. Often students will feel insecure about their presentation, and will therefore not put the effort in to improve it. (UK75)

This kind of guidance can be drawn upon by educators within the school who are not confident in their literacy expertise, and this shared approach means that a common set of strategies is adopted to support struggling writers. I will explore these kinds of shared approaches to student feedback in further detail in the subsequent section on *uniform feedback mechanisms*.

Finally, part of considering aforementioned literacy measures beyond test achievement as well as adopting effective interventions to support struggling literacy learners is having awareness that programmes and interventions employed within the school to enhance literacy test scores may have unintended negative side effects. Zhao (2017) noted that while 'it is universally accepted in medicine that any intervention can have unwanted effects that can damage the person it intends to heal' (p. 2), the same consideration is often not given to such measures in educational contexts. This means that 'evidence' in education 'focuses exclusively on proving or disproving the effectiveness of an intervention' with it remaining 'extremely rare to find a study that evaluates both the effectiveness and adverse effects of a product, teaching method, or policy in education', leaving the author to note that 'I have not yet found an educational product that comes with a warning label carrying information such as "this program works in raising your students' test scores in reading, but may make them hate reading forever"' (p. 4).

Simply, when you roll out an intervention, you will need to keep an eye on how the intervention impacts on students' skills, knowledge and attitudes, both in relation to the intended benefit, but also beyond. If spending hours on an intervention that helps struggling students to recognise and spell words from an approved vocabulary test list improves their performance on high-stakes testing, but also leads to less time being given to other, perhaps more important facets of literacy, the use of such interventions should be questioned. In particular, interventions that improve test scores but significantly decrease student motivation should be reconsidered (see Carr, 2020, for further explanation); if the intervention continues to be adhered to, you will need to take action to counter the side effects, so that the short-term benefits of the intervention do not ultimately outweigh longer term harm.

School literacy policies should detail approaches for whole-school support of struggling literacy learners, including reference to internal and external supports as applicable, with all teachers explicitly responsible. These should ideally address skill acquisition issues as well as engagement issues as required. Implications of collocated issues should be considered. Whole-school strategies to support struggling students should be articulated. This may include explanation of some recurring issues experienced by students with agreed and pragmatic approaches to supporting students detailed so that a common approach can be employed to support struggling literacy learners across the school.

10. The plurality of literacies

As detailed in Chapter 2, the range of literacies a WSLP could include is diverse, however, school literacy policies from Australia tend to be very limited in scope. If you feel that a narrow approach is sufficient to meet the learning needs of your students, or if you already have policies and plans addressing other kids of literacies and wish to avoid duplication, you can follow a similar approach. However, I wanted to raise the possibility of considering a broader range of literacies either directly in the policy, or as focused appendices to be read and implemented in parallel with the policy.

While UK policies also had a relatively narrow scope in their inclusion of a plurality of literacies, they did typically have greater consideration of information literacy. For example, UK4 included this section on information literacy:

Reading for information

Reading for the purposes of study requires specific skills. It is linked to the skill of Managing Information ... whereby children access, select, record and communicate information. Through modelled, shared and guided reading we will develop the following skills:

- extracting information from books using the contexts pages or index
- classifying information by alphabetical order
- posing questions for their research
- using dictionaries
- using a search engine on the internet
- using reference material such as encyclopaedias, atlases, directories, timetables, brochures, etc
- formulating questions which require a search for information
- skimming a text to get an impression of what it is about

- scanning a text to search for specific information
- making notes, selecting what is relevant and appropriate
- distinguishing between fact and opinion in evaluating information.

This excerpt makes visible the connection between information literacy and literacy skills such as reading comprehension, and it is clear to see how building information literacy skills will also support learning in other subjects such as humanities and social sciences.

UK policies also typically gave greater consideration to the intersection of literacy and other areas of the curriculum. UK12 considers how the subject area drama intersects with literacy to offer student benefit:

> We value the role that drama can play in helping children access, explore and respond to a variety of texts. From the time children enter our school they are given opportunities to engage with texts through a range of dramatic devices, such as hot-seating, role-play and reader's theatre. Drama enables children to enter and explore unfamiliar environments, times and cultures. By presenting texts in a dramatic way, children learn that literature can be made public, shared and interactive.

In a similar vein, UK4 includes the following in relation to ICT and literacy:

> **ICT**
>
> We aim to make maximum use of ICT across the curriculum to promote the pupils' literacy skills, as well as developing competence in ICT skills. This involves the use of computers, the Interactive White Board and also the possibilities offered by the wide range of audio- visual materials, graphics, radio and television broadcasts available.
>
> Pupils will have ample opportunities to gain confidence in the use of ICT, for example in using word processors for drafting, using spreadsheets and databases, and using CD-ROM and the Internet to research and communicate, incorporating the 5 E's.
>
> The children's work will be used to enhance the school's website.
>
> The range of ICT resources available include:
>
> - Desktops and Laptops with access to C2K network
> - Interactive Whiteboards

- CD-ROMs
- Internet access
- Audio players with a variety of spoken texts
- T.V., video, DVD players with a variety of material

> ICT will be used to enhance literacy skills, not just within the programme of study for Literacy and Language, but as an integral feature of all programmes of study.

Given that Digital Literacy is one of the General Capabilities in the AC alongside literacy (ACARA, 2022a), this UK example has clear relevance for Australian WSLP creation. Not only does UK4 show how ICT use can build both literacy and ICT skills, but it also considers how ICT can be used to develop literacy across the curriculum. It is also worth noting that this 2011 policy is clearly dated in reference to the technological affordances it mentions, highlighting that to include the intersection between ICT and literacy in your policy in a meaningful way, you will need to be willing to regularly revise this component of the policy to incorporate evolving technological affordances. I do not urge greater screen time for students who are already spending large portions of their school day engaging with technology (as explored in Merga, 2016a; Merga & Williams, 2016), rather I suggest that in some cases, it may be ideal to be more intentional in this ICT use so that literacy skills are receiving attention in ICT use across the curriculum.

Furthermore, in Australian policies there was very little consideration of disciplinary and content area literacy. While further focus is also needed in UK counterparts, in some cases there is consideration of disciplinary literacy. For example, in relation to the development of spelling and vocabulary across the school, the policy for UK16 recommends that educators 'display key vocabulary in context, ensuring a disciplinary approach to literacy'. UK73 considers how the skill of writing is key for learning in subject areas beyond English:

> Writing has close links with other areas of the curriculum, for example expressive arts and creative writing, science and functional writing and social studies and critical literacy. Inter-disciplinary studies are likely to involve both research and a strong element of presentation, and provide valuable opportunities to extend language skills.

This second point has more of a content-area literacy focus than a disciplinary literacy focus, and as I explored in Chapter 2, both are important. As also noted in Chapter 2, schools need to identify the breadth of literacies to be included in their policies, to decide what will be privileged. They should then explicitly plan for literacy learning across all subjects, either directly within the policy or in subject-related appendices, and this planning needs to consider content area literacy focus and disciplinary literacy focus. This planning needs to promote student learning through use of texts to meet disciplinary goals 'in the context of disciplinary practices' (ILA, 2017, p. 3). This approach recognises that 'basic reading and writing processes do not adequately prepare students for advanced participation in each discipline' (p. 4), which is why building disciplinary literacy is important at both primary and secondary schooling levels.

> Under a disciplinary literacy approach, students use discipline-specific frameworks for the same two critical tasks:
>
> 1. Interpreting texts: In mathematics class, students might evaluate and critique solutions like a mathematician would; in history class, students might corroborate evidence across sources like a historian would; in a nutrition class, students might compare and contrast food labels like a nutritionist would; and so forth in each discipline.
> 2. As students learn to read and evaluate texts like somebody in their discipline would, they can also engage in critique of these texts. For instance, in science class, students might use their knowledge of scientific methods and scientific principles to critique an online text that advertises a dubious product that claims miraculous 'research-based' results.
> 3. Composing and revising texts: What constitutes 'good writing' in one discipline may not be considered 'good writing' in another. For instance, an English teacher might expect his students' poems to meet one set of criteria (e.g. inclusion of metaphors), whereas a horticulture teacher might expect her students to create plant taxonomies that meet an entirely different set of criteria (e.g., inclusion of superordinate and subordinate categories). (ILA, 2017, p. 4)

The WSLP needs to consider how core skills such as essay writing or oral presentation delivery can be strategically fostered across disciplinary areas, in ways that reflect disciplinary norms, and drawing upon discipline-appropriate textual sources.

School literacy policies need to consider literacy beyond a narrowed conceptualisation in order to meet learning objectives across the range of disciplines. You should consider planning for building content area literacy and specific disciplinary literacy, as well as weighing up the benefits for including other literacies described in Chapter 2 either directly within the text or as appendices. You can also consider how the ICT and literacy General Capabilities can be mutually developed across the curriculum.

11. Pandemic responsiveness

As per the dates listed in Tables 1 and 2, the vast majority of the policies analysed to inform this book were written pre-pandemic, so it is not surprising that there is little informing material available that demonstrates responsiveness to literacy issues arising from the pandemic in WSLPs. This is a gap that you can fill in order to enhance the relevance of your WSLP.

I hope that by the time this book is published in 2023, the impact of the pandemic on students literacy learning has declined. However, educators will still need to mitigate negative impacts of prior pandemic-related effects on student learning as I will outline further in this section. Whether you consider pandemic-related issues in the body of your policy, or as a related appendix, it is important that all documents written or revised from this point consider the realistic prospect of further impacts, given the likelihood of the emergence of further variants which may be less responsive to vaccinations developed for earlier strains (Egui et al., 2021).

First, the biggest impact on student literacy going forward is likely to be education interruption. Future education interruption that may be anticipated from virulent future variants can be whole school, where learning ceases or shifts to remote form. As we have noted in our recent paper, and as has been observed in the past, education interruption in COVID-19 'often entails a shift to remote, home learning that may be supported by educators and family members to widely varying degrees', which is why we used 'the term "education interruption" rather than "education cessation", as interruption encompasses both stoppage and hindering of an activity' (Merga, Malpique et al., 2021, p. 1139). If schools are not closed, education interruption can also be individual, where a student or close contact contracts COVID and must isolate, or where a student experiences COVID illness which necessitates cessation in learning. It is impossible to predict the extent of future education interruption that will impact on individual and group learning in the future, though its occurrence can be viewed as virtually certain, and therefore it should be considered in planning.

We also cannot ignore the reality that previously experienced education interruption is likely to already have had an impact on students' literacy learning. Researchers have begun to explore the impact of COVID-19 on student learning, and predictions for the ongoing effects are dire (Azevedo et al., 2020; Kuhfeld et al., 2020). Children may have lost 'more than a full year's worth of learning from a three-month school closure', putting them 'behind the curriculum' on re-entry to school, and meaning that they may 'fall further behind as time goes on' (Kaffenberger, 2021, p. 1). Simply returning to learning as designed prior to the education interruption is not advised, with Kaffenberger (2021) stressing the importance of reducing curricular pace on reopening and covering any learning opportunities that were missed before moving on, reducing ambition for broad curricular coverage and focusing instead on the building of foundational skills. By far, the group most vulnerable to negative outcomes of education interruption are our students from disadvantaged backgrounds. It can be contended that 'in regular times schools play a role as a "Great Equalizer" – they provide a single learning environment and integrated peer groups for children from different backgrounds', and the 'pandemic puts this role of schools at risk' (Agostinelli et al., 2022, p. 9).

Specific effects of the pandemic on student literacy learning are beginning to be captured by the research. We found ourselves in an unanticipated position on a research project in the early days of the pandemic. We were working on a project designed to capture data on teachers' experiences of teaching writing in primary schools, and these schools were suddenly hit with pandemic conditions which saw interruptions to schooling across states and territories, through these varied greatly between locations (Sacks et al., 2020).

While the pandemic impacted upon our original plans for data collection, it also put us in the unique position to be able to capture data on the impact of COVID-related education interruption on the teaching of writing in Australian primary schools.

From our survey of 310 primary school teachers, most respondents felt that COVID had impacted upon writing instruction delivered to their students (Merga, Malpique et al., 2021). Teachers focused on the following points in their explanation of the impacts they experienced:

- **Interruption, regression and curricular adjustment**
  There was less time for writing instruction. There was a focus on familiar tasks and skills rather than introduction of new ones. In some cases, there was no writing instruction during periods of education interruption. Routines were interrupted and planned curricular delivery needed adjustment. Children's writing skills regressed, and new material covered online had to be re-taught once classrooms reopened.
- **Limitations on instructional approach**
  There was less explicit instruction and limited learning facilitated through peer interaction. Teachers adjusted their instructional approaches, such as through creation of instructional videos to explain key features of writing.
- **Device reliance and limitations**
  Students may have unequal and unreliable access to devices and internet within their homes. Not all students had access to online learning, and some had their learning supported by telephone or physical delivery of learning materials. Students became reliant on device-related supports (for example, spell check) rather than developing the skills and approaches needed to perform these tasks. Lower achieving students were not always available for support sessions designed to assist them. Teachers of children too young to independently use devices for learning at home found device reliance particularly challenging.
- **Meeting individual needs**
  Differentiation was often not possible, and provision of individual support and feedback was limited.

- **Parent support**
  Parents needed to act as home schooling education supports and to facilitate students' device use. Parents were not necessarily equipped or available to be educators. Parents were not always fluent English language speakers able to support writing in English. Parents needed teacher support and instruction to be able to support home schooling. Where parents provided heavy assistance to their children, teachers were unsure about students' real progress.
- **Wellbeing and motivation**
  Teacher wellbeing was affected by the pressures of adapting their modes of delivery and supporting families to learn from home. Student anxiety and stress impacted upon their learning. Student motivation was lower. Teachers also had to deal with parental stress.
- **Positive outcomes**
  Positive changes to writing instruction focused on increased support from colleagues for planning and sharing of resources.
- **Assessment**
  Teachers found it difficult to assess student learning in writing during this time, and manner of assessment changed. The cancellation of high-stakes NAPLAN testing of writing was viewed as a positive.

These points are adapted from Table 2 (pp. 1144–1145) in Merga, Malpique et al. (2021). For an example of what each of these themes looked like in the text responses of our respondents, I encourage you to view the original table in the open access paper.

For the purposes of your policy, at school level you can use these data to consider how you will mitigate the impacts of education interruption, with a particular focus on planning to support your vulnerable students. Depending on your school circumstances, these planned measures to mitigate education interruption may vary widely, and may include but not be limited to the following:

- **To meet possible future needs, how will the school facilitate adequate resourcing of all students to enable remote literacy learning?**

For example, where your school does not require 1:1 devices, and homes within the community are known to lack resourcing, this may involve raising and putting aside funds for the acquisition of take-home wi-fi enabled devices to be borrowed for students whose learning will be hindered due to a lack of devices within the home.

- **What are the key foundational learnings from the curriculum for each year level that must be taught?**
  A far lighter 'essentials' curriculum can be extracted from the AC for focus in return to learning. You will also need to assess the extent to which content covered during previous periods of educational interruption was learned, and cover this ground again as needed to avoid students falling through the cracks.
- **How can explicit instruction in literacy be supported more effectively in periods of educational interruption?**
  Adequate resourcing will be part of the mitigating strategy, and further research is needed in this area, and you may also wish to further investigate and potentially invest in technologies which can more efficiently facilitate this in remote schooling if required and appropriate.
- **How will you prevent students from becoming overly reliant on digital affordances such as spelling checkers, and typing rather than handwriting?**
  A balanced emphasis on both transcription modes will be needed, and both student and parent education to limit the use of assistive technologies such as spell checkers may need to be delivered. If students have become dependent on these affordances during periods of educational interruption, strategies to wean them off them may be required.
- **How will you support differentiation in literacy learning during educational interruption?**
  There will need to be careful inclusion of literacy learning activities with sufficient scope to allow all students to participate and learn, and both group and individual student feedback mechanisms may need to be revisited to ensure that they are sufficiently targeted and regular.

- **How can parent support be harnessed to support student literacy learning during educational interruption?**
  Schools may need to increase their parent education engagements where possible, highlighting that parent intervention during student assessment can be detrimental to collecting meaningful data about student learning. They may also need to concentrate a greater portion of their time with students who do not have home supports to ensure that these students do not have their disadvantage compounded.
- **Are school libraries sufficiently staffed and resourced, and are there mechanisms in place to provide high quality home reading materials to students during times of education interruption?**
  Given that availability of books in the home is associated with educational benefits (Evans et al., 2010), ensuring that the library is ready and able to ensure that students in home with limited reading materials are not disadvantaged is essential.

School literacy policies need to consider the effects of previous pandemic-related education interruption as well as seek to mitigate the impacts of reasonably expected future education interruption, given the uncertain times that we are living through. By concentrating on a remedial and simplified curriculum on return from significant periods of education interruption, students are less likely to fall behind in their literacy learning trajectories. This section poses additional questions for you to ponder when planning to mitigate the impacts of COVID-related education interruption.

12. Research evidence base

It can be contended that school policies in general 'are forged in a crucible that mixes political realities, practitioner wisdom, technical expertise and whatever can be extracted from research' (Cuban, 1984, p. 2), and this quote has maintained relevance over time. Evidence-based education and policy planning should ideally be informed by robust educational research evidence. Drawing on research to make decisions around what to include and exclude in a WSLP can increase the likelihood that the policy will have a positive impact.

But what is evidence based education, and what constitutes evidence based practise? Allen et al., (2021) note that 'evidence-based practices are well established practices or interventions that have undergone a rigorous evaluation process and demonstrated effectiveness with specific population groups, for example, certain school communities, year levels or students with particular needs', and 'rather than relying on the pendulum swings of fads and opinion, evidence-based practice relies on significant and reliable evidence, obtained by rigorous, replicable methods' (p. 4). However, in reality, it is really not that simple.

We know that research evidence often significantly lags behind the needs of schools, and current COVID-related constraints on conducting research in schools are going to further exacerbate this issue. Methods sufficiently rigorous to ensure a credible research base, such as the use of randomised controlled trials in schools, 'are simply not realistic in the current uncertain climate' (Merga, Mat Roni, Loh & Malpique, 2021 p. 339).

For research to be undertaken and have the opportunity to undergo 'a rigorous evaluation process' (p. 4) and demonstrate effectiveness (Allen et al., 2021), it needs to be funded. When funding is secured from industry, commercial interests can strongly dictate which areas of research are able to accrue a critical mass of evidence, significantly influencing the research focus that is privileged. Now that we have the potential for government intervention over what is given external funding through Australian Research Council grants, political interests can also shape which educational research in Australia can be funded, and thus undertaken (Nature editorial team, 2022). This means that in current times, you will predominantly see Australian research in areas aligning with industry and political interests.

Who gets to decide which practices are *best practice*? Ideally it should be the end users (schools), but strong data literacy will be needed so that practitioners can understand exactly what the research is saying, as well as its limitations, in order to make decisions about what constitutes best practice. Educational researchers stress the utility of their work, but unless the educators reading their work are experts in understanding concepts such as statistical significance, sample size, and the limitations of different methods, what constitutes an evidence-based practice might be very subjective indeed. Also, even practices that have relatively strong research support may be subsequently debunked, so we can only ever claim to follow best practice based on available evidence.

There is also a serious issue with knowledge mobilisation between researchers and schools. Researchers need to learn from schools, and allow the needs of schools to shape their research, rather than exclusively chasing their own pet practices and theories. The knowledge and interests of schools needs to be shared in active exchanges with researchers.

Furthermore, the point of most educational research is to lead to real-world gains in learning and teaching, however educational researchers are not necessarily good at sharing their findings in ways that resonate with classroom teachers. There is a growing desire for educational research associations to bridge the gap between research and translation, for example, as articulated by the British Educational Research Association (BERA, 2018):

> Educational researchers should communicate their findings, and the practical significance of their research, in a clear, straightforward fashion, and in language judged appropriate to the intended audience(s). Researchers have a responsibility to make the results of their research public for the benefit of educational professionals, policymakers and the wider public … (p. 18)

Despite this desire, there may be little practical support in universities for this kind of research communication, regardless of the positive position they may claim to hold on the matter (Merga, 2021d; Merga & Mason, 2021).

This is really problematic given that time-poor classroom teachers and school leadership may rarely have time to deeply read academic literature on literacy research. This work may be somewhat inaccessible to them anyway, as academic journal articles are written to be consumed by other academic researchers and may therefore be very jargon rich, with limited connection to pragmatic application in the classroom. The reality is that educators 'may infrequently take advantage of educational research findings, and researchers may fail to draw on teachers' craft knowledge to contribute to a professional knowledge base' (Joram et al., 2020, p. 1). Thus it is unsurprising that while WSLPs mentioned supporting policies, mention of supporting research was rare.

The reality is that only a limited body of research in education manages to span the divide between academia and the classroom. In addition, there are very few practices that have robust evidence to support their implementation across diverse contexts. Taking into account the limitations of the available research, you will need to determine what degree of supporting evidence is considered sufficient at your school level.

The next challenge is to consider how this evidence should be incorporated in your WSLP. A document heavily bogged down by academic quotes and citations is simply not going to be desirable for a working policy in most contexts. However, particularly where the school is innovating beyond its prior practices, such as when adopting a new approach to literacy intervention or development of a whole-school reading culture, some reference to recent peer-reviewed materials that substantiate that the school is pursuing research supported practice in this regard may enhance the rigour of the document. It may also inspire confidence in interested stakeholders, such as parents.

Where your WSLP claims to be following a research supported path, at least some connection to that research should feature. For example, AU58 claims to be using 'an evidence-based and effective early literacy program'; where there is an explicit claim of evidence-based or research-supported practice, a reference or link to supporting evidence should be provided. This is particularly important, given the tendency for some commercial educational products to claim they are evidence-based, but under closer scrutiny, the evidence base has been generated in ways that do not satisfy basic credibility criteria, as I explore further in Chapter 7 . It will also be useful to defend the school's use of a programme or practice if this link between the decisions promoted in the policy and extant evidence is established. As I contended earlier in this book, literacy is contentious. Even if later on you find out that a programme is not effective for whatever reason, if you made the decision to use it based on the best available knowledge at that time, and substantiated this approach by linking to this evidence, it can potentially insure you against criticism to some extent, even when the programme fails. Given how changeable and controversial literacy is, this level of protection seems sensible.

Furthermore, as I have explored in detail elsewhere, very bad decisions have been made in schools that fly in the face of currently available research-supported understandings of best practice, such as 'decisions to remove all paper books in libraries and replace them with devices' (Merga, 2022a, p. 71). Just as you teach your students not to make key decisions based on opinions alone, considering the available research before making big decisions that can impact on student literacy learning and engagement is key. However, I recognise that research literacy is a learned skill, and that to be able to identify and interpret research, and gauge its applicability to unique teachers and teaching contexts is not easy. This is why some research has flagged the potential value of a research curator within a school, 'who would search for, vet, and present research literature, adapting it to individual teachers and their educational setting' (Joram et al., 2020, p. 9). To support staff to take on this role, or perform this role individually, professional development opportunities may be needed.

Some of the key possible uses of research to support your policy are as follows:

- To justify a new approach to literacy teaching within the school
- To justify use of specific literacy interventions to support struggling literacy learners
- To inform best practice in implementation of a new approach or intervention
- To show that your policy is responsive to current understandings of best practice
- To inform any grant proposals your school may produce to win funding related to initiatives featured in the literacy policy.

You should consider the available research base when planning for implementation of new innovations in the teaching of literacy. In some cases it may be prudent to show justification for new directions taken in literacy teaching or interventions.

13. Handwriting and typing

The transcription skills of handwriting and typing are both essential to enable students to communicate effectively. Writing is 'one of the most powerful tools used to communicate our knowledge, emotions and beliefs, across distance and time' as well as being 'a fundamental part of the school curriculum as an outcome and as a means to demonstrate learning across subjects and grades' (Malpique & Pino-Pasternak, 2017, para. 1). This means that when student literacy is being measured, students' transcription abilities will always be directly or indirectly implicated in their performance. For example, when a young student with proficient handwriting skills but poor typing ability is given an online writing assessment, they may perform well below their actual writing ability level because their typing is slow and inaccurate.

While a WSLP cannot include everything, I contend that attention to both forms of transcription should be explicitly given, particularly as insufficient attention is often applied to developing these essential writing skills in schools. Research suggests that 'writing and writing instruction in most classrooms are inadequate', and 'these findings were generally universal, applying across countries and grades' (Graham, 2019, p. 279). Including handwriting and typing in the WSLP can draw attention to their importance, and ensure that these skills are developed across the curriculum.

The majority of Australian WSLPs did not include handwriting. Of the eighty-three Australian WSLPs that I analysed, twenty-five mentioned handwriting, compared with fifty-seven of the eighty-three UK documents, suggesting that you are more than twice as likely to find consideration of handwriting in a UK policy than an Australian policy.

For example, UK1 includes a handwriting chart with lower case letters, capital letters and numbers, as well as guidance on basic letter shapes. It also includes explicit 'aims' for handwriting:

1. To know the importance of clear and neat presentation in order to communicate meaning effectively
2. To write legibly in both joined and printed styles with increasing fluency and speed
3. To have a correct pencil grip
4. To know that all letters start from the bottom except v, w, o, r, finish at the top
5. To form all letters correctly
6. To know the size and orientation of letters. (UK1)

Secondary school educators reading this may question the purpose of such material for inclusion in their school's WSLPs, but given that some students enter high school without the ability to produce legible handwriting, this kind of guidance can be useful at both primary and secondary school levels. Furthermore, the impact of Presentation Effect can have an ongoing influence on student performance which is research supported (Graham et al., 2011).

> Consider, for example, a situation where students are asked to share what they know about a given topic on a written test. According to the Presentation Effect, a test response that is less legible will receive a lower score for content than the same paper written more legibly. (Santangelo & Graham, 2016, p. 226)

In addition, research suggests that when students (aged 9–14 years) need to independently generate text while also producing writing that is legible, this results in the production of less legible work than that produced by the same students on a simple copying task (Fogel et al., 2022). This suggests that as demands on students' writing increase, their legibility may suffer, highlighting the importance of continued attention on handwriting practice.

Similar to UK1, UK6 devoted a separate (though not complete) page to handwriting in their policy, noting that 'children progress through a variety of developmental stages before they have the necessary hand eye co-ordination, fine motor skills and visual discrimination to produce a conventional handwriting style', and that the school aims 'to promote handwriting which develops from an early print to an individual writing style which is neat, swift and legible. Handwriting should demonstrate knowledge of lower and upper case letter formation, size and spacing.' It also details the handwriting approach followed within the school.

In addition to the many real-world benefits that strong typing skills offer young people, the shift to online NAPLAN literacy testing in Australia has made this skill more important to schools concerned with improving their NAPLAN performance, so it was surprising that only four WSLPs out of the eighty-three analysed even mentioned typing. For example, AU21 recognised the need for attention on typing, noting that 'students need to develop their word processing skills through typing programs and using Microsoft Word'. Perhaps the low frequency of consideration of typing related to the fact that

NAPLAN was not online or transitioning to online mode when the older WSLPs in the sample were written. While this lack of consideration was unexpected given schools' aforementioned reliance on high-stakes testing, this was still more coverage than in UK documents, so this is one area in which we cannot look to the UK for examples.

Furthermore, remote schooling resulting from COVID-19 educational interruption, and the likelihood of its recurrence in the future as discussed in the previous section on pandemic responsiveness, means that improving students' typing proficiency is more important than ever. This set of circumstances has:

> forced teachers, students and families to rely more on technology-based forms of communication, not as a complement to traditional teaching conducted in the classroom, but as the unique means of teaching through computers, tablets, or smartphones, whenever schools, or whole systems, go into lockdown.
>
> This raises very important questions about students' abilities to communicate effectively through keyboarding or touch-typing and about the pedagogical strategies needed by educators to continue teaching writing (either on pen and paper or on keyboards) through distant synchronous activities (learning at the same time, in real time, such as during videoconferencing) or asynchronous activities (learning not occurring at the same time such as via email or set online class assignments). (Malpique, 2020, paras. 2–3).

As such, WSLPs should include planning for teaching and learning across both transcription modes from the early stages of school, right up to the end of secondary school, given that the impact of transcription skills on young people's ability to demonstrate their attainment across the curriculum will be ongoing. Furthermore, as aforementioned, for pandemic responsive planning, schools need to closely consider how student progression across both modes of transcription can be sustained during periods of education interruption.

> Given the importance of both handwriting and typing for enabling students to demonstrate their achievement at primary and secondary schooling levels, these transcription skills warrant inclusion in your WSLP.

14. Uniform feedback mechanisms

In the earlier section on support for struggling literacy learners, I described specific content in WSLPs that could support teachers to help struggling students. The adoption of uniform feedback mechanisms published in the policy is one way that this can be done.

On a pragmatic level, some WSLPs focused on whole-school approaches to providing feedback on literacy that enabled students to experience consistency across learning areas. For example, AU64 included an 'agreed whole school approach to editing' of student writing, along with a supporting table that 'contains editing marks that are utilized by the whole school'. The seven specified marks included required students to do one of the following:

- Start a new paragraph
- Check case of the letter (capital or lower case)
- Correct the spelling
- Add something
- Check punctuation
- Delete/take out something
- Check word choice. (AU64)

This simple strategy for working toward uniformity of editing approach across the school could support students who struggle with feedback literacy, for whom inconsistency in feedback across teachers can be problematic. It is also a useful way of seeing how a whole-school approach can be practically operationalised. This document also detailed an 'agreed whole school approach to reading' as well as an 'agreed whole school approach to writing'.

Similarly, UK policies included whole-school marking policies (for example, UK2), with secondary school UK8 including a simple appendix that can be used across the school. It includes agreed symbols for teacher annotation, explaining that 'to ensure good practice and to standardise marking across the school, it is recommended that teachers follow a common set of annotation symbols', and these relate to the following.

- A good point
- A good point showing real insight

- Inaccurate or poorly supported
- Detail missing; further explanation required
- Irrelevant material
- Underline key word or key point
- Confusing or incorrectly applied material
- New paragraph required
- Spelling error
- Grammar error
- Capital letter
- Full Stop. (UK8)

Unlike the Australian example, this UK example provides guidance for annotation not simply concerned with student errors: it also includes symbols to provide positive feedback to students. However, it also does not take for granted that teachers across the curriculum will be comfortable providing feedback on issues relating to literacy, so it additionally provides the following guidance.

> It is important not to tick (✓) too often; especially if overall mark awarded does not reflect a high standard of work. It is recommended that underlining (_) is used to indicate a key point being made.
>
> It is important that work is well marked and annotated, but it is not useful to a pupil to have every spelling mistake highlighted; especially weaker spellers. A sea of red or green pen is off putting and often detracts from key points being made. It is recommended that some key words are highlighted for spelling and then a comment is placed on the work to indicate the need for pupils to proof read and/or use a dictionary to aid spelling improvement. (UK8)

As such, the pragmatic whole-school guidance given in this UK document considers student motivation and engagement in parallel with the building of skill and knowledge in literacy.

One striking aspect of some UK literacy policies in comparison with their Australian counterparts was the sheer level of detail devoted to adopting a whole-school approach to literacy feedback. For example, UK16 is a ten-page document, and three of these pages are devoted solely to a whole-school policy on feedback.

This includes the following features:

- A comprehensive definition of how feedback is conceptualised within the school
- Aims of feedback.
- Underpinning principles of feedback.
- Type and frequency of verbal, written, peer, self and group feedback.
- A common set of symbols for feedback annotations.
- A plan for monitoring of, and evaluation of the effectiveness of feedback.

As such, there is scope for Australian documents to give far more consideration to whole-school literacy feedback mechanisms than currently typically seen.

> School literacy policies can include uniform feedback mechanisms for assessment of literacy across subject areas and year levels. These should take into account provision of feedback for fostering literacy skills, but also student engagement and motivation.

15. Literacy for ages and stages

Students' literacy needs do not only reflect their literacy knowledge and skill levels, they also to some extent reflect the specific ages and schooling stages they are at. Little consideration was given in Australian documents to the delivery of literacy learning experiences related to literacy needs related to specific ages and stages. For example, while it is expected that Australian WSLPs for secondary schools will be silent on early childhood literacy, greater consideration of the needs of these young learners was expected to be seen in Australian policies for primary schools.

UK policies paid more attention to literacy needs and different phases of learning, perhaps because this is reflective of the UK education system, which addresses student learning in relation to Key Stages. For example, UK40 noted that in EYFS (Reception) which is the Australian equivalent of kindergarten, 'children are given opportunities to speak and listen and represent ideas in their activities; use communication, language and literacy in every part of the curriculum; and, become immersed in an environment rich in print and opportunities to communicate'.

What this will look like is then further explored:

> ... children have daily Letters & Sounds lessons to develop skills like blending and segmenting in preparation for early reading and writing. A wide range of exciting Learning Zones provide children with opportunities to develop their communication, language and literacy skills on a daily basis with a focus on child initiated activities. As well as a Writing Area, which provides children with a range of materials with which to experiment and practice mark marking/letter formation (and eventually to practice taught skills), other Learning Zones are enhanced to provide children with the opportunity to read and write in a range of contexts. A range of resources in the outdoor area, including a mud kitchen menu and writing belts, provide valuable opportunities to engage children in writing for pleasure. In the outdoor area children have constant access to Reading and Writing sheds which are filled with engaging, exciting resources that children can use independently. They also have access to a vast range of texts, including fiction and nonfiction. Children enjoy daily 'story time' so they become familiar with stories and authors and begin to develop a love of reading.
>
> Adult led activities in EYFS are usually linked to stories, poems or nursery rhymes or to cross curricular Topics. From when they start school, children learn that writing can have a range of purposes and they begin to explore the features of different types of writing. (UK40)

Other documents such as UK45 also dedicate a notable portion of the policy to addressing the unique literacy needs of young students.

In addition to early childhood literacy, whole-school literacy policies that include students in secondary schooling years may also consider the inclusion of the unique literacy needs of children in the middle and upper years of schooling. For example, my 2018 book covers some of the unique literacy engagement issues facing children in the middle years of schooling (Merga, 2018).

Your policy may wish to include details specific to literacy relating to key learning stages within schooling, such as the particular needs of young children in the early childhood years if applicable.

Things to never include

I have been reticent to deprecate features of the WSLPs that I analysed, coming from outside their school context. However, bearing in mind that every document included for analysis in this book was freely and easily available online as a result of a Google search using very generic keywords, I was sometimes surprised by what I found.

First, in some policies there were images of students. This could be fine if student and parent approvals were sought for publication of such images where they could be accessed by literally anyone with internet connection, so it might not be an issue. That said, I would stress that images of students should not be included in publicly available documents unless approvals from both students and their parents have been secured.

Second, I was surprised to read a policy that identified (by name) twelve underachieving children (UK32) along with their literacy scores and comments on their learning trajectory. While the included data is important internal information to support communication around student achievement, as a complete stranger outside the school, I should not be able to access specific literacy scores of named students from the UK. This information should never be made publicly available.

Bearing in mind that as I have previously explained, your policy reflects the values of your school, respecting the privacy of the students in your school is a key consideration. As I have explained elsewhere, even where communications are limited to within the school community, 'information about students' research contributions, attitudes and achievements need to be shared with close consideration given to its possible impact on how these students are seen within the school, by their peers and by their teachers' (Merga, 2022a, p. 75). Please do not share images or information about your students within or beyond your school community without consideration of possible impacts upon the students.

CHAPTER 5

Managing the development and implementation of whole-school literacy

Developing, revising and implementing a WSLP all involve managing change. To drive lasting change within your school, close attention needs to be given to how this change will be facilitated, and you may wish to consider adopting a strategic approach.

Often a new course is charted unsuccessfully within schools, and Cuban (1984) somewhat humorously described this as 'the familiar pattern for a new school improvement idea in which a burst of romance is followed by frustration and disappointment' (pp. 5–6). To sustain the 'love', it can help to brush up on your change management skills, even if you already have considerable experience designing and implementing whole-school initiatives.

As you can see from the previous chapters, leading a WSLP involves managing key relationships. Indeed, this can be seen in that defining the roles and responsibilities for contribution of diverse stakeholders to the policy and its implementation are a feature of some WSLPs. You will need to build and maintain the buy-in of a broad range of stakeholders within and beyond the school.

To this end, this chapter will draw on key principles of change management in order to support literacy leaders to succeed in this endeavour, going into detail on how to assemble a literacy team, engage school leadership support, and connect with parents and the broader community.

Change management

In leading a WSLP you are a facilitator of planned organisational change within your school. This change can be conceptualised as 'deliberate activities that move an organization from its present state to a desired future state' (Stouten et al., 2018, p. 752). In your case, perhaps this 'desired future state' is where literacy is genuinely positioned and taught as a whole-school responsibility, and where students' literacy learning is improved.

As you will no doubt be aware if you are an experienced educator, schools can be incredibly resistant to change, whether it be at organisational or classroom level, for many reasons. One key reason is the ongoing stress teachers experience from being continually forced to accommodate change, due to the evolving demands placed upon them by both internal and external forces, whether it be curricular upheaval or the introduction of new external testing mechanisms or modes. Schools face ongoing changes in the communities that they service, student engagement and staffing, and the need to implement educational and specific curricular reforms, amongst myriad additional factors (Louis, 1994). However, it is not only schools that resist change; the whole reason we have such a wide body of change management literature is because making purposeful and sustainable changes in an organisation may be incredibly challenging (Stouten et al., 2018).

As such, stumbling into a change process dictated by a WSLP seems inadvisable. WSLPs should be informed by knowledge of instituting change processes (Culican et al., 2001); attempting to introduce a new approach to literacy learning within a school may be more successful when it is led by someone with an understanding of how to manage change, or at least a commitment to considering change management. This can improve the chances of success, and reduce the detrimental consequences of failed change on the organisational community (Stouten et al. 2018). Even if you have never led a school-wide initiative before, you can use this instance as a good opportunity to both develop and showcase your new and evolving change management skills. This will be beneficial for the school, but also possibly for your personal career plans, as the success of your literacy policy writing and implementation will be at least partly attributed to your change management abilities.

While you may wish to do some further reading around change management, I outline some principles that you can use to inform your leadership approach, as well as your implementation planning. There are many different models that can be drawn upon, though many reform models are not applicable to schooling contexts; 'schools cannot, for example, engage in massive changes in leadership in order to ensure that changes in policy are carried out, as do many businesses in distress' (Louis, 1994, p. 3), though I am sure that if you find your school leadership failing to support the WSLP initiative in your school, you will no doubt wish that this was possible.

Some themes have a degree of consistency across prescriptive models, and I present five herein which are worth your consideration, as they can generally be aligned with the WSLP process. These would look very familiar to you if you attended the 2022 ASLA Summit in Canberra, as I first discussed them in my keynote address then:

1. Assess the opportunity or problem motivating the change.
2. Select and support a literacy team.
3. Formulate and communicate a clear compelling vision of the change.
4. Empower others to act.
5. Identify short-term wins and monitor and strengthen the change process over time (adapted from Stouten et al., 2018).

I will consider these steps in relation to WSLP development and implementation in this chapter.

However, it is important that it is acknowledged that your WSLP prompted change management process will not necessarily follow these steps in this order, or be a neat and smooth journey. Indeed, to some extent, 'change is largely unmanageable', instead being 'messy, uncertain, and circular', and 'full of unpredictable "normal crises" and choices that cannot be anticipated ahead of time' (Louis, 1994, p. 4). As such, you will need to be flexible and forgiving in your approach, and committed to self-reflection, rethinking and regrouping as required across the journey.

1. Assess the opportunity or problem motivating the change

Stouten and colleagues (2018) contend that 'collecting information from all stakeholders is a necessary first step, emphasizing the importance of involving employees in the process' (p. 757). Simply, your school needs to identify:

1. what it is already doing, and
2. what it wants to be doing, and
3. how it will close the gap between the actual and the aspirational.

This can be achieved through a schoolwide audit of students' literacy needs against currently available literacy practices and learning opportunities (Culican et al., 2001; te Riele et al., 2021). This audit can also identify where professional learning and resourcing allocation may need to be guided in order to enhance student literacy skills, knowledge and engagement.

For some of the policies I have seen, the 'problem' is solely a matter of improving performance on high-stakes testing, and measurement of success featured in the policy has aligned with this goal. This is understandable given the aforementioned accountability demands placed on contemporary schools in relation to high-stakes testing. I accept that it is unrealistic to propose that these demands be ignored or side-lined, as schools 'need to respond to the demands of high stakes testing, while considering socio-economic and geographical contexts' (te Riele et al., 2021, p. 3). However, as I have explored previously in this book, it is important that these not be the *only* measurement of success incorporated in the policy. Your literacy policy will be communicating your school's values and beliefs when it comes to literacy. It is unlikely that educators deliberately set out to convey the impression that their schools wholly conflate literacy improvement with test score improvement, but where this is the only measure of improvement taken into account in a WSLP, this is exactly what is being communicated.

Let your stakeholders help you to frame the problem. Getting stakeholder support is absolutely crucial for the success of any WSLP, and success of whole-school approaches to literacy has been attributed to robust consultative processes and relationship building (Marsh & Burke, 1992). It can be contended that all stakeholders involved in the implementation of school policies 'are to some extent policy makers', and 'at all levels, stakeholders reproduce, contest, negotiate and reconstruct' literacy and language policies (Vanbuel, 2021, p. 14). Whatever driving problems you identify, it is good to ask the question: How do other stakeholders view the issue? For example, if many students in your school are struggling with writing performance, getting parent perspectives on their role in supporting their child's writing in the home can add rich information worth consideration.

Your stakeholders need to be involved early and often during policy writing and revision processes, so your literacy team needs to be committed to liaising closely with them. The importance of strong consultative processes is recognised in some literacy policies, with UK33 noting the following.

> This policy is revised regularly in consultation with stakeholders. The nature of the consultation process is dynamic and may be inclusive of, for example: changes in the use and form of verifiable data; staff consultations, especially with the English Department; on-going professional development; continuing links with The Special Educational Needs Coordinator; ratification by the Board of Governors.

As such, school literacy policies need to be created and continually revised through these consultative processes with key stakeholders, so even after the WSLP is written and published, the relationships and communicative exchanges need to continue to be maintained.

The first stage of planning on a WSLP involves the collection of baseline data. Once you have your literacy team assembled and you have agreed on a common understanding of the purpose of the WSLP, you may wish to collect this informing data. You might wish to:

- Conduct a **content analysis** of school documents to identify components that are aligned with the agreed the purpose of the WSLP, and those that may need adjustment to be reflective of the vision being promoted.

- **Interview or survey** teachers, parents, administrators, students and any relevant key external stakeholders to gather information about what works and what might need attention in the policy.
- Assemble and analyse **student assessment data** to identify attitude, skill and knowledge levels and gaps, as well as to gain insight into the needs of specific student groups within the school.
- Where possible and applicable, you may wish to **collect data on the impact literacy issues are having** on learning and teaching, absenteeism and behavioural issues.
- Use these data to **inform** the initial direction of the WSLP (adapted from Boucher, 2001; Cassidy & Kiely, 2008).

Assembling and analysing data to identify attitude, skill and knowledge levels and gaps also creates a baseline snapshot from which future interventions and change can build. It is a point of comparison to show how far you have journeyed and succeeded related to your initial position. Depending on what your intended strategies are going to be in the WSLP, it will pay to be both quite detailed and broad in your data collection at this stage, as this can allow for you to demonstrate that you have met short-, mid- and long-term goals. I will return to this notion of goal setting across these three distances, addressing it in greater detail later in this chapter in relation to monitoring and strengthening the change process.

While working on a WSLP, it is a good opportunity to explore or revisit the literacy resources that you draw upon from the broader community, and to be responsive to their wishes and expectations where practicable. Culican and colleagues (2001) recommend that 'with support from education systems or sectors, schools create outward looking learning communities that promote effective middle years literacy education' by 'valuing and building on literacy practices beyond school', 'connecting school literacy and learning to the wider community', and 'pursuing productive partnerships to enrich literacy and learning' (p. 8). This is another opportunity to forge meaningful connections with parents and the broader community, and demonstrate your valuing of these partners.

This is worth the time and effort, given that 'there is an enormous amount of evidence to indicate that an effective school is one that is proactive and systematic about linking with the home, the previous school, other service providers and the wider community' (Hill & Crevola, 1999, p. 8). I have already discussed defined roles for parents and external partners previously, and these can be negotiated and expanded in consultation with these stakeholders while the policy is being written or revised. There are many formal and informal mechanisms for garnering parental feedback, and parents may greatly appreciate the opportunity to offer their diverse views on how they are willing and able to support student literacy within the home, and how they might support ongoing and new literacy initiatives generated by the school. Baumgartner et al. (1993) found that parents surveyed about homework, tests and grades 'valued education and believed parental involvement was essential', while seeming 'frustrated by the lack of effective parent–school–teacher communication', leaving the researchers to contend that 'to communicate effectively, both parties need to understand each other's perspective' (p. 182). In this vein, rather than tagging in parents to support whole-school literacy initiatives after the fact, once the policy has been published, inviting and valuing their contributions at initial planning phase can be an important step toward facilitating mutual perspective-taking.

It should also be noted UK policies give greater consideration to literacy resources beyond the school. For example, in relation to descriptions of library resources in literacy policies, UK policies were far more likely to mention public and mobile libraries than their Australian counterparts (Merga, 2021a). The scope and nature of this relationship was defined as follows.

> Schools draw on external library services and public libraries as sources of valued resources and literacy expertise. Libraries are sites of broader parental and community outreach around literacy promotion. Students visit public libraries for reading engagement activities and borrowing opportunities. Parents are encouraged to support their child's access to public libraries. (Merga, 2021a, p. 8).

During the writing or revision of the WSLP, you can take the opportunity to audit current external relationships and identify potential new external parties whose involvement with the school can enhance student literacy learning and its resourcing.

2. Select and support a literacy team

In this context, the Guiding Change Coalition described in the literature on change management can be referred to as the literacy team, though in your schools it may wear a different name. This team plays a key role in overseeing the change process relating to the WSLP (Kotter, 1995), and the team should be strategically assembled where possible to ensure it has the right agents to support success of WSLP planning and implementation.

The literacy team leader

You may be reading this book because you are the leader of the literacy team responsible for the writing, revision and implementation of the WSLP. If you are not the leader, you may wish to share this section (and ideally this whole book) with the person who will be leading the initiative in order to support them to succeed.

If you are the leader, given that WSLP design and implementation is by nature a school-wide endeavour, whether you are formally acknowledged as literacy team leader, or if you are informally enacting the role, you constitute middle leadership within your school. This can be a valuable stepping stone if you have further leadership aspirations, a point I will return to throughout this section. Depending on your previous leadership experience, you may need to reflect on your leadership capacity at the outset to optimise your chances of success.

If you have limited leadership experience you should not necessarily be discouraged from venturing into *teacher leadership* as the leader of a literacy team developing or revising a WSLP. The growing body of literature on teacher leadership is responsive to increasing interest in how educators can drive change and improve teaching and learning within schools, and teachers have often been expected to take on leadership roles to support educational improvement since the 1980s. It can be contended that teacher leadership relates to 'teacher participation in educational improvement endeavours, teacher learning in communities of practice and teacher influence beyond the classroom' and:

> … the act of participating in educational improvement endeavours can be understood as comprising practices such as: interacting with other school members around school reform efforts, striving for pedagogical excellence,

> confronting barriers in the school's culture and structures, translating ideas into actions, participating in decision-making, taking the initiative and leading school improvement. The act of learning together in communities of practice comprises practices such as learning together with colleagues, collaborating with colleagues, facilitating communities of learning, growing and developing professionally and being enquiry-based. The act of extending influence beyond the classroom comprises practices such as encouraging others to improve their professional practice, nurturing a culture of success and demonstrating professionalism. (Lai & Cheung, 2015, p. 676)

Teacher leadership can very much be something learned through practice, and your leadership views and practices will expand in scope through experience (Sinha & Hunscin, 2017). One study found that while participants did not begin with a self-perception that they were teacher leaders, through the process of leading they ultimately both saw themselves and were regarded by others as such (Sinha & Hunscin, 2017). This is why if you are seeking to build your leadership capacity as an educator, taking on the role of the leader of a literacy team working on a WSLP can be an important step in developing your capacity for leadership, which may not otherwise be realised.

Clearly, starting at a point of relatively low confidence may be a norm, with confidence subsequently being development from the experience of success in the leadership role (Sinha & Hunscin, 2017). This suggests that while entering the leadership role with confidence in your leadership capacity is desirable, it is not necessarily essential, as this confidence can potentially be developed through the process. Schools' 'focus should extend beyond identifying or waiting for the emergence of the next teaching superhero to lead' (Smylie & Eckert, 2018, p. 572); rather, a novice can step into the role and learn through practice, ideally with the leadership development support of a mentor within the school if possible.

However, I do not suggest that you go into this role completely green, as it is likely that you will need some leadership and change management training. In relation to the leadership of a whole-school literacy approach, Hill and Crevola (1999) contend that 'teachers selected for this role need professional development that goes beyond gaining a better understanding of literacy and classroom teaching and includes training in being a coach, a mentor and a lead learner' (p. 9). Both the training and the experience itself will also enable you to form a cogent argument about your leadership abilities going forward, potentially enabling you to move into future leadership roles within the school if that is your aim.

To lead change within a school, and lead this team successfully, you will need to draw on some of the characteristics of effective teacher leadership. Much of the literature on leadership within schools is focused on the principal's leadership, though there has been growing interest in other forms of leadership within the school in recent times. I assume that in most cases, the leader of the literacy team is going to be a teacher, whether classroom or library based, and it can be argued that 'teachers are uniquely positioned to promote change within schools because they are well versed in the complexities involved with teaching' (Wenner & Campbell, 2017, p. 134). Harris and Jones (2019) note that recent research argues that teachers should hold a far more influential role in policy formation and strategic decision making, and that teachers need to 'become the instigators, creators and implementors of educational change' (p. 123). They contend that 'teachers as the co-constructors of educational change and key contributors to policy making is an idea that is long overdue in many education systems', and 'where teachers are genuinely at the forefront of educational reform and co-constructing change, the net result can be both positive and empowering' (Harris & Jones, 2019, p. 123).

While this book does not delve deeply into leadership styles, the literature suggests that to be an effective teacher leader, some personal characteristics will serve you. Of course, your success will not be solely dependent on these personal characteristics, but it is worth taking them into account at the outset. You may need to be both willing and able to do the following:

- Disrupt traditional hierarchies within your school, and exert your leadership with confidence in order to be a credible leader who can weather difficulties and resistance (Wenner & Campbell, 2017).
- Shift mindsets, 'building trust and providing support to enable staff to change the mindset from "this is what I do" to "this is what we do"', and 'facilitate "bottom up" change' which involves 'supporting teaching staff to drive change and encouraging shared ownership' (te Riele & Stewart, 2020, p. 2).

- Demonstrate strong interpersonal skills to win over this level of support, and encourage staff to buy-in to the endeavour.
- Commit to ongoing learning and introspection, as leading these kinds of initiatives involves personally embarking on 'a continuous learning journey, full of adaptations, pointing to different styles of leadership' (Gear & Sood, 2021, p. 762). This journey will enable you to develop a plurality of leadership approaches, rather than a monotonal effort.
- Ensure you engage school leadership to clearly demonstrate their support for the literacy team and its leadership, as this support can be integral to success (Beer et al., 1990; Wenner & Campbell, 2017).

This final point is crucial; if you do not already have a strong positive relationship with your Principal and the other high-level leaders within your school, you should work on this immediately. As noted by Smylie and Eckert (2018), 'teacher leadership development can become such a compelling focus that it is easy to forget the important role that principals play in its success or failure' (p. 571), so of all of the external factors that you need to manage to ensure your success, it can be contended that this relationship is pivotal. It is also the case that some school cultures could be more likely to lend success than others, with te Riele and Stewart (2020) suggesting that 'collaborative and collegial school cultures, built on teamwork and trust' can be 'helpful for fostering a whole school approach' (p. 1). Given the strong influence that leaders have on influencing and shaping school culture (Merga & Mason, 2019), it is essential to have their active and committed involvement.

The team members

You may find yourself in a position to assemble, or at least influence the assembly of the literacy team responsible for the writing, revision and implementation of the WSLP. This section of the book will be useful in informing what to look for. Ideally, you need a group of educators who:

- can work well in a team and sincerely support the WSLP initiative across the life of the policy
- can influence school leadership and engage their ongoing support

- can liaise effectively with key stakeholders within the different strata of the school (across learning areas in secondary school, across early/middle/upper primary contexts in primary school)
- can liaise effectively with key external stakeholders and build these relationships to benefit the literacy learning of your students
- come from diverse areas within the school, representing diverse roles across the school (Boucher, 2001).

To this end, you are looking for individuals with the following characteristics.

Team players. Not all teachers are comfortable working in teams (Johnson, 2003), and establishing a literacy team that can work well together may be very easy, or easier said than done depending on where you work, and who you work with. Of course, as aforementioned, your leadership approach will be integral to the success of the team, and even 'team players' will not want to cooperate with you if your leadership style has a negative impact on them. One of the interesting things I have noticed both working and doing research in schools is that while many have supportive cultures, others have competitive, adversarial and even hostile staffing environments. You can take two 'like' schools, from a similar socio-economic, geographic contexts, and the atmosphere in the staff room is completely different.

What kinds of traits should you be looking for? I have done some research on effective collaboration in school settings, and you should look for people who actively enact the following (adapted from Merga, 2019d):

1. **Respectful communication**
   Look for people who can listen and respond respectfully to colleagues at different levels of seniority and power. Try to recruit those who at least try to understand the perspectives of others from beyond their groups within the collegial setting. Your team members will need to show respect for expertise and perspectives of others, particularly those teaching outside their learning area or year groups.
2. **Goal setting and planning**
   You need practical people who are planning oriented, not aspirational people who come up with ideas that are not realistic, and who are not interested in being pragmatic.

3. **Open and flexible mind-sets**
   That said, you also need to have team members who are willing to completely revise their views on an idea should evidence or implementation dictate that their current position is wrong. Flexibility and humility are key attributes. The teacher who has shown strong reluctance to be adaptive in the past will probably not work well on the team.

4. **Student-centred approaches with student benefit as the shared goal**
   Look for the kinds of educators who really know their students, who are actively responsive to student interests and issues, and who have open lines of communication with their students. Your policy will need to meet whole school, group and individual needs of students, so bringing team members on board who have a good understanding of what these are will be useful.

5. **Personal advocacy and capacity for advocacy**
   In your efforts to create a conflict-free group, avoid exclusively recruiting staff with retiring and compliant dispositions. You will need your team member to be able to see a place for themselves within the team, and to be able to confidently advocate for what they can offer the policy and the collaborative process of its creation, revision and implementation. You will also need them to be positive ambassadors for the policy.

6. **Generosity and capacity**
   Many educators are time poor, and some schools will not be able to afford to give adequate workload relief, which means you may be reliant on the organisational citizenship behaviours (OCBs) of staff to get the job done. This is an interesting research area in human resources that relates to the 'tendency that many of you have to work overtime for free and do a lot of invisible labour that extends way beyond your defined professional role' (Merga, 2022a, p. 136). If that sounds rather exploitative, it is, but the reality is that in many schools, due to resourcing or leadership issues, this is the only way the job will get done. You will need to recruit team members who have the time and commitment to see the initiative through.

7. **Willingness to evaluate collaboration and provide supportive critical feedback**
   Team members should be able to both give and receive constructive criticism in their roles. You need the kind of team members who have a good sense of humour and self-awareness, and who can create an environment where it is safe to articulate concerns and issues without irrevocably damaging collaborative relationships. While senior staff will be able to offer valuable experience, do not discount the value of early career staff who may bring a fresh perspective.

8. **Holding diverse positions and viewpoints**
   You need a diverse team because you have diverse students, with diverse needs, and a diverse team is most likely to be able to understand these. In addition to the obvious need for team members from different social and ethnic backgrounds, you need educators from mainstream and specialist contexts and across year groups. In the secondary school context, you will also need key representatives from across the learning areas, and in both primary and secondary contexts you will need to work with available support staff if applicable. In all contexts, bringing on board a member of the school leadership team could enhance the traction and influence of your work.

Roles of the literacy team

Once you have your team, it is time to allocate roles. The team are going to be the WSLP leaders within the school, so in addition to the aforementioned leadership training that may benefit the leader of this team, the individual members selected for this team may also need leadership training (Hill & Crevola, 1999).

Some school literacy policies in the UK closely focused on the purpose of the literacy team that you might want to draw upon when considering the overall purpose of your team and its individual members. For example, UK66 dedicates over half a page of their nine-page document to naming the team and outlining its responsibilities. Furthermore, it states:

Each department should nominate one member of staff to support the development of literacy in their subject areas by working with the Literacy Team. The purpose of the Literacy Team is:

- To develop a shared vision of literacy in the Academy
- To initiate and lead literacy development throughout the Academy including for example the appointing of Literacy Mentors amongst pupils
- To update and review the whole-school literacy policy as appropriate
- To drive good practice in the teaching and learning of literacy and within departments
- To develop good practice in the monitoring and evaluation of literacy in the Academy
- To advise staff on good practice resources and methodology
- To help organise staff training
- To organise literacy events in the Academy
- To communicate literacy goals to staff
- To involve external advisors in the process. (UK66)

Once you have decided on the overarching purpose of the team and its responsibilities, where applicable specific individual responsibilities may be allocated.

Leadership support

As aforementioned, mobilising energy must involve garnering the support of the school leader. Your leader may be supportive, apathetic or hostile toward the initiative, or all three at different times, but you need to win them over as far as possible as they are the gatekeepers who can enable or block the project (Heller & Firestone, 1995).

If a whole-school approach to literacy that goes beyond lip service is new to your school, even supportive and knowledgeable leaders may need support to help to facilitate this change. In addition, not all leaders will necessarily be willing champions of this change. For example, many school leaders in secondary schools may not support struggling literacy learners' literacy development across the curriculum (Merga, Mat Roni & Malpique, 2021a).

We noted:

> for school leaders to have impetus to intervene in order to build whole school cultures supportive of reading across all learning areas, the need for this must be acknowledged; perhaps Australia's national curricular positioning of literacy as a general capability is not enough to ensure that this is realized in schools. While there may be numerous root causes, including the aforementioned competing demands on schools and leadership, it is also possible that leadership does not fully realize the need for this approach. (Merga, Mat Roni & Malpique, 2021a, p. 545)

While it is not a given that you will have strong leadership support, you will need to secure it as far as possible. Research suggests that the support of the school administration can play a key role in fostering and enabling teacher leadership in a school (Bellibaş et al., 2020), so for your leadership of a WSLP to thrive, ideally you need your principal's strong support.

Hill and Crevola (1999) highlight the importance of leadership, and the possible need for targeted professional development, describing the value of:

> investing in professional development for principals to assist them exercise their role as instructional leaders. Whole-school design approaches depend to an extraordinary degree on the leadership provided by the principal and senior administration of the school, since only they are in the position to make sure that each of the design elements is attended to and brought into alignment. (p. 8)

If your leadership does not have the time, interest or capacity to upskill through professional development, and it is clear that they need additional training, the literacy policy team will need to come up with creative ways of ensuring that at the very least, leadership has access to information that can support them to perform their role effectively.

Again, this is why it will be useful to recruit at least some staff who already have a strong, positive existing relationship with school leadership onto the literacy team, and they may be more effective conduits of information that you may wish to impart, which will be particularly important if your school leaders do not have the time or the inclination to undertake further training in this initiative. You may need to share this book with your school leadership, though of course, as that is no guarantee it will be read. Given that school leaders are time poor, it may be more practical to share key findings verbally with your principal in the form of a short presentation. Successful literacy policy implementation is typically a result of strong support from school leadership, sufficient resourcing and time being dedicated, and initial and ongoing staff development (May & Wright, 2007).

Buy-in from all

Beyond assembly of the team, and winning over and training leadership as required, you need to think about engaging your educators more broadly. Analysis of barriers to implementation of WSLPs has found that involving all teachers to some extent in the development of the policy may be crucial to its success (May & Wright, 2007). It has been contended:

> In relation to these difficulties, the issue of teacher 'buy-in' is crucial, and the level of buy-in from teachers is largely dependent on the nature of the process undertaken in implementing a school language policy. In short, a school language policy needs to be both carefully thought through and carefully managed if all staff are to be convinced of its merits. (May & Wright, 2007, p. 373)

Te Riele and colleagues (2021) found that 'once a critical mass of staff members had tipped the balance in favour of change, the school community tended to move into a phase of consolidating practice, going beyond only externally driven quality control' (p. 8), and the move toward initiating or consolidating a WSLP can involve a shift to greater collectively, with school leaders acknowledging that the 'work involved in effecting the structural and cultural shifts required for staff to move from working in isolation to working together' (p. 10). Eroding silos in secondary school may be particularly challenging, and not just because secondary teachers are used to working within their disciplinary teams rather than across whole-school groups. The nature of the AC is that while it expects realisation of General Capabilities such as literacy as previously discussed, the curriculum itself is highly bounded and there are few opportunities for cross-curricular learning on a topic. Working together might not feel natural at all given these constraints.

Furthermore, we know that educators constantly face a barrage of judgement, so it can be *very easy* to put them off side and lose their support, and if your colleagues do not see the point of your policy, they are never going to use it, and it may as well not exist. It becomes just another expectation in an increasingly overwhelming succession of bureaucratic hurdles.

There is also the issue of vulnerability. On one hand, you need to win your colleagues over to support your policy. On the other, they are key resources that need to be supported, and you will need to find out where your teaching staff sit in relation to confidence and competence in literacy instruction. Inviting them to be open about gaps in their knowledge that can be supported by professional learning to be planned for within the policy can be seen as intrusive and threatening depending on how it is enacted. This is about building capacity, not fault-finding. This is also why it is so important to choose literacy team members who have strong interpersonal skills and supportive rather than overtly critical dispositions.

Finally, you need your educators to commit for the long haul. The implementation of whole-school literacy initiatives can be a 'slow, complex, and ongoing process of incremental organisational change in which ongoing effort and optimism are key', requiring 'a long-term commitment to achieve deep and lasting cultural change through ongoing collaborative professional learning. It is "always a work in progress" because "there's always more to improve on … always more to do"' (te Riele & Stewart, 2020, p. 3).

3. Formulate and communicate a powerful vision of the change

This involves developing a clear and motivating vision for the reason for change which imagines specific end goals. While literacy is positioned in the AC as a whole-school responsibility, you need a 'school-specific vision' for what this will look like for you (Louis, 1994, p. 5). You will generate this vision with your stakeholders' needs and values in mind.

This work is not separate from work on the WSLP; as per Chapter 3, you might include a rationale and goals in your WSLP anyway. This also flows on from the data collected when assessing the opportunity or problem motivating the change as previously described. As per Chapter 3, the rationale goes beyond defining literacy, instead articulating the shared beliefs, values and goals of your school in relation to the WSLP. It shows a clear understanding of the current situation in your school, as well as the progress that you are seeking to make. As such, no two visions for change will be identical across schools. It is your opportunity to draw attention to the importance of literacy principles and policy, and the purpose of the endeavour. When this is informed by the perspectives of stakeholders, and responsive to current context and data, it will be most meaningful.

When you subsequently communicate this vision to your stakeholders, you need to consider that stakeholder endorsement of this vision can be responsive to the extent to which it resonates with their beliefs and values. Whether or not they are committed to the projected outcomes of the change you are proposing, and the effectiveness with which the vision is communicated will be 'essential for generating awareness' as well as 'support for change' (Stouten, 2018, p. 760). You may wish to devise a communications strategy to ensure that your co-constructed vision reaches all intended stakeholder audiences, and avoiding exclusionary jargon will be important.

In the *final thoughts* section of this book I discuss readability considerations. If you are intending to communicate your vision with audiences within and beyond the school who may not have strong English literacy, you will need to take this into account in all interactions with stakeholders, including but not limited to communicating the vision. If you do not adjust the accessibility of your content, you will only reach the highly educated parents, and not those marginalised parents with lower English literacy, limiting the value and broad applicability of the feedback provided. I also encourage you to consider multi-modal ways of sharing both your vision and your policy to improve its accessibility. For example, you might communicate your vision via video with multi-lingual subtitle options for linguistically diverse communities, and provide opportunities for face to face exchanges of ideas.

4. Empower others to act and commit

Empowering others to act is crucial, and it relates to supporting employees to problem solve, removing obstacles to change, and encouraging their investment and participation in the change initiative (Stouten et al., 2018). You must allow for opportunities for teachers to make a really meaningful contribution to the WSLP and its implementation, and this point is particularly pertinent for those leaders who struggle to delegate, and who prefer to pursue their own vision with the support of others.

The WSLP that you co-create also cannot be static and intractable. There needs to be 'flexibility for teachers to adapt agreed practices to their own skills, style, and students' (te Riele & Stewart, 2020, p. 2), which will enable teachers to tailor the requirements of WSLP to their students' unique needs, feel that their own professional judgement is being respected, and foster a sense of 'collective responsibility' for the success of the WSLP (p. 3). You also need to build readiness for change in your teachers, and this should focus on increasing teacher satisfaction, avoiding overwhelming additions to teachers' workload, fostering an atmosphere of confidence and trust, and demonstrating a sincere exchange of expertise between the schools' teachers and the literacy team (Kondakci et al., 2017).

Ideally commitment to WSLP planning and implementation within your school should outlive the tenure of any one staff member. If teachers are excluded from investing early and often in the creation of the WSLP, this can weaken the sustainability of the initiative. Boucher (2001) described the stunning moment when she realised that the literacy reform initiative she had introduced was not going to succeed without her stewardship after she resigned from the school where it was implemented:

> That summer, the whole staff participated in a professional development opportunity at which the presenter asked them to describe their reading program. The audience, the entire staff with whom I had worked, was silent. Not one of them could explain the program, nor could they state the purpose of the four-year reform initiative. I realize now that I broke one of the most important reform rules: we didn't develop the program, I developed the program ... The purpose of the reform must influence everyone's every decision; everyone should be moving in the same direction and understand why. It would appear that in my case I kept all of that to myself. In sum, my failure to build internal capacity resulted in a multi-year struggle for the school to regain ownership and direction.
>
> If the staff had had collective ownership and understanding of the literacy program reform initiative, then the program would have continued to develop and improve even though I had resigned. (p. 4)

Your educators need to be co-owners of the initiative who are sufficiently knowledgeable of and inspired by the WSLP and its implementation to advocate for it in your absence; its success or failure should not be entirely dependent on you or any other person. Encouraging co-ownership through co-construction may not be sufficient in itself to ensure the change will be successfully achieved, as not everyone will be in an equal position to contribute, and even those who do might not fully grasp what will be needed to implement and sustain the change (Beer et al., 1990). However, where this step is taken and supported by strong leadership, change is more likely to be successful (Beer et al., 1990).

Excluding teachers from a sense of ownership over the initiative could have unexpected negative consequences. While there has been limited research that looks at the impact of moving toward whole-school literacy approaches on teacher attrition, the extant research suggests that such initiatives may have positive or negative impacts. A small US study by Bueker (2005) found that 'a whole-school literacy reform model' can influence 'teachers and their career decisions', and 'all of the teachers had strong feelings on how the implementation influences school climate, student performance, and their own personal and professional lives' (p. 409). Given that you certainly do not want your roll out of the WSLP to send your colleagues running out the door, you will need to give close attention to mitigating the trigger factors identified in this research, with some teachers reporting 'feelings of disempowerment and increased workload attributed to the model' (p. 395).

It was interesting to note that in this study, experienced teachers particularly felt disempowered, as though their experiences and expertise were devalued in the impetus for change (Bueker, 2005). One teacher of fifteen years was quoted as saying:

> I think you see teachers retiring, leaving in general, because they don't feel they're able to teach anymore. They feel they have to ... it's constantly having another curriculum shoved down your throat. ... I think some teachers are just feeling, 'You know what, I'm not ready to go down this road again. I'm done.' (Bueker, 2005, p. 405)

So how can you optimise engagement with all of your teachers and prevent attrition? The following, partly adapted from Bueker (2005), may help:

1. **Extend community.**
   Provide opportunities for informal discussion and community building within and beyond the school.

2. **Spread out training.**
   Do not overwhelm your staff by delivering a high concentration of training at the early stage of the initiative; instead, build a professional development training plan that extends over time.
3. **Keep the load down.**
   Limit additions to the administrative load of teachers, whether the relate to data collection or other facets of implementation.
4. **Increase teachers' knowledge.**
   Provide clear and accessible training on why a whole-school approach can yield better outcomes than current practices.
5. **Increase principals' knowledge.**
   Principals may also need training to provide the right kind of leadership to support this change.
6. **Value the educator knowledge base.**
   Provide more than cursory recognition of the expertise your teachers can bring to the initiative. Encourage, showcase and reward their contributions.

Gauging the current knowledge and skill base of teachers will help you to target professional development in required areas. For primary school teachers, teachers' literacy instruction capacity needs to be noted in relation to proficiency in literacy instruction both in subject English and beyond. For secondary school staff, you will need to capture ability to foster both disciplinary and content area literacy, as well as capacity to support any whole-school interventions supporting students requiring literacy-related teaching adjustments.

In the secondary context, as I have mentioned previously, it is crucial that you manage to get educators from across the curriculum onboard, and ideally in the team. This may also involve working closely with the HoLAs or disciplinary representatives to map out what disciplinary literacy skills and knowledge are needed. This should be relatively straightforward, given that as previously illustrated, the AC already includes some information about what these look like. However, in consultation with their staff, these disciplinary informants will need to take the next step and plan for implementation and learning. If they are already comprehensively addressing disciplinary and content area literacy in their classroom and meeting the needs of students with specific literacy needs, this step will simply be a matter of making this pedagogy visible and possibly incorporating this within the policy, or an appendix to the policy. However, if up to this point, addressing disciplinary and content area literacy has been aspirational rather than actual, and/or there has been a prevailing assumption that students who struggle with literacy are not the responsibility of teachers in disciplines beyond English, you will be looking to foster a change. If this is you, this may feel like an overwhelming proposition, and you will need leadership support as well as adequate time and resourcing to lead to this kind of change.

Part of empowering others to act is developing and promoting teachers' change-related ability and knowledge (Stouten et al., 2018). This is concerned with the professional development of staff to enact the WSLP, which I have explored in previous chapters, but also to feel safe to attempt to do so. You need to create and maintain an environment in which it is 'psychologically safe to make mistakes and learn from them' so that teachers feel confident in moving outside their comfort zones and trying new things (Stouten et al., 2018, p. 765). This may be particularly pertinent for secondary school teachers who have never explicitly taught content area literacy skills in their subject before, and who may have played a passive rather than active role in supporting struggling literacy learners. You will need to support your teachers and collect ongoing feedback to determine what further support you can provide, in all relevant areas, from resourcing to professional development, while ensuring that you allow for enough time to acquire knowledge and skills (Stouten et al., 2018) so that your staff do not feel overwhelmed.

5. Identify short-term wins and monitor and strengthen the change process over time

You know from the previous sections that your WSLP is going to need to include thoughtful implementation planning. DoEWA's (2021) whole-school literacy implementation model includes reference to 'target setting, milestones and evaluation', and this facet of the change management literature draws attention to the need to include clear and meaningful goals that are met in short-, mid- and long-term oriented time frames. You may even want to explicitly categorise your goals as such in the plan, so that all of your stakeholders know when to expect to see the initiatives built into the WSLP come to fruition.

In engaging your team of educators to stay the course on the implementation of a WSLP, at least up to the evaluation period, they need to see some indicators that the ship is headed in the right direction, even if it is not realistic to see land yet. As noted by Kotter (1995), 'creating short-term wins is different from hoping for short-term wins'; 'the latter is passive, the former active' (p. 65). Actively creating achievable short-term goals leads to the opportunity to identify short-term wins and use them as reinforcement of change progress. This can very motivating, as these short-term successes can:

- positively reinforce the literacy team's efforts
- demonstrate that the vision is realistic and can be practically enacted
- convince those parties within the school who are cynical and resistant to change that it is possible
- provide key achievements that can be promoted externally to sustain commitment of stakeholders beyond the school (partly based on Stouten et al., 2018).

The key aim in goal setting at all three time frames is viability. It is essential that you be realistic in your goal setting, and this will involve careful consideration of when it is practical to expect to see change in relation to the strategies you are introducing in the WSLP.

> While measuring the impact of your intervention on student achievement as well as student engagement can be useful, it is crucial that you be aware that you need to allow several months to see movement in this regard; it is not something that will change in a few weeks or months. Engagement changes (concerned with reading attitudes and frequency) will typically be detected before you see changes in achievement. Therefore, you should be able to track changes in volume of reading, frequency of reading and attitudes towards reading before you see meaningful shifts in student performance, so you should not limit your measures to performance only. Setting realistic goals is so important. For example, you are almost certainly not going to see a significant improvement in student reading comprehension three weeks after rolling out an intervention. (Merga, 2022a, p. 74)

I have previously touched on how to measure and set goals for strategies to promote literacy improvement and engagement in my other work, and earlier in this chapter I briefly noted the importance of potentially capturing quite a wide range of data at the earliest stages of the WSLP. As I have noted elsewhere, 'you can't claim to have implemented a successful approach unless you can prove that there has been a shift in however you're measuring change at school level' (Merga, 2022a, p. 73). While policies are already collecting data on student performance on assessments as noted earlier in this book, depending on the nature of your strategies and the intended outcomes, you may wish to collect data on numerous other areas.

For example, you may decide to increase student access to books and opportunities for sustained self-selected reading experiences as one small part of your broad WSLP. As I have noted previously:

> if you are looking to increase access to books in your school by giving all students weekly access to the library during class time, you need to find out what their current levels of access are so that you can demonstrate that what you did made a difference ... just because a class has timetabled access to the library, this does not necessarily align with actual levels of access to the library, as school library professionals have reported that these timetabled sessions may be often interrupted due to other curricular demands ... As such, observing and recording access of each class over a period of months may be far more accurate than relying on what has been timetabled as a measure of current frequency of access prior to the intervention. (Merga, 2022a, p. 73)

There are many possible goals that can be attached this this approach, but I will narrow the focus here on *just one goal* at each level, and keep the planning and data collection at a minimum for each, so you can see possible planning and related data collection requirements. As a note of caution, the need to have demonstrable short-term wins should not lead you to preference short-term goals over those that require a longer time period to come to fruition, but are of equal or greater value.

Short-term goal: *Seeing an increase in student book borrowing from the library.* To achieve this goal, you will need to have access to baseline student book borrowing data to compare with subsequent data collected at a near future point in order to track an improvement that can be celebrated. For example, you might collect borrowing data at the start of an intervention in the WSLP which sees an increase in students' access to libraries during class time shift from monthly to weekly access, and then compare it with data collected one month after this implementation has rolled out. You may also want this goal to be revisited at mid- and long-term points, so while it is a short-term goal, changes may also compound beyond the short-term point.

Midpoint goal: *Seeing a positive shift in your students' attitudes toward reading.* Your WSLP may include a range of strategies to improve students' attitudes toward reading for pleasure. For example, this may involve increasing opportunities for students' silent reading for pleasure during class time from weekly to daily, such as in the programme recently rolled out at Queenwood school (Collins et al., 2022). You will need to have collected baseline data around your students' reading engagement just prior to WSLP implementation for comparison. This can be collected through surveys, where students state their agreement with statements on reading enjoyment on a Likert type scale, which will lead to quantitative (numerical) data that can then be compared with a midpoint repeat survey.

1. Collecting these data anonymously improves the likelihood of student honesty in responses, but if you want to compare the baseline results to midpoint results, you will need to assign students with an anonymous code that may be difficult to manage for many reasons (for example, see Audette et al., 2020) so that you can match their initial response to their later response.
2. Alternatively, you can also compare attitude scores in the whole cohort at baseline to midpoint, but the cohort needs to stay the same; this is a less methodologically rigorous approach, but may be preferable depending on your resourcing constraints, and it means that students' anonymity can be genuinely preserved.
3. As another option, instead of collecting baseline and mid-term data, you can ask students at the midpoint to reflect on whether they believe that increasing opportunities for students' silent reading for pleasure changed their attitudes toward reading. On one hand this is the least rigorous for a number of reasons, including the fact that it relies on recall, but on the other, students are providing insights specific to their perceptions of the efficacy of the intervention (increased opportunities for students' silent reading).

Long-term goal: *Seeing improvement in students' reading comprehension after WSLP implementation.* Again, this is a matter of collecting baseline data around your students' reading comprehension just prior to WSLP implementation, where the WSLP includes measures for enhancing students' reading comprehension such as increasing students' exposure to reading aloud (Westbrook et al., 2019), or increasing opportunities for reading comprehension improvement across disciplines. You will then compare the baseline with subsequent reading comprehension performance after a long interval to allow for improvement. You will then match these data to individual student data, or look for whole (identical) cohort changes as per previous.

Given that as previously mentioned, it will be virtually impossible to control for all other factors; because your students are not isolated monkeys learning in a lab as part of a randomised controlled trial, you will not be able to establish *causation* (see Mat Roni et al., 2020). However, it should be plausible to find correlation supporting the benefits of the WSLP, with the limitations of correlation acknowledged. Also, where WSLP includes many research-supported measures to enhance reading comprehension, as it *should*, you will not be able to determine which (if any) of the approaches or interventions has had the greatest impact on the improved outcomes.

When you are looking to meet your goals, collection of quantitative data is not the only means by which to demonstrate goal achievement. Another advantage of setting multiple goals in relation to one strand of your initiative is that it can also enable the collection of different kinds of data, which may appeal to diverse stakeholders.

> When you mix it up and collect both quantitative and qualitative data, this makes for rich reading, and also sometimes the qualitative data will capture a change that is less apparent in the quantitative data and the reverse. For example, I might collect changes in students' attitudes towards reading on scales in a survey (quantitative), but I might also want to interview a random selection of students to collect some rich description around any changes to their attitudes, also to collect feedback on how I could improve the programme for the next iteration (qualitative). (Merga, 2022a, p. 74)

Measuring goal achievement through diverse data sources enables you to tell a detailed story about what has been achieved through policy implementation, as well as pinpoint any areas requiring revision in order to enhance the efficacy of the policy.

Related to this planning for short-, mid- and long-term goals, I was interested to see some documents literally planning for planning (for example, UK46). UK32 includes the following, for example:

> **Planning**
>
> We have detailed whole school schemes of work for literacy based on the Northern Ireland Literacy Framework. These are available in STAFF – WHOLE SCHOOL LITERACY PLANNING AND EVALUATIONS. Each year band plans according to long term, medium term and short term criteria. The long term plans are determined by the Northern Ireland Literacy Strategy and the Literacy Framework. The medium term plans are done on a termly basis and the short term plans are fortnightly. (These fortnightly plans are evaluated reflectively and inform each future plan to ensure value added teaching and revision if necessary).
>
> Creative writing weeks are incorporated into planning schedules in an effort to enhance and develop the writing skills of our children. Please see planners for more detail regarding this.
>
> We also have detailed literacy arrangements for each year band in order to facilitate movement of teachers across year bands or introduction of new/substitute teachers. These arrangements detail all areas of literacy and the practice within that year band. These arrangements were written by teachers in conjunction with literacy co-ordinators.
>
> Please see arrangements for each year band in Appendix 6. Planning links are made with parents via tips as to how they can help their child reach their potential (see homework overview appendix 7 and Newsletter see appendix 8). Our website is used effectively to help parents and we are currently building up our bank of parenting tips. Some of these include recordings of aspects of literacy guided reading lessons, book lists, phonics recordings, suggested apps and digital links.

Not only does this policy articulate planning expectations for short-, medium- and long-term planning, it also plans to optimise connections between parents and the school in order to support student learning at home. Consider planning for planning in your WSLP.

Avoid drowning

Policy development and implementation is a gargantuan task. You will need to monitor and strengthen the change process over time by 'continuing to invest resources (leader time and effort, staffing, and money) in the change process to remind people of the urgent character of the change and keep the pace moving' (Stouten et al., 2018, p. 766). This involves evaluating and adjusting the WSLP as needed, taking stakeholder feedback on board. This may seem like an interminable investment, particularly given that educators and leaders in schools are already under the pump, with high rates of attrition (Mason & Matas, 2015). It is true that 'writing policy documents, including identifying the appropriate data to inform these policies, provides yet another potentially onerous task for school staff' (Allen et al., 2021, p. 2). It is essential that the literacy team and its leadership continue to identify emerging and ongoing needs for time and resourcing, and that these needs be affectively communicated to school leadership in a timely manner to ensure that they are met.

CHAPTER 6

A possible structure

I was initially reluctant to include this structure, as I do not want to be prescriptive, and as I have reiterated throughout this book, I believe that what structurally works for one school may be a poor fit elsewhere. However, I know that some readers will prefer me to distil the analysis and research I have outlined up to this point into something very simplistic and easy to pick up and use, which can then be shaped as well as justified down the track by reference to the more detailed explanations also provided in this book. Including this chapter also enables people lacking the time or inclination to read a whole book on WSLP to simply skip to the good part of the story, though they will be missing out on the opportunity to understand the logic and research informing this dénouement.

Based on what I have covered up this this point, here is a possible structure that you could use as a frame for your WSLP. Again, you do not have to use this approach, as there may be a more effective structure that is more responsive to your context and needs.

The order in which you present the information, and what you choose to include or exclude in your context is also entirely up to you, and will be reflective of what works best for your planning team, and your school.

In addition, if you are using this structure to revise an existing WSLP, don't forget to update any references to the AC so that your WSLP reflects the current version.

Title: (Name of your school)'s Whole-school Literacy Policy

Date of publication/approval: day/month/year

Review cycle/date: (cycle length; for example, every two years), month/year (next review due)

Parties responsible: (titles; for example, Literacy Committee, Curriculum Leader English, Student Committee and so on)

Information about the school

- Who will be reading this policy? Consider all internal and external stakeholders who will be accessing this policy, and provide information that will meet their needs.
- What should readers know about your school in order to understand the strengths and needs of the school community as they relate to students' literacy learning?
- What contextual details are needed give the reader a sense of the school culture, and how this might impact on its orientation toward literacy? Include relevant geographic, socio-economic, cultural, linguistic and other factors that may influence literacy learning, as well as details about historical and current literacy initiatives.

Information about the literacy team

- Who are the people on the team? Include the names and titles of the team responsible for policy creation, and their roles, in policy development, support of implementation, and subsequent evaluation/review. Ideally in secondary schools this team should not be limited to English teachers only, or the capacity to build content area and disciplinary literacies will be limited.
- Who is the leader of the literacy team, and how will they support their colleagues' efforts to promote literacy across the school?

Definition of literacy

- This needs to go beyond a cut/paste from the AC and consider the plurality of literacies and whole-school literacy. How is literacy is defined within your school?
- What are the key shared terms that will be used in discussion of literacy (these can be listed in detail in an appendix)?
- Which literacies will this policy focus on? Will literacy development occur in mutual development of other General Capabilities? What is whole-school literacy?

Rationale and goals

- What are the broad goals of the school? How are these related to shared understandings the school holds around the importance of literacy principles and policy?
- Why is whole-school literacy important?
- In a general sense, what are the unique or key literacy needs of key ages and stages within your school (for example, early childhood, middle years etc.)?

Explicit literacy targets and implementation planning

- What are the literacy targets to be attained through WSLP implementation? What will successfully reaching literacy targets look like (i.e. how will you evaluate success)? Do not limit this section to increases in student performance on high-stakes testing. For example, what literacy targets do you have in relation to educator professional development?
- Consider engagement and motivation as well as quantitative attainment goals. How will you enhance students' literacy motivation and engagement? Do you want to build a school reading culture? If yes, how will you do so?
- What planning is needed to address disciplinary literacy needs as well as overarching content area literacy needs? How will general strategy

instruction in literacy be supported across the school? Consider attaching exemplars of discipline specific texts to the WSLP as appendices.

- Have you included transcription skills?
- How will you measure improvement in student literacy engagement, skills and knowledge?

Table 7 shows a possible approach to implementation planning, but you should use the format that works best for you. You do not need to use a table, though many policies do choose to adopt this approach

Table 7: Example of implementation planning

Overarching priorities	Literacy targets	Strategies/ activities for attainment	Launch date (if applicable)	Responsible parties and roles	Measures of success S: Short-term, <3 months M: Mid-term, 3-9 months L: Long-term, >9 months
Build a whole-school reading culture	Increase opportunities for silent reading for pleasure within the school	Whole-school reading after lunch every Wednesday Mobile book carts to support book choice on Wednesdays Timetabling for twice-weekly library visits for every class	At the beginning of Term 2 At the beginning of Term 2 From Week 4 of Term 1	Initiative led by Library Manager in the library and supported by all classroom teachers Student library monitors will run the mobile book carts, restocking them, recording borrowing, and taking the cart to classrooms during the reading period	Survey of students' attitudes toward reading shows improvement (pre initiative surveying compared with six months post implementation) (M)
	Teacher book talks to model reading engagement	School assemblies will begin with a teacher from across disciplines sharing a brief spiel about a book they recently enjoyed Duplicate copies of the book will be available in the library	At the beginning of Term 2 Ongoing, two weeks' prior to assembly days	All teachers will have the opportunity to do this through the year. Teachers should notify Library Manager of selected book at least two weeks in advance so copies can be acquired for student borrowing	An increase in student borrowing rates of teacher promoted books as measured at two months, six months and 12 months post implementation. (S,M,L)

Roles and responsibilities

- While these may be allocated in implementation planning, you may also wish to include a section that details the roles and responsibilities of key stakeholders. Who are the responsible parties for planning and implementation? What is their role?
- Provide a clear description of the role of the classroom teacher in fostering whole school literacy.

Assessment of progress

- How will student attainment in literacy be assessed? Include literacy measures beyond test achievement.
- Include uniform feedback mechanisms for assessment of literacy across subject areas and year levels.

Interventions, enrichment and accommodations for students with specific needs

- What explicit strategies will you employ across subject areas and year groups for identifying struggling students?
- What are some of the common specific issues that teachers must accommodate to support student literacy attainment in your school (for example, EAL/D, dyslexia etc.)? What whole-school measures/interventions will support these students? Content on intervention programmes should include the name of the programme, year levels where it may be implemented, a summary of the nature of the programme and what is involved, mechanisms of assessment of success of the programme, responsible parties for implementing the programme, and how students will be identified for inclusion in the programme.
- Consider consulting the recent research to include evidence and support for your approach to meeting the needs of struggling literacy learners across the whole school.
- For teachers with limited knowledge of how to support struggling literacy learners, you might want to include appendices with explanation of some common issues experienced by students with

agreed and pragmatic approaches to supporting students detailed so that an agreed approach can be employed to support struggling literacy learners across the school.

Ongoing professional development for educators

- What are the specific literacy related professional development needs of your staff? How will you plan to meet them? How will you identify student needs and related teacher knowledge gaps?

Resources and the library

- What resources will you need in order to realise the planning within this policy? Consider including a list of key resources as an appendix if desirable.
- What is the role of the school library and staff in building and sustaining student literacy? Are current library staffing and resourcing levels sufficient to enable the library to function as a key literacy facility within the school?
- Are there grants/other funding sources that the school will attempt to win in order to fund new literacy initiatives to expand resourcing capacity? For schools facing resourcing challenges, planning for grant applications to expand literacy resourcing capacity can be a mid-term goal.

Defined roles for parents and external partners

- How will parents and external partners be expected to support the realisation of this policy? How will the school sustain meaningful communication with these stakeholders?
- What kinds of data need to be collected from these partners to ascertain their capacity as external supports and their views toward literacy? You may wish to include outreach and training for external partners in your implementation planning in order to build engagement and capacity.
- If applicable, does your policy include learning opportunities for parents of both primary and secondary school aged children to foster early and ongoing literacy learning and engagement within the home?

Transition support

- How will you support students to make transitions, and how will this be a whole-school responsibility?
- How will you ensure that staff are adequately prepared to support these shifts, and that communication around student literacy learning needs is clear at both large (for example, from primary to secondary school) and smaller (for example, from year to year within school) key transitions?

Pandemic responsiveness

- What measures will your school take to mitigate literacy learning loss in further pandemic related education interruptions for individuals and whole classes?
- How can any literacy learning loss already sustained through education interruptions (if applicable) be addressed?

Policy evaluation and review planning

- How will you know if this policy was useful? How will you identify areas to address in review and evaluation?
- Who will be responsible for this process? What will policy evaluation and review look like in your school?

Links with policies

- What are the relevant internal and external policies that should be read in parallel with this document? Include links or hyperlinks to these policies, or include as an appendix to this policy. This might also appear at the beginning of the document.

CHAPTER 7

Final thoughts

You have probably already noticed that I have given attention to a vast array of issues relating to the WSLP and its delivery, however this book provides a structure without dictating what your priorities should be. It is likely that you as a reader will feel that this book falls short on the areas of *specific* interest to you. Arriving at Chapter 7, you might be thinking 'Why wasn't there more on (insert your area of interest)?' For example, the reader from the library may wish for more information about the role of the library in whole-school literacy leadership, and the reader from the science classroom might wish for further information about content and disciplinary literacy teaching in this subject area.

If you are in a primary or secondary school, you may have wanted more content specifically focused on your schooling years. It is a limitation of this book that I do not consistently provide identifying details about the age range or related school type where I quote or paraphrase from their WSLP. I decided on this approach as I wanted to preserve the anonymity of the schools associated with the publicly available WSLP documents cited in this book. There are some schools (particularly remote Australian schools) that have a specific age range that would make it easily identifiable. In future works I may decide to juxtapose what is on offer at primary and secondary levels if it serves a need, but for the purposes of this book I was writing for both audiences, and while I have pointed out distinguishing issues and features throughout, I did not want this juxtaposition to be the focus of this work.

Giving sufficient depth to all considerations to meet diverse reader needs cannot be realistically achieved in one book. While you may wish to use this book to inform your approach, other reading and training can furnish these further needs. For example, if a key issue in your school community is meeting the needs of EAL/D learners who struggle with listening skills, you will need to draw on the work of others who focus on this specific need in order to flesh out your WSLP. Likewise, if your school has many students who seem to be experiencing ongoing issues with poor phonemic awareness, you will need to look more closely at the implications for whole-school literacy approaches that relate to meeting this need. This book aims to provide a workable frame, but for the fleshing out of the frame, I hand over to you, the school-based experts, to do the further work to construct a WSLP that will be entirely responsive to your unique needs. This book may fall short of providing everything you need to design and implement a WSLP, but I have done the best I can to provide what I hope is a helpful foundation for you.

Rather than summarising what you have already read, this chapter ties up the book by addressing some of the practical elements of writing your WSLP, including some questions that may have lingered in your mind as you read through the previous sections. For example, it encourages the literacy team to answer questions such as 'Is this policy easy to read?', and includes related supportive tools such as readability indicators. I also make a wish list for future research in this area, some of which you may be interested in undertaking. Finally, I make a request of you, my reader.

Is my policy the right length?

How long should your policy be? As previously noted, the level of depth and complexity in these policies varied dramatically, so there is no standard, accepted length. For example, AU34 was a two-page literacy policy for a primary school. It included a one-sentence rationale, ten dot-point guidelines, eleven dot-points on implementation and one sentence on evaluation (including a set date for scheduled review). As might be imagined, it was very general in nature.

When it comes to length, as per Tables 1 and 2 previously, and Figure 1 below, UK documents were typically much longer than their Australian counterparts. While 57.8 per cent of Australian WSLPs were four pages or less, only 7.2 per cent of UK documents were this short. The majority (54.2 per cent) of UK documents were more than nine pages long.

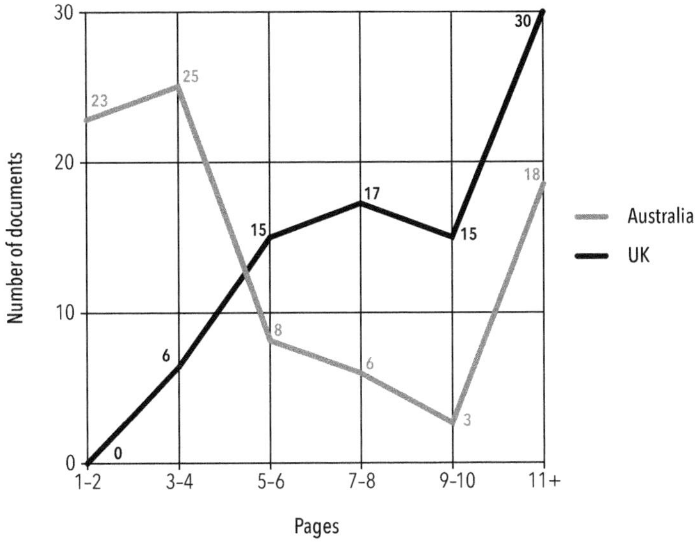

Figure 1: Length of whole-school literacy policies (Australia/UK)

This means that this is one of those 'how long is a piece of string?' questions. I doubt that there are many one or two page documents that have sufficient depth and complexity to meet the needs of Australian schools. However, a document that is very long may also not often be read in its entirety, and even if the document is very long, it is important that it remains clear and concise. It is more important that you carefully select the content to include and exclude based on your schools' needs rather than seek to meet an arbitrary length requirement. If you find that your WSLP is getting ridiculously long, consider moving some of the content to appendices.

Is my policy easy to read?

Readability matters. I know that staff within a school are typically highly literate, but they are unlikely to be the only consumers of your WSLP, and it is important that literacy plans and policies are easy to read so that they are fit for use (Marsh & Burke, 1992). If the policy is jargon dense and can only be understood by the English Department, it will be of little use across the school. To this end, regardless of who is leading policy development, the team should make sure that the policy is subject to readability critique across the learning areas of the school, perhaps in a focus group setting, so that it can be simplified as required.

It would also be quick and easy to run it through a readability tool online to make sure that it is not being pitched at a very complex level. This is as simple as accessing a free readability tool such as SMOG online and pasting in the text (in chunks if necessary) to determine how difficult to read your policy is. It will take about ten minutes, and certainly be worthwhile if it means that colleagues less confident in literacy instruction are then able to access and use the policy. The SMOG tool is easy to find online (Readability Formulas, n.d.) and see Ferguson et al. (2021) for more information on readability tools.

You might need a little bit of assistance in interpreting the readability results. Bear in mind that for text to be readable by the *general public*, text should be reported as being as close to being readable by a nine year old as possible. As the readability formulas are usually calculated in relation to US or UK schooling years, your text needs to be evaluated by the SMOG tool as being at Year 4 (UK), Year 5 (Australia) or Grade 5 (US) level (Ferguson et al., 2021). Do not be shocked if your policy is much harder to read than you expected.

Also, depending on the intended audience of your policy, a higher readability level may be acceptable. For example, you may wish for your WSLP to be targeted at your university-level educated colleagues, and prepare a more readable 'explainer' document for your parents, many of whom will need the text to be graded at a level suitable for the general public as described previously.

Do we need an expert consultant?

You probably do not need an expert or academic consultant to support you to create your WSLP as you have a wealth of expertise already in your staff (Luke, 2003). With some extra research and close internal consultation, you will be able to bring together a valuable document that is contextually responsive.

Consultants often have limited lenses on literacy, the tiny gardens that we carefully cultivate. This can work for you if your students have a common skill gap. For example, if most of your students struggle with writing, engaging an academic consultant who is an expert in writing could work for you. They should be knowledgeable about the recent research on practical measures for improving writing performance, and identifying the difficulties with writing that need to be addressed.

However, do not underestimate the capacity you already have within your school. You have knowledge that those of us who work in academia do not have. As soon as academics such as I leave the primary or secondary school classroom, our practical understanding of the needs of students is affected. Our tendency to specialise in a key research area or areas increases our value in speaking to these areas of knowledge, but cannot be extrapolated to expertise in literacy more broadly.

For example, I often work with schools who are seeking to build a reading culture or improve literacy engagement, but I know that reading engagement is just a part of the bigger picture when it comes to improving the complex range of skills and knowledge that underpin student literacy (for example, Kim, 2020). I also have a slightly bigger and more varied 'garden' than some highly specialised researchers, as I have also undertaken research that focuses on issues beyond reading engagement. These include, but are not limited to the needs of struggling literacy learners in secondary schools (see Merga, Mat Roni & Malpique, 2021b), initial teacher education and professional development (see Merga et al., 2020), wellbeing in schools (see Merga, 2021b), workforce issues impacting upon school library professionals (see Merga, 2019b), and issues relating to student writing (see Merga, Malpique et al., 2021), amongst numerous other literacy concerns. That said, I still have many gaps in my specialised literacy knowledge, and I lack the rich practical knowledge of a teacher who has spent thirty years in a primary or secondary schooling environment.

If you do decide to engage a consultant to focus on a key area, try not to lose sight of the bigger picture. When it comes to improving achievement in student literacy, schools should avoid a '"quick fix" approach focused on materials and one-stop workshops with "experts"', which is often unfortunately favoured over 'a longer-term view focused on teachers' knowledge' (Asselin, 2003, p. 53). The 'quick fix' approach:

> de-skills teaching by promising results from 'foolproof' packages and one-time workshops. Educators are being pressured to purchase expensive commercial reading programs that are marketed to raise test scores ... Research has shown that the traditional lecture or workshop by a person outside the school culture has limited value, yet it persists. It is interesting that the quick-fix approach appeals most to those stakeholders from outside of classrooms. (Asselin, 2003, p. 53)

It is tempting to buy into a one size fits all approach, but this is only appropriate if you work in a school where all of the students are experiencing the same issues with literacy. My previous research suggests that this would be quite unusual, given that most secondary English teachers feel that their struggling literacy learners are facing diverse challenges at both group and individual levels (Merga, 2020b).

If you do engage a consultant to support you in this process, you will need to find one who is willing to consider the literacy needs of *all* of your students, while paying particular attention to your struggling literacy learners. They will need to be willing to listen to you and responsive to your unique school context, and not assume that an approach they used at a previous school will yield the same results in a new environment. You need to develop a WSLP that can be used, and that fits your school, so theoretical and abstract conceptualisations of literacy should be kept to a minimum. You will need to engage someone who is pragmatic and interested in literacy for real world uses beyond theories.

Somewhat ironically, given that I am an education researcher, I need to note that I do not believe that research always has the answers. Like Cuban (1984), I understand that 'policymakers face practical dilemmas which research findings often prove inadequate or irrelevant' (p. 4), so while we should benefit from the expertise of researchers where possible, you are actually the education expert within your school as an experienced educator knowledgeable of your schools' needs and context.

The only exception to this contention is evaluation. Given the tensions between conflict of interest, professional achievement, accountability and external expectations, evaluating your own WSLP can be problematic, and this may be particularly contingent on what you seek to do with this knowledge. As such, you may wish to engage a consultant to facilitate the evaluation stage of your WSLP, and you will need to reach out to them before implementation. While there is still a degree of conflict of interest as they are employed by you, they will need to be professionally objective in their determination of the success of your WSLP, and in order to propose any adjustments that might need to be made to increase its efficacy moving forward. You do not *need* to engage a consultant for this stage, however if you have the funds, it may be a worthwhile investment, particularly if you wish to share your WSLP and the journey your team embarked upon to create and implement it in public forums such as educational, literacy or library conferences, or if you intend to use your leadership of the WSLP for promotional purposes. Being able to say that it has been externally evaluated and found to have delivered student benefit will confer credibility. The consultant may also be able to spot something in the data that was hidden from you due to your close proximity with the WSLP and the school.

Further research needed

During my writing of and promotion of this book I have tried to draw attention to the importance of literacy as a whole-school responsibility (for example, Merga, 2022b). If you are in educational research, or considering moving into this area, even if just to complete a higher degree by research, you might want to look at WSLPs. As I have previously mentioned, there are not a lot of researchers in this area, looking at these policies, and given that many schools spend time and resourcing to develop them, here are a few of the priority areas for research that can have a strong real world benefit.

Research question: Do schools actually use their WSLPs?
Why it is needed: Due of a lack of evaluation and monitoring, it is hard to know the extent to which WSLPs have been actually put into practice at individual teacher and departmental levels within schools, and there is often a lack of adequate attention of evaluation and monitoring in WSLPs as previously explored (Beverton & Sewell, 2002). We need to know if WSLPs are even being enacted, or if like so many other initiatives and policies, they are simply another bureaucratic output that gathers dust. Where WSLPs were hardly used, we need to understand why, as implications can prevent schools wasting time and resourcing that are already scarce.

Research question: What elements or interventions in WSLPs are most strongly associated with positive transformation within schools, and how is this reflective of school context/composition?
Why it is needed: As this book clearly demonstrates, schools have a wide range of choices about what elements to include in their WSLP. As I have insisted throughout, I doubt a one size fits all approach will work, so we need to know which facets best serve which schools. Schools will have this knowledge through their experiences implementing WSLPs, and researchers need to learn from them.

Research question: To what extent are Australian schools positioning literacy as a whole-school responsibility?
Why it is needed: It is commonly speculated that Australian schools do not take this curricular positioning of literacy as a whole-school responsibility very seriously, and this is in part confirmed by the weak focus on literacy across the curriculum in Australian WSLPs that I found in the analysis that I undertook in order to write this book. We need to find out how common it is for schools to have a WSLP orientation that extends beyond the aspirational, and where this is the case, the extent to which this approach has been imbedded in the scope of practices and structures within a school, including but not limited to the WSLP.

Research question: Where schools have successfully transitioned into a whole-school approach to literacy, to what factors do they attribute this success?
Why it is needed: One of the reasons I wrote this book was the paucity of available information on how to practically enact a whole-school approach to literacy. I would love for future editions of this book to be able to weave in the accounts, experiences and data from schools that have *successfully* transitioned to a whole-school approach to literacy. I would like to undertake research that:

1. Determines what success looks like in this context. What is a demonstrated genuine school wide commitment to literacy? How can we assess and measure this?
2. Identifies recurring factors that schools identified were crucial to this success.

3. Analyses these factors and identifies further enabling and constraining forces behind these factors, to provide practical guidance for schools looking to transition to a whole-school approach to literacy.

Note about commercial educational products

Many schools will have 'go to' commercial educational products that work well in their school, which may be mentioned or heavily drawn upon in a WSLP. I have avoided naming commercial educational products, even though the documents I analysed in this book did often include references to these resources.

I have avoided inclusion of specific commercial educational products for the following reasons:

1. This book does not wish to endorse any particular commercial educational products. Just as the concept of literacy itself is constantly reimagined, reshaped and extended, the availability, usefulness, quality and variety of commercial educational literacy products also constantly changes over time.
2. The educational value of some of these products is very questionable indeed. Like researchers in the UK, I am concerned by the proliferation of private companies selling schools 'literacy catch-up schemes' which claim to have 'evidence-based' solutions (Innes et al., 2021, p. 9); however, on closer investigation these are often very poorly research supported. Evaluations of the educational benefit of products are often conducted by the manufacturer rather than an external party, and where an external party is employed, funding is still provided by the manufacturer, with conflict of interest unavoidable in both instances.
3. Products can have widely varying utility in different schools; what works wonders in one school may be of no use in another.

While I have avoided mention of commercial educational products, this does not mean that I am against their judicious use. I am aware that some products can be very helpful within schools, and support students to higher levels of attainment in literacy. Use what works in your school community, and keep an eye on the evolving peer-reviewed research around best practice in literacy learning so that you can avoid falling for the latest aggressively marketed but poorly substantiated products, and you can identify new products that can genuinely support student literacy learning.

A final request

I really hope that you found this book useful. If you use this book to help you to write or revise your WSLP, please shoot me an email or tag me on Twitter and let me know how it went.

Please let me know:

1. how you used the book
2. what aspects of the book were useful
3. what aspects of the book were missing, or needed further consideration
4. any interesting developments that arose during your WSLP journey.

I want this book, and future iterations to be as useful to the end user as possible, while being grounded in the available research. If possible, I would love for future editions to include your own real-world experiences and reflections (with anonymity optional if you prefer). Your views will be greatly appreciated. Thanks for your interest in my research.

References

Agostinelli, F., Doepke, M., Sorrenti, G., & Zilibotti, F. (2022). When the great equalizer shuts down: Schools, peers, and parents in pandemic times. *Journal of Public Economics*, *206*, 104574, 1–10.

Aharony, N. (2009). Librarians' attitudes towards marketing library services. *Journal of Librarianship and Information Science*, *41*(1), 39–50.

Angelo, D. (2013). Identification and assessment contexts of Aboriginal and Torres Strait Islander learners of Standard Australian English: Challenges for the language testing community. *Papers in Language Testing and Assessment*, *2*(2), 67–102.

Alford, J., & Windeyer, A. (2014). Responding to national curriculum goals for English language learners: Enhancing reading strategies in junior high school content areas. *Journal of Immersion and Content-Based Language Education*, *2*(1), 74–95.

Allen, K. A., Reupert, A., & Oades, L. (2021). Implementing school policy effectively. In K. A. Allen, A. Reupert, & L. Oades (Eds.), *Building Better Schools with Evidence-based Policy* (pp. 1–9). Taylor & Francis.

Andrade, H. L. (2019). A critical review of research on student self-assessment. *Frontiers in Education*, *4*, 1–13.

Asselin, M. (2003). Improving literacy education through professional study: The leadership role of the teacher-librarian. *Teacher Librarian*, *31*(1), 53–54.

Audette, L. M., Hammond, M. S., & Rochester, N. K. (2020). Methodological issues with coding participants in anonymous psychological longitudinal studies. *Educational and Psychological Measurement*, *80*(1), 163–185.

Australian Bureau of Statistics (ABS). (1997). *4228.0 – Aspects of Literacy: Assessed Skill Levels, Australia, 1996.* www.abs.gov.au/AUSSTATS/abs@.nsf/Lookup/4228.0Main+Features11996? OpenDocument=

Australian Bureau of Statistics (ABS). (2013). *Programme for the International Assessment of Adult Competencies, Australia.* www.abs.gov.au/statistics/people/education/programme-international-assessment-adult-competencies-australia/latest-release#data-download

Australian Curriculum, Assessment and Reporting Authority (ACARA). (n.d.-a). *English: Aims.* www.australiancurriculum.edu.au/f-10-curriculum/english/aims/

Australian Curriculum, Assessment and Reporting Authority (ACARA). (n.d.-b). Literacy in the learning areas. *In Literacy (Version 8.4).* www.australiancurriculum.edu.au/f-10-curriculum/general-capabilities/literacy/

Australian Curriculum, Assessment and Reporting Authority (ACARA). (n.d.-c). *English: Rationale.* www.australiancurriculum.edu.au/f-10-curriculum/english/rationale/

Australian Curriculum, Assessment and Reporting Authority (ACARA). (n.d.-d). *Curriculum version history.* www.australiancurriculum.edu.au/about-the-australian-curriculum/#

Australian Curriculum, Assessment and Reporting Authority (ACARA). (2014). *My School Fact Sheet.* www.acara.edu.au/verve/_resources/FAQs_2014.pdf

Australian Curriculum, Assessment and Reporting Authority (ACARA). (2021a). *National assessment program — literacy and numeracy achievement in reading, writing, language conventions and numeracy: National report for 2021.* ACARA.

Australian Curriculum, Assessment and Reporting Authority (ACARA). (2021b). *General capabilities. Digital literacy (previously ICT). Consultation- introductory information and learning continua.* www.australiancurriculum.edu.au/media/7024/gc_digital_literacy_ict_capability_consultation_curriculum.pdf

Australian Curriculum, Assessment and Reporting Authority (ACARA). (2022a). *Digital literacy.* https://v9.australiancurriculum.edu.au/f-10-curriculum/general-capabilities/digital-literacy?element=0&sub-element=0

Australian Curriculum, Assessment and Reporting Authority (ACARA). (2022b). *What's changed in the new Australian Curriculum?* https://v9.australiancurriculum.edu.au/resources/stories/curriculum-changes

Australian Curriculum, Assessment and Reporting Authority (ACARA). (2022c). *Literacy.* https://v9.australiancurriculum.edu.au/teacher-resources/understand-this-general-capability/literacy#accordion-85833852f3-item-6dc9a03bf4

Australian Curriculum, Assessment and Reporting Authority (ACARA). (2022d). *Literacy: About the general capability.* https://v9.australiancurriculum.edu.au/content/dam/en/curriculum/ac-version-9/downloads/general-capabilities/general-capabilities-literacy-about-the-general-capability-v9.docx

Australian Curriculum, Assessment and Reporting Authority (ACARA). (2022e). *General capabilities downloads*. https://v9.australiancurriculum.edu.au/downloads/general-capabilities

Australian Curriculum, Assessment and Reporting Authority (ACARA). (2022f). *Health and Physical Education propositions*. www.australiancurriculum.edu.au/f-10-curriculum/health-and-physical-education/key-ideas/

Australian Curriculum, Assessment and Reporting Authority (ACARA). (2022g). *Personal and Social capability*. https://v9.australiancurriculum.edu.au/f-10-curriculum/general-capabilities/personal-and-social-capability?element=1&sub-element=0

Australian Institute for Teaching and School Leadership Limited (2011). *Australian Professional Standards for Teachers*. Education Services Australia.

Australian School Library Association (ASLA). (2014a). *Evidence guide for teacher librarians in the highly accomplished career stage*. www.asla.org.au/resources/Documents/Website%20Documents/evidence-guide_ha.pdf

Australian School Library Association (ASLA). (2014b). *Evidence guide for teacher librarians in the proficient career stage*. https://asla.org.au/resources/Documents/Website%20Documents/evi- dence_guide_prof.pdf

Australian School Library Association (ASLA). (2018). *What is a teacher librarian?* https://asla.org.au/what-is-a-teacher-librarian

Australian School Library Association (ASLA) and Australian Library and Information Association (ALIA) (2016). *Statement on Teacher Librarians in Australia.* https://asla.org.au/resources/Documents/Website%20Documents/Policies/policy_tls_in_australia.pdf

Avalos, B. (2011). Teacher professional development in teaching and teacher education over ten years. *Teaching and Teacher Education, 27*(1), 10–20.

Azevedo, J. P., Hasan, A., Goldemberg, D., Iqbal, S. A. & Geven, K. (2020). *Simulating the potential impacts of COVID-19 school closures on schooling and learning outcomes: A set of global estimates*. Washington, DC: World Bank. www.worldbank.org/en/topic/education/publication/simulating-potential- impacts-of-COVID-19-school-closures-learning-outcomes-a-set-of-global-estimates

Baumgartner, D., Bryan, T., Donahue, M., & Nelson, C. (1993). Thanks for asking: Parent comments about homework, tests, and grades. *Exceptionality, 4*(3), 177–185.

Beer, M., Eisenstat, R. A., & Spector, B. (1990). Why change programs don't produce change. *Harvard Business Review, 68*(6), 158–166.

Bellibaş, M. Ş., Gümüş, S., & Kılınç, A. Ç. (2020). Principals supporting teacher leadership: The effects of learning-centred leadership on teacher leadership practices with the mediating role of teacher agency. *European Journal of Education, 55*(2), 200–216.

Beverton, S., & Sewell, G. (2002). Implementing whole school literacy policies. *Education 3–13, 30*(1), 24–29.

Billman, A., & Pearson, P. D. (2013). Literacy in the disciplines. *Literacy Learning: The Middle Years, 21*(1), 25–33.

Boomer, G. (1992). Negotiating the curriculum. In Boomer, G., Onore, C., Lester, N., & Cook, J. (Eds), *Negotiating the curriculum: Educating for the 21st century* (pp. 4–14). Falmer.

Borman, G. D., & Dowling, N. M. (2008). Teacher attrition and retention: A meta-analytic and narrative review of the research. *Review of Educational Research, 78*(3), 367–409.

Boucher, L. C. (2001). Why you can't buy a vegetable garden: Whole-school literacy program reform. *New England Reading Association Journal, 37*(3), 1–9.

Branch, J. L., & Oberg, D. (2001). The teacher-librarian in the 21st century: The teacher-librarian as instructional leader. *School Libraries in Canada, 21*(2), 9–11.

British Education Research Association (BERA). (2018). *Ethical guidelines for educational research* (4th Ed.). www.bera.ac.uk/wp-content/uploads/2018/06/BERA-Ethical-Guidelines-for-Educational-Research_4thEdn_2018.pdf?noredirect=1

Bueker, C.S. (2005). Teachers' reports of the effects of a whole-school literacy reform model on teacher turnover. *The Elementary School Journal, 105*(4), 395–416.

Bullock, A. (Chairman) (1975). *The Bullock Report – A language for life*. Report of the Committee of Enquiry appointed by the Secretary of State for Education and Science under the Chairmanship of Sir Alan Bullock FBA. Her Majesty's Stationery Office.

Burden, R., & Burdett, J. (2005). Factors associated with successful learning in pupils with dyslexia: a motivational analysis. *British Journal of Special Education, 32*(2), 100–104.

Butt, R. (2016). Employment procedures and practices challenge teacher assistants in mainstream schools. *School Leadership & Management, 36*(1), 63–79.

Cambourne, B. (2021). A brief history of 'The Reading Wars'. *EduResearch Matters Blog*. Australia Association for Research in Education. www.aare.edu.au/blog/?p=9488

Campbell, L., Gray, S., MacIntyre, T., & Stone, K. (2020). Literacy, numeracy and health and wellbeing across learning: Investigating student teachers' confidence. *International Journal of Educational Research*, 100, e101532.

Carr, S. (2020). Dampened motivation as a side effect of contemporary educational policy: a self-determination theory perspective. *Oxford Review of Education, 46*(3), 331–345.

Cassidy, A. & Kiely, B. (2008). *Resources for developing a school-wide literacy plan.* Junior Certificate School Programme Support Service. www.pdst.ie/sites/default/files/1136_literacy_plan6.pdf

Cazden, C., Cope, B., Fairclough, N., Gee, J., Kalantzis, M., Kress, G., Luke, A., Luke, C., Michaels, S., & Nakata, M. (1996). A pedagogy of multiliteracies: Designing social futures. *Harvard Educational Review*, *66*(1), 60–92.

Chambers, D. (2015). *Working with teaching assistants and other support staff for inclusive education.* Emerald Group Publishing Limited.

Christensen, C. A. (2005). The role of orthographic-motor integration in the production of creative and well-structured written text for students in secondary school. *Educational Psychology*, *25*(5), 441–453.

Clark, C., & Teravainen-Goff, A. (2020). *Children and young people's reading in 2019.* National Literacy Trust research report. https://cdn.literacytrust.org.uk/media/documents/Reading_trends_in_ 2019_-_Final.pdf

Collins, V. J., Dargan, I. W., Walsh, R. L., & Merga, M. K. (2022). Teachers' perceptions of the benefits and challenges of a whole-school reading for pleasure program. Issues in *Educational Research*, *32*(1), 89–104.

Crevola, C. A., & Hill, P. W. (1998). Evaluation of a whole-school approach to prevention and intervention in early literacy. *Journal of Education for Students Placed at Risk*, *3*(2), 133–157.

Cuban, L. (1984). Transforming the frog into a prince: Effective schools research, policy, and practice at the district level. *Harvard Educational Review*, *54*(2), 129–152.

Culican, S.J., Emmitt, M. & Oakley, C. (2001). *Literacy and learning in the middle years: Major report on the middle years literacy research project.* Deakin University.

Cunningham, A. E. (2005). Vocabulary growth through independent reading and reading aloud to children. In E.H. Hiebert & M.L. Kamil (Eds.), *Teaching and learning vocabulary: Bringing research to practice* (pp. 45–68). Erlbaum.

Daliri-Ngametua, R., Hardy, I., & Creagh, S. (2021). Data, performativity and the erosion of trust in teachers. *Cambridge Journal of Education.* DOI:10.1080/0305764X.2021.2002811

Daniels, E., & Steres, M. (2011). Examining the effects of a school-wide reading culture on the engagement of middle school students. *RMLE Online*, *35*(2), 1–13.

Darmawan, I. G. N. (2020). The changes in attitudes of 15-year-old Australian students towards reading, mathematics and science and their impact on student performance. *Australian Journal of Education*, *64*(3), 304–327.

Department of Education (2014). *Improving literacy and numeracy national partnership final report Western Australia* www.dese.gov.au/teaching-and-school-leadership/resources/improving-literacy-and-numeracy-national-partnership-final-report-western-australia

Department of Education Western Australia (DoEWA) (2021). *An implementation model for whole-school literacy in the secondary school.* Unpublished resource provided on request.

Dix, K., Felgate, R., Ahmed, S. K., Carslake, T., & Sniedze-Gregory, S. (2020). *School libraries in South Australia.* 2019 Census. Australian Council for Educational Research. https://doi.org/10.37517/978-1-74286-583-6

Domina, T., Renzulli, L., Murray, B., Garza, A. N., & Perez, L. (2021). Remote or removed: Predicting successful engagement with online learning during COVID-19. *Socius, 7*, DOI: 10.1177/2378023120988200

Dulfer, N., Polesel, J., & Rice, S. (2012). *The experience of education: The impacts of high stakes testing on school students and their families.* The Whitlam Institute.

Duursma, E. V., Augustyn, M., & Zuckerman, B. (2008). Reading aloud to children: The evidence. *Archives of Disease in Childhood, 93*(7), 554–557.

Eades, D. (2015). Taking evidence from Aboriginal witnesses speaking English: some sociolinguistic considerations. *Precedent*, 126, 44–48. http://classic.austlii.edu.au/cgibin/download.cgi/au/journals/PrecedentAULA/2015/12

Education Standards Authority NSW (n.d.). What is Standard Australian English and why is it 'standard'? https://ab-ed.nesa.nsw.edu.au/go/aboriginal-english/what-is-standard-australian-english

Eisenbach, B. B., & Greathouse, P. (2020). Enhancing students' mental health literacy through the paratext of two middle-level novels. *Voices From the Middle, 28*(2), 15–17.

Eguia, R. T., Crawford, K. H., Stevens-Ayers, T., Kelnhofer-Millevolte, L., Greninger, A. L., Englund, J. A., & Bloom, J. D. (2021). A human coronavirus evolves antigenically to escape antibody immunity. *PLoS pathogens, 17*(4), e1009453.

Evans, M. B. (2018). The integration of reading, writing, speaking, and listening skills in the middle school social studies classroom. [Doctoral dissertation, Utah State University]. DigitalCommons@USU. https://digitalcommons.usu.edu/etd/7157

Evans, M. D., Kelley, J., Sikora, J., & Treiman, D. J. (2010). Family scholarly culture and educational success: Books and schooling in 27 nations. *Research in Social Stratification and Mobility, 28*(2), 171–197.

Faggella-Luby, M. N., Graner, P. S., Deshler, D. D., & Drew, S. V. (2012). Building a house on sand: Why disciplinary literacy is not sufficient to replace general strategies for adolescent learners who struggle. *Topics in Language Disorders*, 32(1), 69–84.

Fajardo, M. F. (2015). A review of critical literacy beliefs and practices of English language learners and teachers. *University of Sydney Papers in TESOL*, 10, 29–56.

Fenwick, L. (2010). Initiating and sustaining learning about literacy and language across the curriculum within secondary schools. *Australian Journal of Language and Literacy, 33*(3), 268–283.

Ferguson, C. & Merga, M. K. (2021). How can an adult literacy tutoring program help participants build confidence and meet their goals? *Australian Journal of Language and Literacy*, *44*(1), 75–83.

Ferguson, C., Merga, M. K., & Winn, S. (2021). Communications in the time of a pandemic: The readability of documents for public consumption. *Australian and New Zealand Journal of Public Health*, *45*(2), 116–121.

Fogel, Y., Rosenblum, S., & Barnett, A. L. (2022). Handwriting legibility across different writing tasks in school-aged children. *Hong Kong Journal of Occupational Therapy*. DOI: 10.1177/15691861221075709.

Freebody, P. (2007). *Literacy education in school: Research perspectives from the past, for the future*. ACER. https://research.acer.edu.au/cgi/viewcontent.cgi?article=1001&context=aer

Garoni, S., Edwards-Groves, C., & Davidson, C. (2021). The 'doubleness' of transition: Investigating classroom talk practices in literacy lessons at the end of primary school and the beginning of secondary school. *Australian Journal of Language and Literacy*, *44*(2), 62–75.

Gear, R. C., & Sood, K. K. (2021). School middle leaders and change management: Do they need to be more on the 'balcony' than the dance floor? *Education Sciences*, *11*(11), 753–765.

Gee, J. P. (2000). The new literacy studies and the social turn. *Situated Literacies: Reading and Writing in Context*, 2, 180–196.

Gewirtz, S., Maguire, M., Neumann, E., & Towers, E. (2021). What's wrong with 'deliverology'? Performance measurement, accountability and quality improvement in English secondary education. *Journal of Education Policy*, *36*(4), 504–529.

Gilbert, L., Teravainen, A., Clark, C., & Shaw, S. (2018). *Literacy and life expectancy: An evidence review exploring the link between literacy and life expectancy in England through health and socioeconomic factors*. National Literacy Trust.

Goodwyn, A., & Findlay, K. (2003). Shaping literacy in the secondary school: Policy, practice and agency in the age of the National Literacy Strategy. *British Journal of Educational Studies*, *51*(1), 20–35.

Goss, P., & Sonnemann, J. (2016). Widening gaps: *What NAPLAN tells us about student progress*. Grattan Institute.

Graham, S. (2019). Changing how writing is taught. *Review of Research in Education*, *43*(1), 277–303.

Graham, S., Harris, K. R., & Hebert, M. (2011). It is more than just the message: Presentation effects in scoring writing. *Focus on Exceptional Children*, *44*(4), 1–12.

Graham, S., & Rijlaarsdam, G. (2016). Writing education around the globe: Introduction and call for a new global analysis. *Reading and Writing*, *29*(5), 781–792.

Guerriero, S. (2014). *Teachers' pedagogical knowledge and the teaching profession*. OECD Publishing. www.oecd.org/education/ceri/Background_document_to_Symposium_ITEL-FINAL.pdf

Gutierrez, A., Lowe, K., & Guenther, J. (2021). Indigenous student literacy outcomes in Australia: a systematic review of literacy programmes. *Asia-Pacific Journal of Teacher Education*, *49*(1), 37–60.

Hammond, J., & Macken-Horarik, M. (2001). Teachers' voices, teachers' practices: Insider perspectives on literacy education. *Australian Journal of Language and Literacy*, *24*(2), 112–132.

Hand, B. M., Alvermann, D. E., Gee, J., Guzzetti, B. J., Norris, S. P., Phillips, L. M., Prain, V. & Yore, L. D. (2003). Message from the 'Island Group': What is literacy in science literacy? *Journal of Research in Science Teaching*, *40*(7), 607–615.

Hannant, K., & Jetnikoff, A. (2017). What do students need to know about writing for science in the middle years? *Literacy Learning: The Middle Years*, *25*(1), 53–65.

Harris, A., & Jones, M. (2019). Teacher leadership and educational change. *School Leadership & Management*, *39*(2), 123–126.

Heller, M. F., & Firestone, W. A. (1995). Who's in charge here? Sources of leadership for change in eight schools. *The Elementary School Journal*, *96*(1), 65–86.

Hill, P. W., & Crevola, C. A. (1999). Key Features of a whole-school, design approach to literacy teaching in schools. *Australian Journal of Learning Difficulties*, *4*(3), 5–11.

Hofer, S. I., Holzberger, D., & Reiss, K. (2020). Evaluating school inspection effectiveness: A systematic research synthesis on 30 years of international research. *Studies in Educational Evaluation*, *65*, e100864.

Humphrey, S., & Robinson, S.H. (2012). Using a 4x4 framework for whole school literacy development. In J. Knox (Ed.), *To boldly proceed: Papers from the 39th International Systemic Functional Congress* (pp. 81–86). Sydney: Organising Committee of the 39th Systemic Functional Conference.

Hutton, J. S., Horowitz-Kraus, T., Mendelsohn, A. L., DeWitt, T., Holland, S. K., & C-MIND Authorship Consortium. (2015). Home reading environment and brain activation in preschool children listening to stories. *Pediatrics*, *136*(3), 466–478.

Independent Teacher Workload Review Group (2016). *Eliminating unnecessary workload around planning and teaching resources*. https://assets.publishing.service.gov.uk/government/uploads/system/uploads/attachment_data/file/511257/Eliminating-unnecessary-workload-around-planning-and-teaching-resources.pdf

Information Literacy Meeting of Experts. (2003). *The Prague declaration: Towards an information literate society. National Commission on Library and Information Science; National Forum on Information Literacy & UNESCO*. http://www.unesco.org/new/fileadmin/MULTIMEDIA/HQ/CI/CI/pdf/PragueDeclaration.pdf

Innes, M., Gunter, H. M., & Armstrong, P. (2021). Researching literacy policy: Conceptualizing trends in the field. *London Review of Education, 19*(1), 1–15.

International Literacy Association (2017). *Content area and disciplinary literacy strategies and frameworks*. www.literacyworldwide.org/docs/default-source/where-we-stand/ila-content-area-disciplinary-literacy-strategies-frameworks.pdf?sfvrsn=e180a58e_6

Jennings, J. L., & Lauen, D. L. (2016). Accountability, inequality, and achievement: The effects of the No Child Left Behind act on multiple measures of student learning. RSF: *The Russell Sage Foundation Journal of the Social Sciences, 2*(5), 220–241.

Jerrim, J., Lopez-Agudo, L. A., & Marcenaro-Gutierrez, O. D. (2020). Does it matter what children read? New evidence using longitudinal census data from Spain. *Oxford Review of Education, 46*(5), 515–533.

Johnson, B. (2003). Teacher collaboration: Good for some, not so good for others. *Educational Studies, 29*(4), 337–350.

Jones, S. L., & Lee, E. A. (2014). Literacy-related professional development preferences of secondary teachers. *Alberta Journal of Educational Research, 60*(2), 245–263.

Joram, E., Gabriele, A. J., & Walton, K. (2020). What influences teachers' 'buy-in' of research? Teachers' beliefs about the applicability of educational research to their practice. *Teaching and Teacher Education, 88*(2), 1–20.

Kaffenberger, M. (2021). Modelling the long-run learning impact of the Covid-19 learning shock: Actions to (more than) mitigate loss. *International Journal of Educational Development, 81*, 102326, 1–8.

Keay, J. K., Carse, N., & Jess, M. (2019). Understanding teachers as complex professional learners. *Professional Development in Education, 45*(1), 125–137.

Kim, Y. S. G. (2020). Toward integrative reading science: The direct and indirect effects model of reading. *Journal of Learning Disabilities, 53*(6), 469–491.

Kondakci, Y., Beycioglu, K., Sincar, M., & Ugurlu, C. T. (2017). Readiness of teachers for change in schools. *International Journal of Leadership in Education, 20*(2), 176–197.

Konza, D. (2011). Phonics. *Research into practice*. Government of South Australia. www.ecu.edu.au/__data/assets/pdf_file/0012/663699/SA-DECS-Phonics.pdf

Kotter, J.P. (1995). Leading change: Why transformation efforts fail. *Harvard Business Review, 73*(2), 59–67.

Kuhfeld, M., Soland, J., Tarasawa, B., Johnson, A., Ruzek, E. & Liu, J. (2020). Projecting the potential impact of COVID-19 school closures on academic achievement. *Educational Researcher, 49*(8), 549–565.

Lai, E., & Cheung, D. (2015). Enacting teacher leadership: The role of teachers in bringing about change. *Educational Management Administration & Leadership, 43*(5), 673–692.

Lance, K. C., & Kachel, D. E. (2018). Why school librarians matter: What years of research tell us. *Phi Delta Kappan, 99*(7), 15–20.

Lance, K. C., & Maniotes, L. K. (2020). Linking librarians, inquiry learning, and information literacy? *Phi Delta Kappan, 101*(7), 47–51.

Ledger, S., & Merga, M. K. (2018). Reading aloud: Children's attitudes toward being read to at home and at school. *Australian Journal of Teacher Education, 43*(3), 124–139.

Lewandowsky, S., & van der Linden, S. (2021). Countering misinformation and fake news through inoculation and prebunking. *European Review of Social Psychology*. DOI: 10.1080/10463283.2021.1876983

Lewis, M., & Wray, D. (1999). Secondary teachers' views and actions concerning literacy and literacy teaching. *Educational Review, 51*(3), 273–281.

Lewis, M., & Wray, D. (2001). Implementing effective literacy initiatives in the secondary school. *Educational Studies, 27*(1), 45–54.

Loh, C. E., Ellis, M., Paculdar, A. A., & Wan, Z. H. (2017). Building a successful reading culture through the school library: A case study of a Singapore secondary school. *IFLA Journal, 43*(4), 335–347.

Long, L., MacBlain, S., & MacBlain, M. (2007). Supporting students with dyslexia at the secondary level: An emotional model of literacy. *Journal of Adolescent & Adult Literacy, 51*(2), 124–134.

Louis, K. S. (1994). Beyond 'managed change': rethinking how schools improve. *School Effectiveness and School Improvement, 5*(1), 2–24.

Lu, W. & Cross, R. (2014). Making sense of mixed messages: Literacy within the Australian Curriculum. *Literacy Learning: The Middle Years, 22*(2), 41–50.

Luke, A. (2003). Making literacy policy and practice with a difference. *Australian Journal of Language and Literacy, 26*(3), 58–82.

Luke, A., Dooley, K., & Woods, A. (2011). Comprehension and content: Planning literacy in low socioeconomic and culturally diverse schools. *The Australian Educational Researcher, 38*(2), 149–166.

Luke, A., & Woods, A. F. (2009). Critical literacies in schools: A primer. *Voices from the Middle, 17*(2), 9–18.

Lynch, A. (2009). Changing schools: How policy implementation can impact on the literacy learning of mobile students. *Australasian Journal of Early Childhood, 34*(2), 47–53.

MacCullagh, L. (2014). Participation and experiences of students with dyslexia in higher education: a literature review with an Australian focus. *Australian Journal of Learning Difficulties, 19*(2), 93–111.

Mackenzie, N. & Hemmings, B. (2014). Predictors of success with writing in the first year of school. *Issues in Educational Research, 24*(1), 41–54.

Mackey, T. P., & Jacobson, T. E. (2011). Reframing information literacy as a metaliteracy. *College & Research Libraries, 72*(1), 62–78.

Malpique, A. A. (2020). In these pandemic school days handwriting still matters! *EduResearch Matters.* www.aare.edu.au/blog/?tag=anabela-malpique

Malpique, A., & Pino-Pasternak, D. (2017). To empower students with effective writing skills, handwriting matters. *The Conversation.* https://theconversation.com/to-empower-students-with-effective-writing-skills-handwriting-matters-81949

Malpique, A. A., Pino-Pasternak, D. & Roberto, M. S. (2020). Writing and reading performance in Year 1 Australian classrooms: Associations with handwriting automaticity and writing instruction. *Reading and Writing, 33*(3), 783–805.

Marsh, V., & Burke, J. (1992). A whole school approach to literacy: Chisholm Primary School (ACT). *Australian Journal of Language and Literacy, 15*(1), 7–26.

Mason, S., & Matas, C. P. (2015). Teacher attrition and retention research in Australia: Towards a new theoretical framework. *Australian Journal of Teacher Education, 40*(11), 45–66.

Mat Roni, S., & Merga, M. K. (2019). Using an artificial neural network to explore the influence of extrinsic and intrinsic variables on children's reading frequency and attitudes. *Australian Journal of Education, 63*(3), 270–291.

Mat Roni, S., Merga, M. K., & Morris, J. E. (2020). *Conducting quantitative research in education.* Springer.

May, S. (2007). Sustaining effective literacy practices over time in secondary schools: School organisational and change issues. *Language and Education, 21*(5), 387–405.

May, S., & Wright, N. (2007). Secondary literacy across the curriculum: Challenges and possibilities. *Language and Education, 21*(5), 370–376.

McIntosh, S., & Vignoles, A. (2001). Measuring and assessing the impact of basic skills on labour market outcomes. *Oxford Economic Papers, 53*(3), 453–481.

McKenna, M. C., Kear, D. J., & Ellsworth, R. A. (1995). Children's attitudes toward reading: A national survey. *Reading Research Quarterly, 30*, 934–956.

McPherson, M. (2020). The influence of teacher librarians' personal attributes and relationships with the school community in developing a school library programme. *School Libraries Worldwide, 26*(1), 136–150.

Meeks, L., Madelaine, A., & Stephenson, J. (2020). New teachers talk about their preparation to teach early literacy. *Australian Journal of Learning Difficulties, 25*(2), 161–181.

Merga, M. K. (2013). Should Silent Reading feature in a secondary school English programme? West Australian students' perspectives on Silent Reading. *English in Education, 47*(3), 229–244.

Merga, M. K. (2014a). Peer group and friend influences on the social acceptability of adolescent book reading. *Journal of Adolescent and Adult Literacy, 57*(6), 472–482.

Merga, M. K. (2014b). Exploring the role of parents in supporting recreational book reading beyond primary school. *English in Education, 48*(2), 149–163.

Merga, M. K. (2014c). Western Australian adolescents' reasons for infrequent engagement in recreational book reading. *Literacy Learning: the Middle Years, 22*(2), 60–66.

Merga, M. K. (2014d). Are Western Australian adolescents keen book readers? *Australian Journal of Language and Literacy, 37*, 161–170.

Merga, M. K. (2014e). Are teenagers really keen digital readers?: adolescent engagement in ebook reading and the relevance of paper books today. *English in Australia, 49*(1), 27–37.

Merga, M. K. (2015a). Access to books in the home and adolescent engagement in recreational book reading: Considerations for secondary school educators. *English in Education, 49*(3), 197–214.

Merga, M. K. (2015b). 'She knows what I like': Student-generated best-practice statements for encouraging recreational reading in adolescents. *Australian Journal of Education, 59*(1), 35–50.

Merga, M. K. (2016a). 'Bring Your Own Device': Considering potential risks to student health. *Health Education Journal, 75*(4), 464–473.

Merga, M. K. (2016b). 'I don't know if she likes reading': Are teachers perceived to be keen readers, and how is this determined? *English in Education, 50*(3), 255–269.

Merga, M. K. (2017a). Interactive reading opportunities beyond the early years: What educators need to consider. *Australian Journal of Education, 61*(3), 328–343.

Merga, M. K. (2017b). Becoming a reader: Significant social influences on avid book readers. *School Library Research, 20.* https://files.eric.ed.gov/fulltext/EJ1160840.pdf

Merga, M. K. (2017c). What would make children read for pleasure more frequently? *English in Education, 51*(2), 207–223.

Merga, M. K. (2018). *Reading engagement for tweens and teens: What would make them read more?* ABC-CLIO.

Merga, M. K. (2019a). *Librarians in schools as literacy educators: Advocates for reaching beyond the classroom.* Palgrave McMillan.

Merga, M. K. (2019b). Do librarians feel that their profession is valued in contemporary schools? *Journal of the Australian Library and Information Association, 68*(1), 18–37.

Merga, M. K. (2019c). How do librarians in schools support struggling readers? *English in Education, 53*(2), 145–160.

Merga, M. K. (2019d). Collaborating with teacher librarians to support adolescents' literacy and literature learning. *Journal of Adolescent & Adult Literacy, 63*(1), 65–72.

Merga, M. K. (2020a). School librarians as literacy educators within a complex role. *Journal of Library Administration, 60*(8), 889–908.

Merga, M. K. (2020b). 'Fallen through the cracks': Teachers' perceptions of barriers faced by struggling literacy learners in secondary school. *English in Education, 54*(4), 371–395.

Merga, M. K. (2021a). The role of the library within school-level literacy policies and plans in Australia and the United Kingdom. *Journal of Librarianship and Information Science.* DOI: 10.1177/09610006211022410

Merga, M. K. (2021b). Libraries as wellbeing supportive spaces in contemporary schools. *Journal of Library Administration, 61*(6), 659–675.

Merga, M. K. (2021c, November 26). *Leading reading in your school: From literacy policy positioning to TikTok* [Closing keynote presentation]. School Library Association of Victoria (SLAV) Conference School Libraries Powering Literacy, Melbourne, Victoria and Online. https://slav.org.au/event-4122652

Merga, M. K. (2021d). The academic labour of knowledge mobilization: What scholarly publishers need to know. *Learned Publishing, 34*(4), 655–665.

Merga, M. K. (2021e). How can Booktok on TikTok inform readers' advisory services for young people? *Library & Information Science Research, 43*(2), e101091.

Merga, M. K. (2022a). *School libraries supporting literacy and wellbeing.* Facet Publishing.

Merga, M. K. (2022b). Every teacher needs to be a literacy teacher – but that's not happening in most Australian schools. *The Conversation.* https://theconversation.com/every-teacher-needs-to-be-a-literacy-teacher-but-thats-not-happening-in-most-australian-schools-184557

Merga, M. K., & Booth, S. (2017). Investigating debates around racism in sport to facilitate perspective transformation in the secondary English classroom. *Journal of Transformative Education, 15*(3), 184–202.

Merga, M. K., & Gardiner, V. (2018). The role of whole-school literacy policies supporting reading engagement in Australian schools. *English in Australia, 53*(3), 37–50.

Merga, M. K., & Ledger, S. (2018). Parents' views on reading aloud to their children: Beyond the early years. *Australian Journal of Language and Literacy, 41*(3), 177–189.

Merga, M. K., & Ledger, S. (2019). Teachers' attitudes toward and frequency of engagement in reading aloud in the primary classroom. *Literacy, 53*(3), 134–142.

Merga, M. K., Malpique, A., Mat Roni, S., Valcan, D., & Ledger, S. (2021). Teachers' perceptions of the impact of COVID-19 on writing instruction in Australia. *Issues in Educational Research, 31*(4), 1138–1155.

Merga, M. K., & Mason, S. (2019). Building a school reading culture: Teacher librarians' perceptions of enabling and constraining factors. *Australian Journal of Education, 63*(2), 173–189.

Merga, M. K., & Mason, S. (2021). Perspectives on institutional valuing and support for academic and translational outputs in Japan and Australia. *Learned Publishing, 34*(3), 305–314.

Merga, M. K., Mason, S., & Morris, J. E. (2019). 'The constant rejections hurt': Skills and personal attributes needed to successfully complete a thesis by publication. *Learned Publishing, 32*(3), 271–281.

Merga, M. K., & Mat Roni, S. (2017). The influence of access to eReaders, computers and mobile phones on children's book reading frequency. *Computers and Education, 109*, 187–196.

Merga, M. K., & Mat Roni, S. (2018a). Children's perceptions of the importance and value of reading. *Australian Journal of Education, 62*(2), 135–153.

Merga, M. K., & Mat Roni, S. (2018b). Empowering parents to encourage children to read beyond the early years. *The Reading Teacher, 72*(2), 213–221.

Merga, M. K., Mat Roni, S., Loh, C. E., & Malpique, A. (2021). Revisiting collaboration within and beyond the school library: New ways of measuring effectiveness. *Journal of Library Administration, 61*(3), 332–346.

Merga, M. K., Mat Roni, S., & Malpique, A. (2021a). School leadership and whole-school support of struggling literacy learners in secondary schools. *Educational Management Administration & Leadership, 49*(3), 534–550.

Merga, M. K., Mat Roni, S., & Malpique, A. (2021b). Do secondary English teachers have adequate time and resourcing to meet the needs of struggling literacy learners? *English in Education, 55*(4), 351–367.

Merga, M. K., Mat Roni, S., & Mason, S. (2020). Teachers' perceptions of their preparedness for supporting struggling literacy learners in secondary English classrooms. *English in Education, 54*(3), 265–284.

Merga, M. K., & Williams, R. (2016). The role of health educators in mitigating health risk from increasing screen time in schools and at home. *Asia-Pacific Journal of Health, Sport and Physical Education, 7*(2), 157–172.

Mol, S. E., & Bus, A. G. (2011). To read or not to read: a meta-analysis of print exposure from infancy to early adulthood. *Psychological Bulletin, 137*(2), 267.

Montagni, I., Ouazzani-Touhami, K., Mebarki, A., Texier, N., Schück, S., Tzourio, C., & Confins Group. (2021). Acceptance of a Covid-19 vaccine is associated with ability to detect fake news and health literacy. *Journal of Public Health, 43*(4), 695–702.

Nathanson, S., Pruslow, J., & Levitt, R. (2008). The reading habits and literacy attitudes of inservice and prospective teachers: Results of a questionnaire survey. *Journal of Teacher Education, 59*(4), 313–321.

National Literacy Trust (2018) *The Secondary Literacy Research and Policy Guide 2018/2019*. London: National Literacy Trust.

Nature editorial team. 2022). Australia must abolish law that allows politicians to veto research grants. *Nature*, *605*(7908), 7. https://doi.org/10.1038/d41586-022-01200-5

Neri, N. C., Guill, K., & Retelsdorf, J. (2021). Language in science performance: do good readers perform better? *European Journal of Psychology of Education*, *36*(1), 45–61.

Ness, M., Merga, M.K., Torres, J.E. & Chambre, S.J. (2022). The essential leadership of school librarians. *International Literacy Association*. www.literacyworldwide.org/docs/default-source/where-we-stand/the-essential- leadership-of-school-librarians.pdf?sfvrsn=f80c5216_6

Newsum, J. M. (2020). Leading from the shadows: School librarian leadership. In C. J., Craig, L. Turchi, & D. M. McDonald (Eds.). *Cross-Disciplinary, Cross-Institutional Collaboration in Teacher Education* (pp. 221–239). Palgrave Macmillan.

Ofsted (2013). *Improving Literacy in Secondary Schools: A Shared Responsibility*. Ofsted.

Ofsted (2022). *School inspection handbook*. www.gov.uk/government/publications/school-inspection-handbook-eif/school-inspection-handbook

Organisation for Economic Co-operation and Development (OECD). (n.d.). *Evaluation and assessment frameworks for improving school outcomes*. OECD Publishing. www.oecd.org/education/school/46927511.pdf

Organisation for Economic Co-operation and Development (OECD). (2010). *PISA 2009 results: Executive summary*. OECD Publishing.

Parker, R. (1985). The 'Language across the curriculum' movement: A brief overview and bibliography. *College Composition and Communication*, *36*(2), 173–177.

Parsons, A. W., Parsons, S. A., Malloy, J. A., Gambrell, L. B., Marinak, B. A., Reutzel, D. R., & Fawson, P. C. (2018). Upper elementary students' motivation to read fiction and nonfiction. *The Elementary School Journal*, *118*, 505–523.

Perelman, L. (2018). *Towards a new NAPLAN: Testing to the teaching*. Analysis & Policy Observatory. http://apo.org.au/system/files/139796/apo-nid139796-698251.pdf

Readability Formulas (n.d.). *The SMOG Readability Formula, a Simple Measure of Gobbledygook*. https://readabilityformulas.com/smog-readability-formula.php

Reeves, S., Exley, B., & Dillon-Wallace, J. (2018). Secondary school English teachers caught in the NAPLAN Fray: Effects of the disparate responses. *English in Australia*, *53*(1), 24–32.

Reimers, F. M. (2022). *Primary and secondary education during COVID-19: Disruptions to educational opportunity during a pandemic*. Springer.

Rice, S. (2014). NAPLAN results don't tell us the whole story. *The Conversation*. https://theconversation.com/naplan-results-dont-tell-us-the-whole-story-30715

Roberts, P. (1995). Defining literacy: paradise, nightmare or red herring? *British Journal of Educational Studies*, *43*(4), 412–432.

Rood, R. E. (1989). Advice for administrators: Writing the attendance policy. *NASSP Bulletin*, *73*(516), 21–25.

Rowley, I. (2019). Ofsted: What curriculum evidence will they need? *SecEd*. www.sec-ed.co.uk/best-practice/ofsted-what-curriculum-evidence-will-they-need/

Rutherford, L., Singleton, A., Derr, L. A., & Merga, M. K. (2018). Do digital devices enhance teenagers' recreational reading engagement? Issues for library policy from a recent study in two Australian states. *Public Library Quarterly*, *37*(3), 318–340.

Sacks, D., Bayles, K., Taggart, A. & Noble, S. (2020). COVID-19 and education: How Australian schools are responding and what happens next. *PwC Australia*. www.pwc.com.au/government/government-matters/COVID-19-education- how-australian-schools-are-responding.html

Sadusky, A., Reupert, A. E., Freeman, N. C., & Berger, E. P. (2021). Diagnosing adults with dyslexia: Psychologists' experiences and practices. *Dyslexia*, *27*(4), 468–485.

Sanfilippo, J., Ness, M., Petscher, Y., Rappaport, L., Zuckerman, B., & Gaab, N. (2020). Reintroducing dyslexia: early identification and implications for paediatric practice. *Pediatrics*, *146*(1), e20193046.

Santangelo, T., & Graham, S. (2016). A comprehensive meta-analysis of handwriting instruction. *Educational Psychology Review*, *28*(2), 225–265.

Schleicher, A. (2019). *PISA 2018: Insights and interpretations*. OECD Publishing.

Sinha, S., & Hanuscin, D. L. (2017). Development of teacher leadership identity: A multiple case study. *Teaching and Teacher Education*, *63*, 356–371.

Smylie, M. A., & Eckert, J. (2018). Beyond superheroes and advocacy: The pathway of teacher leadership development. *Educational Management Administration & Leadership*, *46*(4), 556–577.

Snow, P., de Bruin, K., & Graham, L. (2021). Reading instruction and support. In K. A. Allen,, A. Reupert, & L. Oades (Eds.), *Building Better Schools with Evidence-based Policy* (pp. 118–124). Taylor & Francis.

Softlink (2021). *Australian School Library Survey Report 2020*. www.softlinkint.com/downloads/2020_Softlink_School_Library_Survey_-_Australian_Report.pdf

Spichtig, A.N., Pascoe, J.P., Gehsmann, K.M., Gu, F., & Ferrara, J.D. (2022). The interaction of silent reading rate, academic vocabulary, and comprehension among students in grades 2–12. Reading Research Quarterly. DOI:10.1002/rrq.457

Sroka, M. (2021). 'It depends where i am in my life, whether i love reading or not': Challenges to fostering strong personal reading lives and why it matters. *Language Arts Journal of Michigan*, *37*(1), 63–72.

Standards and Testing Agency. (2018). *Information for parents: 2018 national curriculum tests at the end of key stages 1 and 2*. https://assets.publishing.service.gov.uk/government/uploads/system/uploads /attachment_data/file/694765/Information_for_parents_-_2018_national _curriculum_tests_at_the_end_of_key_stages_1_and_2.pdf

Stanovich, K. E. (2009). Matthew effects in reading: Some consequences of individual differences in the acquisition of literacy. *Journal of Education*, *189*(1–2), 23–55.

Steele, C. M. (2020). Teaching Standard Australian English as a second dialect to Australian Indigenous children in primary school classrooms. [Doctoral dissertation, The University of Melbourne]. Minerva Access. https://minerva-access.unimelb.edu.au/handle/11343/267354

Stouten, J., Rousseau, D. M., & De Cremer, D. (2018). Successful organizational change: Integrating the management practice and scholarly literatures. *Academy of Management Annals*, *12*(2), 752–788.

Suarez-Lledo, V., & Alvarez-Galvez, J. (2021). Prevalence of health misinformation on social media: systematic review. *Journal of Medical Internet Research*, *23*(1), e17187.

Sullivan, A., & Brown, M. (2015). Reading for pleasure and progress in vocabulary and mathematics. *British Educational Research Journal*, *41*(6), 971–991.

Tasmanian Government. (2018). *Tasmania's Literacy and Numeracy. Framework*. https://documentcentre.education.tas.gov.au/Documents/Literacy-Numeracy-Framework-2018.pdf

Tasmanian Government. (2022). *Literacy framework consultation paper released*. www.premier.tas.gov.au/site_resources_2015/additional_releases/literacy_framework_consultation_paper_released

te Riele, K. & Stewart, S. (2020) *Whole school approaches to literacy fact sheet 3/2020*. Peter Underwood Centre. https://eprints.utas.edu.au/35385/1/3-2020_%20WholeSchool%20Aprroaches%20to%20T_L.pdf

te Riele, K., Stewart, S., & Stratford, E. (2021). Whole school change for literacy teaching and learning: purposes and processes. *Language and Education*. DOI: 10.1080/09500782.2021.1944182

Thomas, D. P. (2020). Rapid decline and gender disparities in the NAPLAN writing data. *Australian Educational Researcher*, *47*(5), 777–796.

Thompson, G. (2014). NAPLAN, My School and accountability: Teacher perceptions of the effects of testing. *International education journal: comparative perspectives*, *12*(2), 62–84.

Thompson, P. A., Hulme, C., Nash, H. M., Gooch, D., Hayiou-Thomas, E., & Snowling, M. J. (2015). Developmental dyslexia: predicting individual risk. *Journal of Child Psychology and Psychiatry*, *56*(9), 976–987.

Thomson, S., De Bortoli, L., Underwood, C., & Schmid, M. (2019). *PISA 2018: Reporting Australia's Results: Volume I Student Performance*. Australian Council for Educational Research.

Thorbjørnsen, J. M. H. (2020). European perspectives on local literacy plans: A comparative study of Norwegian primary schools and the EU high-level group of expert on literacy. [Master's Thesis, University of Oslo, Oslo].

Tigert, J. M., & Leider, C. M. (2021). Beyond the 'core': preparing art educators to meet the needs of culturally and linguistically diverse students. *TESOL Quarterly*. DOI:10.1002/tesq.3040

Townsend, D., Carter, H., & Knecht, R. (2022). What's the purpose? A mixed-methods exploration of purposes for reading in secondary classrooms. *Reading & Writing Quarterly*. DOI: 10.1080/10573569.2022.2046220

Vanbuel, M. (2021). How stakeholders see the implementation of language education policy: a Q-study. *Current Issues in Language Planning*. DOI:10.1080/14664208.2021.1928427

Vanbuel, M., & Van den Branden, K. (2020). Each primary school a school-based language policy? The impact of the school context on policy implementation. *Language and Education*, *35*(1), 42–59.

Vanderlinde, R., Dexter, S., & van Braak, J. (2012). School-based ICT policy plans in primary education: Elements, typologies and underlying processes. *British Journal of Educational Technology*, *43*(3), 505–519.

Vansteelandt, I., Mol, S. E., Caelen, D., Landuyt, I., & Mommaerts, M. (2017). Attitude profiles explain differences in pre-service teachers' reading behavior and competence beliefs. *Learning and Individual Differences*, *54*, 109–115.

Walpole, S., Justice, L. M., & Invernizzi, M. A. (2004). Closing the gap between research and practice: Case study of school-wide literacy reform. *Reading & Writing Quarterly*, *20*(3), 261–283.

Weekes, P. (2014). From dot points to disciplinarity: The theory and practice of disciplinary literacies in secondary schooling. [Doctoral dissertation, University of New England]. Research UNE. https://hdl.handle.net/1959.11/16965

Weldon, P. R. (2016). Out-of-field teaching in Australian secondary schools. *Australian Council for Educational Research policy insights #6*. https://research.acer.edu.au/cgi/viewcontent.cgi?article=1005&context=policyinsights

Wenner, J. A., & Campbell, T. (2017). The theoretical and empirical basis of teacher leadership: A review of the literature. *Review of Educational Research*, *87*(1), 134–171.

Westbrook, J., Sutherland, J., Oakhill, J., & Sullivan, S. (2019). 'Just reading': the impact of a faster pace of reading narratives on the comprehension of poorer adolescent readers in English classrooms. *Literacy*, *53*(2), 60–68.

Wigfield, A., & Eccles, J. S. (2000). Expectancy – value theory of achievement motivation. *Contemporary Educational Psychology*, *25*, 68–81.

Wilson, R. & Carabetta, G. (2022). COVID and schools: Australia is about to feel the full brunt of its teacher shortage. *The Conversation*. https://theconversation.com/covid-and-schools-australia-is-about-to-feel-the-full-brunt-of-its-teacher-shortage-174885

Wise, K., MacDonald, A., Badham, M., Brown, N. & Rankin, S. (2022). Interdisciplinarity for social justice enterprise: intersecting education, industry and community arts perspectives. *The Australian Educational Researcher*. DOI: 10.1007/s13384-022-00516-5

Zhao, Y. (2017). What works may hurt: Side effects in education. *Journal of Educational Change*, *18*(1), 1–19.

Zhao, Y. (2020). Two decades of havoc: A synthesis of criticism against PISA. *Journal of Educational Change*, *21*, 245–266.

Index

Milton Keynes UK
Ingram Content Group UK Ltd.
UKHW051813131123
432470UK00026B/725

9 781923 116061